OREGON OR BUST

Volume 2

OREGON OR BUST

Volume 2

Amazing True Short Stories from the Descendants of the Oregon Trail Pioneers and Articles about the Indian Wars, the Gold Rush, Outlaws, Vigilantes, Prehistoric Indian Tribes, Empire Builders, and Settlers of the Great Northwest---and More!

Gentry W. Cutsforth

ISBN: 149290872X
EAN: 9781492908722

This book was printed in the United States of America.

CONTENTS

Introduction 1
Note: Pioneer stories #1 - 175 and additional articles have been previously published in "*OREGON or BUST*" – Volume 1.

176 Duck Too Difficult for Half-Breed Joe 4
177 Preacher's Long Legs Ridiculed by Indian Women.................... 6
178 Whitewash Destroys Accounts on Walls 7
179 Chief Plenty Belly Raises Plenty Cain.. 7
180 Girl's Father Objects to Suitor's Business 9
181 Strange Coincidence Happens to Couple 10
182 Father's Decease No Grief to Youngster 11

Starvation, Near Starvation, Malnutrition, and Dehydration: How are These Physical Conditions Different? 13

183 Terrible Creature Sends Lad to Tree 16
184 White Cow Causes Row with Indians 17
185 Indian Turns Nudist When Shower Arrives 19
186 Men Reap Reward for Kindly Deed 21
187 Uninvited Visitors Disdain Milk Diet 22
188 Scotchman's Shield Comes in Handy 24
189 Prickly Cactus Brings Return of Livestock............................... 25
190 Pretty Kitty Visits Unsuspecting Child 27
191 Girl Sobs in Vain to Save Doomed Man.................................. 27
192 Quick Action Saves Children from Fire................................... 29

'Grandma' Tabatha Moffatt Brown
Part 1: A Story of Pioneer Courage and a Woman who's Buckskin Needles Built a University in Oregon 31

193 Strategy Obtains Release of Woman 38
194 White Man Smart; Also Smart Injun.. 40
195 Death Extended as Matter of Kindness..................................... 41

'Grandma' Tabatha Moffatt Brown
Part 2: Concluding a Story of Great Pioneer Courage, Determination and Humanitarian Generosity 42

196 Vagrants Frightened When 'Corpse' Speaks 51
197 Sweetbriar Tells of Charming Romance 54
198 Was This Pioneer Settler Chagrined? 55
199 Brief Ceremony—but It Worked 56
200 White Man Regrets Ardent Flirtation 57

Columbia River "Medicine Rock" 59

201 Indian Woman Asks for Gift of Child 63
202 Folks Shocked When Woman Rides Horse 64
203 Old Yellow Pooch Faithful to Boots 65
204 Danish Folk Learn to Love Country 66
205 Lucky Strike Len Given Phony Cigar 67
206 Father Defends His River Toll Bridge 68
207 Telephone Lad Feels Wrath of Subscriber 70

Northwest Empire Builders: Ben Holladay
An Empire Builder Deserted by His Friends 72

208 Three Panthers Frighten Man into Full Retreat 79
209 Hearse Prized by Pleased Indians 80
210 Twin Santa Clauses Visit Eager Children 81
211 Jokester Almost Sends Militiamen to Battle 82
212 White Man's Bicycle Astonishes Indian 84
213 All Ends Well for Very Capable Liar 85
214 Wolves Chew Pants of Sleeping Pioneer 86
215 Hog Goes West in Most Unusual Way 87

When Oregon Went Berserk: Episode 1 of 6
An Account of Ten Spectacular Years (1855-1865)
When the Northwest was Host to War, Greed and Death 88
Episode 1: No White Man's Life Was Safe 90

216 Minister of Gospel Shocked by Greeting 97
217 Three "Brave" Wolves Scare Missionaries 98
218 Wedding Party Has a Change of Scene 99
219 Gourd Proves Handy for Darning Socks 99
220 Magic Fire Glass Impresses Indians 101
221 Coatless Man Gets Dinner After Delay 103
222 Wandering Indian Aids Suffering Child 104
223 Aunt Polly Resents Mr. Nude Indian 106
224 Chinese Disappear in the Black of Night 107
225 Distressed Mothers Find Babes Mixed 108

Prehistoric Indians of the West: Part 1 of 3
From the Columbia River in Oregon, the Shoshonean linguistic family spread to the land of the Maya 110

226 Indian Attack Foiled by White's Quick Wit 119
227 Whites Fare Badly During Stage Raid 120
228 Clerk Pays Twice for Indian Maiden 122
229 One of Joe Meek's Noted Tales Retold 123
230 Lewelling Developed Many Fine Cherries 125
231 Ponies Offered in Trade for Bride 127
232 Heroism Displayed by Brave Woman 128
233 Boy Falls Victim to Attack of Cougar 129
234 Dire Tragedy Claims Bridal Party Lives 130
235 Bad-Man Example Brings Gun Reform 132

Northwest Empire Builders: George H. Williams
A Statesman of a Bitter Era 134

236 Marriage of Princess Brings Peace Pact 142
237 He Got His Harem, But What a Harem! 144
238 Indians Kept at Bay by Dog's Resistance 146
239 Rogue River Settlers Take Terrible Revenge 148
240 Correspondence Bride Has Great Adventure 150
241 Who Killed Umtux? Still Moot Question 151
242 Free Trader Gets Hand of Princess 153
243 Indian Angry When White Bride Refused 155

244 Bonneville Causes West's First Strike 156
245 Redskins Demand White Man's Dance................................. 157

When Oregon Went Berserk: Episode 2 of 6
An Account of Ten Spectacular Years (1855-1865) When
the Northwest Was Host to War, Greed and Death 160
Episode 2: The White Man's Superior Equipment
and Organization 161

246 Mexican Murderer Pays High Penalty.................................... 162
247 Priest Takes Chiefs on Peace Mission.................................... 165
248 Secrecy Required in Boat Building 167
249 Happy Family Has Terrible Tragedy 168
250 "Forty Thieves" Not Appreciated.. 170
251 Lane and Nesmith Barely Save Necks 171
252 Church Given $\$^{210}$ for Dorion Burial.................................... 173
253 Horse Trade Cause of Early Killing... 175
254 Snakes Driven Out, Says Indian Legend................................ 176
255 Adventurous Trip Made by Youngster.................................... 177

Prehistoric Indians of the West: Part 2 of 3................................ 178

256 Making Dogs Smarter Simple Task... 185
257 Scores Are Wiped Out by Massacre.. 186
258 Wool Fragments Are Made Into Socks................................... 187
259 Girls Get Fright from Indian Fracas... 188
260 Battle of Table Rock Declared to Be Myth............................. 190
261 Broken Friendship Patched by Romance 192
262 Mother Watches Daughters Perish.. 195
263 Lone White Man Puts Indian Band to Rout........................... 196
264 Rawhide Ropes Stop Harassment... 197
265 Funeral Trek Made Across Plains 198

Northwest Empire Builders: Simeon G. Reed
A Versatile Empire Builder and College Founder........................ 200

266 Lost Steer Saves Train From Grief.. 209
267 Wits Rescue Young Pony Express Rider.................................. 210
268 Little Becky's "Big Fish" Story 212
269 Surrender Not Understood by Raiding Party........................ 214
270 Brandy Protected by Unique Cache... 215
271 Farmer Kills Own Pig in Cornfield.. 216
272 Swimmer Loses Pants in Water 217
273 Woman Recounts Early Happenings 219
274 Grave of Indian Hidden by Sheep 220
275 Tragedy Averted by Indian Wife 221

When Oregon Went Berserk: Episode 3 of 6
An Account of Ten Spectacular Years (1855-1865)
When the Northwest was Host to War, Greed and Death 222
Episode 3: The Great "Reckless' Gold Rush................................ 222

276 Melon-Stealing Indians Fooled.. 230
277 Bully's Daughter Saved by Indian 231
278 Cougars No Joke in Pioneer Days 232
279 Initials in Rock Seventy Three Years Found 233
280 Settlers Escape by Clever Ruse.. 233
281 Greenbacks Not Money to Indian 235
282 Liquored Captain Has Good Alibi 236
283 Pioneer Lives to Tell of Scalping.. 237
284 Empty Guns Bluff Indians 238
285 Indians Ransack House for Sugar 239

Prehistoric Indians of the West: Part 3 of 3.................................. 240

286 False Molars Scare Indian 246
287 Rash Horseman Taught Caution 247
288 Indian Raid Only Horses.. 248
289 Boy Didn't Like Indian Girl 249
290 Indian Woman's Recipe Wasn't Pleasing................................ 250
291 Indian Racketeer Gets Sandwiches 251
292 Little Girl Foils Indians' Attack 252

293 Feather Bed Rescued From Bay 253
294 Night Visitor Not Indian 254
295 Teamster Hides Gold in Salt 255

Northwest Empire Builders: Peter French
Part 1 of 2: The Northwest's Greatest Cattle King 257

296 Soft Words Didn't Work 266
297 Indian's Horse Follows Hearse 267
298 This Indian Was Prankster 268
299 Penalty Paid For Murder 269
300 Drunken Indians Get Orders Mixed 270
301 Prospective Romance Goes on the Rocks 271
302 Concomly's Grandson Has Great Travels 272
303 Stampede Upsets Mormon Caravan 273

When Oregon Went Berserk: Episode 4 of 6
An Account of Ten Spectacular Years (1855-1865)
When the Northwest was Host to War, Greed and Death 275
Episode 4: Hostile Indians Became Aggressive 275

304 Patriot Spoils July Fourth Meal 282
305 Enraged Woman Beats Indian 283
306 Indian Woman Drinks Washing Fluid 285
307 Pioneers Escape Indian Attack 285
308 Marauders Leave Trail of Feathers 287
309 McLoughlin Murder Early-Day Mystery 288
310 Marooned Group Nearly Starves 290
311 Making Sauerkraut and Cabbage "Spears" 291

Northwest Empire Builders: Peter French
Part 2 of 2: The Strange Fate of the Northwest's Greatest
Cattle Empire: 294

312 Pie Thief Gets Hot Pepper Cure 302
313 Pioneer Doctor Scalped by Proxy 303
314 Scout Rescues Captive Girl 304

315 Indians Evince Sense of Humor 305
316 Feathers Good Hiding Place 306
317 Pony Substitutes for Slave Maid 308
318 Woman's Shooting Impressed Indians 309
319 Tooth-Shedding Scares Indian 310

When Oregon Went Berserk: Episode 5 of 6
An Account of Ten Spectacular Years (1855-1865) When the Northwest was Host to War, Greed and Death 312
Episode 5: With the Gold Rush Came Men Too 'Smart' to Work for It 313

320 Settlers Foster Indian Romance 319
321 Settler Escapes Death in Creek 320
322 Indian Woman's Finery Shocks Guests 322
323 Teepee Cover Saves Pioneers 323
324 Wife's Relatives Plague Trader 324
325 Indian Scorns Farm Lessons 325
326 This Indian Woman Was Boss 326
327 Old-Timer Recalls Table Rock Battle 327

Northwest Empire Builders: Henry W. Goode
He Made Northwest Lights Shine Brighter 329

328 Indian Covets Dinner Call 337
329 Rescued Indian Shows Gratitude 337
330 Woman's Wig Frightens Indian Woman 338
331 Chinese Innkeeper Parts With Queue 339
332 Indians Battle Among Selves 341
333 Tree Monument to Early Hero 342
334 Powder Blast Scares Indian 343
335 Indian Girl Rejects Parent's Choice 344

When Oregon Went Berserk: Episode 6 of 6
An Account of Ten Spectacular Years (1855-1865) When the Northwest Was Host to War, Greed and Death 346

Episode 6: No Degrees of Crime—Any Crime—
One Punishment—Hanging! 346

336 Dead Man's Glasses Save Pioneer's Life 353
337 Plug of Tobacco Repulses Indian 354
338 Woman Rescues Settlers' Flour 355
339 Horse Raiders Change Minds 356
340 Pioneer Sheriff Has Troubles 357
341 Indian Woman Frightens Herder 358
342 Woman Recovers Stolen Bossy 359
343 Emigrants Rescue Foot Traveler 360

Northwest Empire Builders: Simon Benson
The All Steam Bunyan That was a Mighty Logger 362

344 Governor Was Full of Scraps 370
345 Teamster Hides Watch on Horse 371
346 Daughters Offered as Doctor's Fee 372
347 New-Fangled Gun Scares Indian 373
348 Paint Betrays Horse Thieves 376
349 Trade Brings Dire Results 377
350 Joe Meek's Position Made Big Difference 378

*"It is our **manifest destiny** to overspread the continent allotted by Providence for the free development of our multiplying millions"*

John L. O'Sullivan, 1845

*This attitude of **manifest destiny** was prevalent during the 19th-century period of expansion by Anglo-Saxon Americans that the United States not only could, but was destined to stretch from coast to coast. It helped fuel the western settlement, remove the Native Americans by death or moving them onto reservations, and wars with Mexico.*

Introduction

Volume 2

First of all, I want to thank you for picking up this volume of "Oregon or Bust", be it printed or in digital format. Many readers of Volume 1 have expressed much appreciated praise for the book with comments like these:

"I really like the stories and learned a lot about the Oregon Trail Pioneers that I didn't know before"

"I can't believe what these awesome people went through to get to Oregon"

"I found the book to be a "fun" read."

"I had trouble putting it down"

"After reading one story, the intriguing title of the next lured me on and on until before I realized it, I had read ninety stories"

"I can't wait for Volume 2. I hear it will even be better."

I thank you all for your kind endorsements. Of all the comments, (some from **young** readers, I may report) to me the most surprising statement was that the book is a "**fun**" read. I never thought of it as a fun read, but the person went on to explain that you can read a few stories, come back later and read a few more or even start over or skip around—you are free to do what you want—that makes it more "**fun**". Thanks Dorothy Paris for your explanation.

I recommend that everyone read the introduction to Volume 1, if you haven't already, as it outlines the history of the Oregon Trail Pioneers and explains how their stories were discovered in a 75-year-old scrapbook and then published in these two books for this, and future generations, to enjoy.

As in the first book, in addition to the hundreds of pioneer stories, I have added six more statesmen and developers to the series of articles entitled ***Northwest Empire Builders***. These ambitious men include:

1. **Ben Holladay**—An Empire Builder Deserted by His Friends.
2. **George H. Williams**—A Statesman of a Bitter Era.
3. **Simeon G. Reed**—A Versatile Empire Builder and College Founder.
4. **Peter French**—Part 1: The Northwest's Greatest Cattle King.
Part 2: The Strange Fate of the Northwest's Greatest Empire.
5. **Henry W. Goode**—He Made the Northwest's Lights Shine Brighter.
6. **Simon Benson**—The All Steam Bunyan That Was a Mighty Logger.

Other Articles of Interest

Starvation, Near Starvation, Malnutrition and Dehydration: What are the differences and how does our body react to them?

After repeated references in the pioneer stories of people starving or nearly starving-to-death, or running out of drinkable water while crossing the deserts, I decided to research the subjects and include my own article.

'Grandma' Tabatha Moffat Brown—A true pioneer who nearly starved-to-death with her family on the Applegate Trail in Southern Oregon.

Part 1: A Story of Pioneer Courage and a Woman Whose Buckskin Needles Built a University in Oregon.

Part 2: Concluding a Story of Great Pioneer Courage, Awesome Determination and Humanitarian Generosity.

Prehistoric Indians of the West— A three part series. From the Columbia River in Oregon, the Shoshonean linguistic families have been traced from coast to coast in America and south to the land of the Maya.

When Oregon Went Berserk— Don't miss this **wild** six episode account of the ten spectacular years (1855-1865) when the Northwest was host to war, gold, greed and death.

Episode 1: No White Person's Life Was Safe.
Episode 2: The White Man's Superior Equipment and Organization.
Episode 3: The Great "Reckless" Gold Rush.
Episode 4: Hostile Indians Became Aggressive.
Episode 5: With the Gold Rush Came Men Too "Smart" to Work for It.
Episode 6: No Degrees of Crime-Any Crime-One Punishment-Hanging!

I hope you are now excited and as ready to get started as I am. May your journey into the lives of the Oregon Trail Pioneers be a "fun" read.

Thank you. May God bless you, and may God bless America.

Gentry W. Cutsforth

The westward expansion of the United States is one of the defining themes of 19th-century American history

~ 176 ~

Duck Too Difficult for Half-Breed Joe

Joe was a half-breed who earned his living by operating a portable trading business and doing odd jobs for the settlers on the side. He traveled up and down the country for many miles trading his wares and performing any task that would pay him satisfactorily.

But his Indian nature often asserted itself and many times when the task became too tedious he would walk off and leave the job unfinished.

Joe called at Grandfather's house one afternoon and finding that no one was interested in the goods he had for sale, asked for something to do. A duck had just been killed for the evening meal, so Grandfather took Joe to the woodshed and gave him the job of picking the duck with the instructions that he must not leave before he was finished.

As most everyone knows, a duck is extremely difficult to pick. The afternoon wore on. Four o'clock, 5 o'clock but Joe had not returned from the woodshed. Grandmother began to get anxious. At 5:30 there came a knock upon the back door. There stood Half-breed Joe, pin feathers in his eyes, mouth, nose and hair, not to mention his clothes.

Handing the still unpicked duck to Grandmother, he said: "Pick like hell all afternoon. Here, you finish. I quit!"

GEORGIA TEATS, Portland, Oregon

~ 177 ~

Preacher's Long Legs Ridiculed by Indian Women

I can still see Grandmother's eyes twinkle as she told this story on her circuit rider husband, William Wade Watson.

Going upon his rounds of preaching among the scattered white settlers and tribes of Indians around Olympia, Washington, Grandfather Watson rode a small, short-legged pony. Grandfather was 6 foot 3 himself and of course, his feet almost dragged the ground.

Busy with hewing a home from the forest, Grandfather seldom had time to prepare sermons and practice hymns so he did this en route.

One day he was riding along a forest path loudly singing a hymn from his hymn book when he came upon a group of Indian women picking berries. The one nearest the trail looked at his dangling legs, spat out a mouthful of berries that she was chewing and in great amusement cried out, "Long-legged Jesus man! Hee-hee-hee-hee!"

Immediately the other women took it up and all of them chanted "Long-legged Jesus man!"

Grandfather who thought such jokes of the devil, kicked his horse in the flanks and galloped on, but far down the forest path he could still hear the shrieking laughter of the Indian women.

MRS. IMOGENE HUMPHREY, Salem, Oregon

~ 178 ~

Whitewash Destroys Accounts on Walls

In the early days in The Dalles, Oregon, a man by the name of Waymire opened a general store. Much of the trading was done by bartering and exchanging furs, livestock etc.

In extending credit, Waymire, not being much of a bookkeeper, wrote the names of the customers and the goods bought on credit.

On a trip to Portland to buy supplies, his wife decided to clean up the store during his absence. So she got lime and white-washed the interior of the entire establishment.

When Waymire returned, he was aghast. "I am a ruined man," he cried. "What do you expect me to do now to get our money back?" But his wife told him he could remember most of the accounts and could rewrite them. So, one Sabbath morning Waymire marked the accounts back on the wall.

"I didn't remember all the exact figures," he said, "but I evened up the money so's the ones that are able to pay had a little more and them as warn't had a little less."

MRS. C.M. MARTENS, Vancouver, Washington

~ 179 ~

Chief Plenty Belly Raises Plenty Cain

My father was Superintendent of Buildings (depots, roundhouses, etc.) when the Northern Pacific Railway was being pushed west through Montana.

At the time of this story, the rails had been laid as far west as Thompson Falls, Idaho. It was in the depth of winter—January—and the going was tough. However, telegraph operators had been installed in little stations built at Airlee, Eddy and Horse Plains (now Plains) to facilitate communication. Main headquarters at the time was at Missoula, Montana.

One cold night, with four feet of snow on the ground, a frantic call came over the wires from the lone agent at Horse Plains. "Help! Quick! Indians are on the warpath here! They are breaking down the depot door!"

The agent at Missoula shouted the message through the big construction camp. An engine was quickly coupled to a boxcar. Fifty men grabbed up all manner of firearms, leaped into the boxcar and away they went to rescue the agent at Horse Plains.

It was a freezing ride, and a rough one, the engine doing its furious best over the bumpy new road with the aid of snowplow and spurting sandbox. They roared through Airlee and Eddy as the agents at those stations stood on the platforms waving smoking lanterns at them.

At last they came in sight of Horse Plains and the fifty men in the boxcar clutched their rifles and revolvers. The train ground to a stop. The men jumped out into the snow, but where were the Indians? Not a living being in sight. But, lo! Around the corner of the little depot came old Chief Plenty Belly, known to all as the worst beggar and horse thief in Western Montana. His blanket was wrapped around his ears and he was blowing on his hands and seemed nearly frozen.

"What's the matter here?" called the engineer.

Old Plenty Belly looked up to the cab, and sadly pointed to the station door. "Fella no let me in. I holler lots and poundum door. I try breakum, glass." And he displayed a bloody fist.

The men found the broken window, reached in and unsnapped the catch, crawled through and found the station agent, in a dead faint under his bunk.

REV. JOSEPH P. CLANCY, St. Helens, Oregon

~ 180 ~

Girl's Father Objects to Suitor's Business

Pretty Mary Lucinthe Gardner and the ambitious young dentist, Dr. L. S. Skiff, were very happy when they first fell in love, but the objections of Mary's father, to their marriage, quickly cast a gloom over their youthful dreams.

Parental objections to marriage were common enough back in the 1850s, when it was customary for the suitor to consult the bride's parents, but, as least, it was fair to expect a reason for the refusal.

Abner Davis Gardner, however, who had brought his family to Linn County, Oregon from Iowa in 1853, steadfastly refused to state any reason for his dislike of the young dentist.

It was not fair, the lovers protested. Dr. Skiff came from a good family, had his degree in dentistry since 1849, the year he came to Oregon, and was honorable in every way.

"Tain't any of those things," the elder Gardner at last was forced into saying, "It's jist that he ain't a farmer, and how's he agoin' to keep you when he gets every tooth in the county pulled out?"

Ridiculous as this lack of faith in the future of dentistry appears, it must be kept in mind that at the time an aching tooth was nearly always extracted. Daguerreotypes of our ancestors in their advancing years nearly always showed shrunken mouths due to lack of teeth.

It must be admitted, however, that the stern parent showed little faith in the country itself or he would have expected an ever increasing number of teeth to be extracted.

This was the point on which he at last admitted that he was in error. The influx of settlers into the Willamette Valley continued to increase and as Gardner, in a casual sort of way, inquired about the condition of their teeth, he found an amazing number had cavities.

At last there was no doubt in the father's mind that there was enough business in the country to keep Dr. Skiff pulling and filling teeth all his life. Once this point was settled, he quickly gave the young couple his blessing and a wedding followed.

The newlyweds later moved to Salem, Oregon, where the husband practiced his profession, for many years, on State Street on the site of the present day Patton Block. The supply of aching teeth held out long enough for them to raise two fine sons, Mark and Will.

LESTER HALPIN, Portland, Oregon

~ 181 ~

Strange Coincidence Happens to Couple

In 1856, when Grandmother was a bride of eighteen, she left her home in Elkhart, Indiana to come to Oregon by ox team.

They had trouble with the Indians, and on one occasion their train camped with two other trains for three days until safe to travel. One evening a baby boy 2 years of age fell into a spring and was nearly drowned.

Forty-nine years later, when Grandmother was a widow, living alone in Eastern Oregon, she met and married a man sixteen years younger than she.

One evening as they sat talking over the past, he told her that his parents crossed the plains in 1856 when he was two-years-old and he had been told that once, when they were camped with two other trains, waiting for the Indians to quiet down before going on westward, that he fell into a spring and nearly drowned.

They always felt that it was the same incident both had experienced in 1856.

Mrs. R. E. Emmons, Yakima, Washington

~ 182 ~

Father's Decease No Grief to Youngster

In 1862, when but a little girl of six years, my mother, Mrs. Joshua A. Howard, of Garfield, Washington, crossed the plains with her parents from Iowa to the Walla Walla Valley.

She still vividly recalls many incidents of the long trip, but the one that believe she likes best to relate, goes, with the exception of the names, something like this:

"As we came across the plains we would travel steadily for several days at a time, stopping only for short night camps, until we came to a favorable-looking spot where there was plenty of good grass and water and where there was little likelihood of an Indian attack, and there we would camp for two or three days to allow the cattle to eat and rest.

"At these camps the men took turns standing watch over the stock. When not on guard the men did as they pleased. Some rested and some went hunting and scouting around.

"There was a Smith family in our wagon train, consisting of Mr. Smith, his wife and three or four small children.

"On the first day at one of these rest camps Mr. Smith went hunting. He did not get back to camp that night. When he had not shown up by morning some alarm was felt, as it was thought that he had probably fallen into the hands of some stray band of Indians.

"Scouting parties were organized, however to go in search of the missing man, and late on the third day they found him.

"Smith had killed a coyote and evidently as he stooped to take hold of the dead animal, a pistol which he always carried thrust into the waistband of his pants was accidentally discharged, killing him.

"He was carried back to camp on a crude stretcher, and one of the older men was delegated to break the news to Mrs. Smith. Mrs. Smith, standing beside her wagon with her children clinging to her skirts, received the news of the death of her husband with dry eyes and without even the flicker of an eyelash." 'Put him over there', she said, pointing to a pile of bedding.

"However, little Willie Smith, aged about seven, released his clutch on his mother's dress and began jumping up and down, clapping his hands and shouting at the top of his voice, 'Goody, goody, goody. I'm going to have daddy's knife.'"

Frank Z. Howard, Klamath Falls, Oregon

For a small morsel of food a man will transgress

and swerve from right to wrong. Proverbs 28

Starvation, Near Starvation, Malnutrition, and Dehydration

BY GENTRY W. CUTSFORTH

How are these four physical conditions different? How do our bodies react, and adapt, to long periods without food or water? How is dying of thirst different from dying of starvation?

These are questions I asked myself after reading many of the *Oregon or Bust* stories telling of the early pioneers that traveled the old trails into the Oregon Country back in the 1800s. It seemed that running short of provisions was always of great concern. Many of these folks found repeated rationing of food a necessity due to unexpected delays caused by the weather, road conditions, breakdown of the wagons, illness, exhausted and injured livestock, and even occasionally the birth of a new member of the family. These delays resulted in food shortages that could only be restocked if they could reach the next trading post, if there was one, and if they had any money left to pay for it.

Hunters and trappers who roamed the deserts and wildernesses often found themselves isolated without nourishment or water. Later, the prospectors who poured into the Northwest by the thousands, crazed by gold fever, chose to ignore repeated, emphatic warnings that they would find little shelter from summer heat, frequent rainstorms, winter snow, or freezing temperatures. Prospecting equipment and supplies were unavailable anywhere above Portland on the Columbia River. Game animals were becoming scarce and food provisions were either completely sold out or priced extremely high. For example, the price of a pound of flour at The Dalles was $24. That's $1,200 for a fifty pound sack!

These warnings unfortunately fell on deaf ears. And as expected, hundreds, perhaps thousands, of these rambunctious miners starved, or suffered the devastating effects of being nearly starved, or crippled by malnutrition or dehydration.

Definition of Terms

Starvation is defined as the result of a severe or total lack of nutrients needed by the body for the maintenance of life.

Near Starvation therefore must be a point that is reached where, without food, the body will begin the process of its own destruction as a way to survive.

Malnutrition is normally a condition caused by the consumption of single staple carbohydrates, like rice, without anything else to eat to provide the needed nutrients, resulting in multiple vitamin and mineral deficits that are associated with many serious health related problems.

Children are most susceptible to malnutrition, causing growth retardation, brain dysfunction, an enlarged liver, convulsions, loss of blood pressure, poor wound healing, eventual blindness, poor blood clotting, scurvy, sore mouth and throat, and many other conditions which may slowly lead to death unless healthy foods are carefully administered.

Dehydration is caused by the lack of liquids in the body that are constantly supplied by the blood stream to cells and organs. Death can happen within three days without water, depending upon factors such as your physical size, your health and weather conditions such as heat, precipitation, and wind. Starvation can occur within thirty days.

Some of the terrifying symptoms of dehydration include extremely painful muscle and stomach cramps, pain in other interior organs, terrible headaches, nausea and vomiting, reduced urine in the bladder, reduced blood pressure, delusions, dizziness, delirium, fainting, dry mouth and eyes, unconsciousness, swelling of the tongue, the inability to stand upright or think clearly, and the agony of not being able to swallow. This is one of the worst ways to go.

Adult Starvation

Complete starvation in adults leads to death in 8 – 12 weeks. (Even less for children). The consumption of water will extend life substantially, but only the necessary nutrients and energy in the form of calories will prevent the body from literally feeding off of itself. The body will use its own muscle mass for protein energy to prevent shutting down and complete failure of its organs, one at a time. As muscles break down, nerve cells degenerate and movement is regulated. Weak and painful muscles restrict or even prevent free movement. The ability to seek food and water becomes unbearably difficult or physically impossible. People become disoriented, confused and angry, and may become so desperate they turn on others. We are not ourselves when we're hungry.

In the final stages, adults may experience hallucinations, convulsions, chronic diarrhea, shrinkage and loss of function of the liver, heart, lungs, and sex organs. Anemia, reduction of muscle mass and the resulting pain and weakness, lowered body temperature, extreme sensitivity to cold, immune deficiency, inability to properly digest food if eaten, difficulty concentrating and making decisions, irritability, eventual loss of over 50% of normal body weight, and even more horrid conditions may be experienced from the lack of nutrients in food. Victims often just lie down, give up, and die.

Recovery from "Near" Starvation

Many factors determine the body's recovery from "near" starvation. Obese people have more fat energy stored for the body to use. The severity and length of time of starvation and availability of water to drink are all determining factors for recovery. But chances are there will be lifelong physical problems as a result. Only the long term, carefully prepared treatments that first begin with liquid nourishment should be administered, as the body may not be able to absorb or even tolerate a fully balanced diet. Such treatment is seldom available in the wilderness.

Starvation was one of the greatest worries of the early pioneers. Constant evaluation of their provisions was essential to determine if the daily consumption, without frittering it away, would subsist until they reached their final destination, or the next trading post down the long meandering trail.

The importance of survival was primary to these pioneers. The words "Oregon or Bust' painted on the side of many of their wagons became a compelling reason to "carry on."

GENTRY W. CUTFORTH, Author of "Oregon or Bust"

~ 183 ~

Terrible Creature Sends Lad to Tree

The Pringle family, including seven children, experienced most of the hardships which commonly befell an emigrant family in the trip over the plains from Missouri to Oregon in 1846. Dangers from Indian attacks, mountain fever, fatigue, and shortage of provisions were all part of their lot, but it was the lack of food which led to the following adventure to fourteen-year-old Octavius Pringle.

The family had arrived east of the Cascades when their food was running so low that the problem was becoming serious. Only one riding pony remained in the train—an emaciated old mare—but young Octavius volunteered to ride over the mountains into Salem and return with provisions.

The boy made his way to Salem without mishap. He loaded his animal with all the dried peas and graham flour that she could carry, in her weakened condition, and started back to his family.

After eating his supper, a tin cupful of graham flour mixed with water, he looked around for a place to spread his blanket. He selected the base of a large ash tree thinking that its branches would give a place of safety if necessary.

Imagining a pair of bright eyes staring from the darkness of every bush, he rested fitfully when suddenly there was a crashing in the underbrush. Convinced that it was a bear, Octavius sprang to his feet and bolted up the tree. As he remembered the precious provisions, however, he went back for them. A few moments later the boy was safely perched in the tree with several bags of dried peas and graham flour, and his two blankets.

Literally perched on a branch the young emigrant wrapped the blankets around him and sat listening. The crashing continued at intervals during the night and each time they sent new shivers of fear through the cold and sleepless boy.

As dawn broke, he discovered the noisy animal. It was nothing more than a scrawny old cow which had either strayed away from a wagon train or had been deserted to forage for herself.

A very disgusted lad came down from his perch, "shooed" away the innocent cause of his plight, located his horse, and rode triumphantly, but sleepily, to his family desperately in need of food.

Edgar LaPlante, Portland, Oregon

~ 184 ~

White Cow Causes Row with Indians

During the 1840's, milk was a precious item in Oregon's Willamette Valley. My grandfather (Uncle "Doc" Sitton) settled on his farm, five miles northwest of McMinnville in what is now Yamhill County. Not until several years later, when Uncle Tom Shaden settled just west of McMinnville, did Grandfather taste milk, excepting on his annual trips to Oregon City to get wheat ground and other supplies from Dr. McLoughlin.

When Uncle Tom crossed the plains he worked a large white cow as an ox. This cow was one of the first in the Yamhill country, so all of the settlers went to Uncle Tom's cabin as often as possible for a good meal and a taste of real milk and cream, but most of all, for some real milk gravy.

Imagine the consternation of the settlers when they heard that Indians had killed Uncle Tom's white cow and carried off the meat. As soon as possible about twenty men, including my grandfather, started after the marauders. The trail led north and at the old Indian crossing of the North Yamhill River, about 1½ miles west of the present town of Yamhill, they found where the party had camped and jerked the meat. The ashes were still warm, but signs showed that the Indians had gone eastward.

The settlers followed and early in the morning of the second day, while crossing a grassy opening in the foothills of the Cascades, in what is now Clackamas County, they sighted and caught two papooses with hackamores. The settlers knew they were after horses and that an Indian camp was near. Following a trail that led down to a creek they found the camp. During the skirmish that followed the Indians were soon overpowered, with no casualties except one horse shot from under its rider, as there were only seven in the Indian party.

A council followed. It was decided that the Indians could go on unmolested provided they would return to their people, who lived east of the Cascades, never to return to the Willamette Valley again, and provided the settlers take all the Indians horses, camp equipment--and the jerked meat.

On the return trip the white party should have been in a satisfied state of mind, as they had accomplished their mission. They had rid the valley of the band of marauders, without loss of life, and by agreement had taken the Indians' property, which would compensate the whites for their loss of time and hardships suffered. Yet they were contrary minded, for all that they had done could never return to the little community Uncle Tom's white cow.

J. Fred Brady, Albany, Oregon

~ 185 ~

Indian Turns Nudist When Shower Arrives

In the early days, in the Grand Ronde District of Oregon, a storekeeper there received a shipment of overcoats. They were rough, heavy coats made of horse blankets, gaudy-colored affairs giving a sort of Joseph's coat-of-many-colors impression, but they proved popular with the Indians and soon were nearly gone.

There was one Indian, a long, lean fellow called Charley, who came into the store one day and immediately spied these coats. He asked the price and was visibly disappointed to learn that he did not have enough money to buy one.

Every day thereafter he reappeared to gaze longingly at the dwindling stock of coats. One day, however, when there was only one left he appeared with enough money to pay for it, handed over the cash and donned the coat. It was several sizes too small for him. The sleeves hit him half way to the elbows and it was much too short, but Charley couldn't be bothered about such minor details as he marched proudly forth.

He had been gone but a few minutes when it started to rain. Shortly thereafter the storekeeper looked out and saw how he was returning!

Aside from the shapeless felt hat on his head and his shoes, he was completely naked. Under his arm, wrapped up in his overalls and shirt, was the precious coat, untouched by the rain as Charley galloped toward the shelter of the buildings.

Once there he put on his shirt and pants, oblivious to their dampness, and to several shocked onlookers, blissfully happy that his precious coat had escaped undamaged.

When the storm was over, he put it on once again and cheerfully set forth upon his way.

Kenneth M. Day, Portland, Oregon

~ 186 ~

Men Reap Reward for Kindly Deed

My great-grandfather came across the plains from east of the Mississippi with his parents in a covered wagon and settled down in the Willamette Valley of Oregon. It was there that Great-Grandfather met and fell in love with a young woman in that settlement, and they were married.

The young couple decided to go south to make their home. They journeyed south as far as the Umpqua River Valley. Here they found that a small settlement had sprung up. The Indians were considered friendly so the couple decided to make their home there.

In the winter of 1841, a small band of Indians were living about ten miles up the river from the white settlement. The winter was very severe.

In the worst part of the winter, two old buck Indians from the Indian encampment came stumbling into the white settlement. The

Indians informed the settlers that the greater part of their band was sick and dying from some kind of sickness. They had come to ask for help.

Three men stepped out from among their fellow men and volunteered to go. Great Grandfather was one of the three. They stayed in the Indian camp for a few weeks, helping and giving aid to the sick Indians until they were able to care for themselves. The Indians seemed surprised and angry that only three from the whole white settlement had come to help them.

In the spring of the year following the Indians' illness, a small band of Indians crept silently into the white settlement one night and drove away almost all of the livestock that they could find, except the three white men's stock who had helped them while they were sick. These three men lost nothing.

The next morning the settlers discovered their losses. They organized in a group and went to the place where the Indians had been encamped. They found that the whole Indian band had moved away. Neither the settlement's stock, nor the Indians were ever seen again in that part of the country.

Irma Vance, Powers, Oregon

~ 187 ~

Uninvited Visitors Disdain Milk Diet

My grandparents, coming from Missouri, took up a homestead on what is now known as Fern Ridge, Oregon.

Soon after their crude one-room cabin was built, Grandfather set off for the nearest trading post for their winter supplies and left Grandmother alone with her one, small five-year-old daughter, Emma. Although Grandmother was by nature courageous, the country was wild and new. The dread of the Indians was constantly near her.

A few days after Grandfather had gone, she felt especially nervous, so to take her mind from such brooding, she busied herself by unpacking a few pictures and other little treasures from a trunk she had brought with her from Missouri. She had tacked two or three pictures on the wall and was looking over the other things in the trunk, when a strange sound Emma made caused her to raise her eyes. There were, what seemed to her, Indians standing all over the place.

"As a matter of fact," she would say, with a wry little smile when she used to tell us the story, "when I counted them the second time, there were only five." She collected her wits quickly and realized that they only wanted something to eat.

But she told them she had nothing to eat, which was almost the truth, for a little bread and some milk was all she had in the house. There had been no meat for days. The Indians refused to believe her and insisted, so she set out what bread she had and the only crock of milk.

This apparently made them very angry for they began taking mouthfuls of milk and walking around the room spitting it on the walls, the floor and even on her. She stood watching them, terrified. When finally the milk was gone the Indians left in disgust.

In our attic, is one of the pictures Grandmother had tacked on the wall that day. In one corner is a spot, faded, but recognizable as the splatter from a well-aimed mouthful of milk.

G. A. Drew, Junction City, Oregon

~ 188 ~

Scotchman's Shield Comes in Handy

Jock McLeod was a tall, raw-boned individual, proud of the Scotch ancestry his burry accent proclaimed. Traveling by wagon train from Independence, Missouri, he had established a small cabin in the Northwest wilderness, where he lived with his wife and son, and their hired man.

One morning, the hired man stepped from the house and walked to a spring close by for water. While in the act of filling a pail, he was shot, from behind, with an arrow and pitched forward, face down in the mud, dead. A band of Indians rushed from the woods whooping and yelling, all of them drunk from the effects of whisky traded to them by white renegades After scalping their victim the band rushed toward the house, believing that only the man's wife remained inside.

Jock McLeod, witnessing the whole affair from the window, quickly snatched up an old war shield, a prized possession that had once belonged to his great-grandfather in Scotland. He rushed from the house with the arrows bouncing off his shield like hailstones.

The Indians, bewildered, retreated to the edge of the woods, allowing Jock time enough to retrieve the body of his hired man and carry it back into the house, covered every inch of the way by a gun in the hands of his eleven-year-old son, who was watching from the cabin.

Ludwig Franz, Portland, Oregon

~ 189 ~

Prickly Cactus Brings Return of Livestock

In the spring of 1875, my father, Thomas Henry Look, then a boy of seventeen, with his brother-in-law, Lon Donavon, crossed the plains from Nebraska and settled near Eugene, Oregon.

He was of a very kindly and bashful nature, which proved as asset to him several times, during the following thirty-seven years that he taught school in Oregon and Washington.

One instance, when it particularly proved of value, was while crossing the plains. It was past the noon hour and they were looking for a place where they could stop to prepare their lunch and also have quick grazing for their horses.

They found a spot that seemed satisfactory, so they unhitched their horses, prepared their own lunch, and while eating, Father decided to remove his shoes and stockings to rest his feet.

No sooner were they removed when some Indians appeared on horseback. Father had always lived on the farm and felt kindly toward Indians, a feeling they seemed to sense.

So after exchanging a few friendly words, they rode away. He and his companion watched them, but saw their own horses, that were grazing nearby, join the Indian group and gallop away.

Father jumped up quickly and started after them, forgetting he was barefooted. He was stopped suddenly by numerous cactus needles in his feet. He sat down quickly to extract them, only to sit on more cacti.

He was then in rather an uncomfortable situation, but his sense of humor came to his rescue; he began to laugh. The Indians, observing his predicament and good nature, thought it a good joke and laughed too.

They turned their horses around, sent Father's back to the wagon, and went happily on their way.

Annette L. Dean, Hoquiam, Washington

~ 190 ~

Pretty Kitty Visits Unsuspecting Child

When I was a small girl of seven, I was in the backyard at play when I discovered a pretty kitty crouched under my father's leather shop. I called to the kitty but it wouldn't move, but sat staring at me.

I wanted the kitty badly and ran to have my father come and get it for me. Not realizing what it might be, living so far in the woods, he brought out a gun and killed it. The "kitty" was a young cougar just half grown.

The mother of the cougar, a bigger threat to my life, was killed a few weeks later in the woods nearby.

Jennie Pinkington, Marshfield, Oregon.

~ 191 ~

Girl Sobs in Vain to Save Doomed Man

Ellen Tichenor was the first little white girl to step upon the land at Port Orford, Curry County, Oregon in 1852. The Indians there were very fond of her.

The Indian women presented Ellen with baskets and pretty beaded moccasins and, during the summer months, freshly-gathered berries. She learned to speak their language, which pleased the chief, Tagonecia.

In the summer of 1855, a Coquille River Indian was captured and was charged, on no stronger basis than supposition, with being one of the perpetrators of a massacre that took place on the Coquille River in 1851. He was accordingly sentenced to be hanged. The hanging was to take place from a tree that grew on the edge of Battle Rock.

The day that the Indian was to be hanged was a beautiful one; the town was full of satisfaction and excitement. All were making their way to the rock.

From their temporary reservation at the south end of Port Orford Lake came a slow procession of Indians taking positions on Fort Point, where they could witness the proceedings. Little Ellen Tichenor, playing with her flowers, saw the people gathering. She asked Seth Lount what was the matter. She was told that an Indian was to be hanged. She did not realize what that meant, but was determined to follow the crowd and find out.

The child made her way up the rock and childlike, forced her way to the very front. There stood the Indian by the tree with a rope around his neck. He was speaking and begging for his life.

The child understood his tongue and heard him proclaim his innocence and swear that he was not near the Coquille River at the time of the massacre. She began to realize what was to happen—the Indian had to die. She knew all the white men, and turning to them began to plead for his life.

She cried, begged, and implored. The Indian understood her efforts and his face lit up with hope. Someone angrily asked why the child was not carried away, but the crowd was so dense that there was no getting through.

The child, finding her efforts were useless and unable to stop the proceedings, flung herself on the ground at the feet of the Indian and sobbed uncontrollably. The box was kicked out from under the Indian and his body swung out over the precipice. Little Ellen could only watch in horror as the lifeless body was lowered to the ground.

Ellen married E. W. McGraw, who was Oregon's first United States Attorney. They both lie at rest in the cemetery at Port Orford.

Frank B. Tichenor, Port Orford, Oregon

~ 192 ~

Quick Action Saves Children from Fire

My parents were among those who came to Oregon via covered wagon. When the group that had left Missouri split up, some to go to the California gold fields, others to push on to Oregon, my father chose to earn his living from the soil and established a cabin in the wilderness.

One morning when our parents set out for a neighboring village, being the oldest, I was left in charge of the younger children. They had been gone several hours when the air became thick with the pungent odor of burning wood, and far away on the horizon a great cloud of smoke curled upwards. A forest fire!

As the smoke-laden air became more difficult to breathe, we children huddled together in the cabin thoroughly frightened. At last the crackling of flames reached our ears. I realized that we were doomed unless we could find safer shelter.

Suddenly, Emily, the youngest, suggested that we go down in the well. It had been dry for several seasons.

One by one the children were led from the house and sent down the ladder into the well. At last, when we were all secure within our retreat, the flames reached, and consumed the cabin, and then spread through the dry grass across the small clearing and over the entrance of the well. But we were all saved.

Hours later our parents returned home. They were torn with anguish, expecting to find that we had all perished. Excitement and thankfulness flowed from their mouths as we crawled out of the well-hole one-by-one. Little Emily received the richly deserved praises from everyone for her quick plan that saves our lives.

It was with a light heart that father set to work the next day, building our new home upon a safer, more fertile spot.

JACK MOARLEDGE, Portland, Oregon

'Grandma' Tabitha Moffatt Brown

Part I

A Story of Pioneer Courage and a Woman who's Buckskin Needles Built a University in Oregon

BY LOREN MILLIMAN, Staff Writer,
The Oregonian, January 20, 1935

By all the rules of reason, Grandma Brown should have died enroute to Oregon. That's what the ordinary person would have done, and that's what a good many of her party did do. Just died. But Grandma Brown was made of tougher stuff.

She was sixty-six-years-old when she left Missouri for Oregon to start her life anew. Arriving at Salem on Christmas day, 1846, she took stock of her assets and found a picayune. A 6 ¼ cent piece. That was all. Six and one-quarter cents. Discouraged? Not a bit of it. She bought three steel buckskin needles with that picayune and started sewing. The income from those needles was to grow, and to grow and to make possible the beginning of Pacific University at Forest Grove, Oregon.

Perhaps Grandma Brown faced her future in Oregon so bravely because she had conquered so many handicaps in her recent past. As a young woman, she had been left with three children to care for.

Later, she became so lame from a fall on the ice that she always walked with a decided limp and carried a cane. She had trice faced starvation when wagon train supplies ran out, had suffered a broken arm, the resetting of which she personally supervised.

She and the members of her party had been detoured from the Oregon Trail to the Applegate cut-off in Southern Oregon—a disastrous move that brought the horrors of Umpqua Canyon, where the pioneers struggled and starved through the hub-deep mire.

And when starvation seemed certain, she had gone ahead with Captain John Brown, her 78-year-old brother-in-law, to bring aid to the others. Her aged companion collapsed. They were alone in the woods amidst unseen hostile Indians. How would this 66-year-old woman, riding side-saddle, rescue her companion?

But let Grandma Brown tell her story as she finally did in a fascinating letter, a copy of which today may be read in the white brick library on the oak-covered campus of Pacific University. The letter is addressed to her brother and his wife, Mr. and Mrs. Chester Moffatt, who at that time were living in Claridon, Ohio.

At this juncture, it will be well to mention various persons mentioned in the narrative:

Tabitha Moffatt (Grandma) Brown, writer of the letter, born May 1, 1780; left a widow January 12, 1817, when her husband, Rev. Clark Brown, an Episcopal minister, died.

Orus Brown, her eldest child. Orus came to Oregon in 1843 and returned to Missouri in 1845, to get his mother.

Manthano Brown, her second son. He remained in the East because of illness and because his wife refused to leave her parents.

Pherne Brown Pringle, her youngest child. She and her husband, Virgil K. Pringle, accompanied Grandma Brown to Oregon.

Captain John (Uncle) Brown. A seventy-eight-year-old sea captain, Grandma Brown's brother-in-law, who insisted on accompanying them to Oregon.

Rev. Harvey Clark. He came to Oregon in 1841 as an independent missionary to the Indians and accompanied Orus Brown back to Missouri.

The remarkable letter which tells of Tabitha Brown's soul-trying experiences is dated, "Forest Grove, West Tualatin Plains, Washington County, Oregon Territory, August, 1854." It is addressed to "My Brother and Sister: It is impossible for me to express to you the unspeakable pleasure and happiness your letter of the 29th of June gave me.

"Not hearing from you for so great a length of time, I had concluded myself to be the last one of my father's family remaining here, a pilgrim in the wide world, to complete the work that God intended for me to do. Oh that I could be present with you and Margaret and relate in the hearing of your children the numerous vicissitudes and dangers I have encountered by land and by sea since I parted with you and Margaret in Brimfield! It would fill a volume of many pages. But I will give a few items from the time I left Missouri in April of 1846 for Oregon.

"I expected all three of my children to accompany me but Manthano was detained by sickness and his wife was unwilling to leave her parents. I provided for myself a good ox wagon team and a good supply of what was requisite for the comfort of myself, Captain Brown, and my driver."

When the wagon train set out from Missouri it was gaily decorated. Tabitha Brown had fitted her covered wagon up with a carpet for the floor and a rocking chair for her own comfort. Probably she took along her knitting.

Don't think when you read of her adventures that she was a big, raw-boned woman. Like many of the very determined of her species, she was small and slight and never weighed more than 108 pounds. Blue-gray eyes were set in a delicate face. Her hair was gray. It never turned white. In manner and expression she was always young, those who knew her recorded.

"Uncle John insisted on coming and crossed the Plains on horseback. Orus Brown, with his wife and eight children, and Pherne Brown, with her husband, Virgil K. Pringle, and five children, fitted out their separate families and joined a train of forty more for Oregon, in high expectations of gaining the wished-for land of promise.

"The novelty of our journey, with few exceptions, was pleasing and prosperous until after we had passed Fort Hall. Then we were within eight hundred miles of Oregon City, if we had kept on the old road down the Columbia River. But three of four trains of emigrants were decoyed off by a rascally fellow that came out from the settlement in Oregon assuring us that he had found a new cut-off, that if we would follow him, we would be in the settlement long before those taking the other Old Oregon Trail.

"The idea of shortening a long journey (it was already August) caused us to yield to his advice. He said he would clear the road before us so that we would have no trouble in rolling our wagons after him. He robbed us of what he could by lying and left us to the depredations of Indians and wild beasts, and to starvation.

"Our sufferings, from that time, no tongue can tell. He left a pilot with us who proved to be an excellent man; otherwise we would never have seen Oregon. But God was with us.

"We had sixty miles of desert, without grass or water; mountains to climb, cattle giving out, wagons breaking, emigrants were sick and dying, hostile Indians to guard against night and day to keep from being killed or having our horses and cattle arrowed or stolen.

"We were directed south of Oregon, hundreds of miles into Utah Territory and California; fell in with the Clamotte and Rogue River Indians; lost nearly all our cattle, and passed the Umpqua Mountains twelve miles through."

Mrs. Brown tried to be sure that she kept her prize mare by tying the halter rope around her waist as she sat on her rocking chair in the wagon as the cattle rested. She had taken this precaution after some Indians had made tentative kidnapping attempts. One day, as she sat in her wagon, she pulled on the halter rope and it came back empty into her hand. The Indians had cut the rope and stolen her favorite horse.

"So terrible was the Umpqua Canyon that only a few of the 42 wagons that carried the 150 persons in the train were brought through. Straining cattle, toiling and cursing men bogged down in the defile.

"I rode through in three days at the risk of my life, on horseback, having lost my wagon and all that I had but the one horse I was on. My families were the first that started into the canyon, so they got through the mud and rocks much better than those that came in afterward. Only one wagon came through without something breaking. The canyon was strewn with dead cattle, broken wagons, beds, clothing, and everything but provisions, of which latter we were nearly all destitute.

"Some people were in the canyon two and three weeks before they could get through. Some died without any warning from fatigue and starvation. Others ate of the flesh of cattle that were lying dead by the wayside.

"After struggling through mud, rocks, and water up to our horses' sides, much of the way in crossing this twelve mile mountain, we opened into the beautiful Umpqua Valley inhabited only by Indians and wild beasts. We had still another mountain to cross, the Calipose, besides many more miles to travel through mud, snow, hail, and rain.

"Winter had set in. We were yet a long distance from any white settlement." The word was "Fly, everyone that can, from starvation, except those that are compelled to stay by the cattle to recruit them for further traveling."

Cattle were preferred to horses by the early pioneers because the cows and oxen could nip off mouthfuls of grass and swallow them as they walked. They didn't need to stop and chew each bite as a horse does, but later as the cattle rested, they could lie and chew their cuds.

"Mr. Pringle and Pherne insisted upon my going ahead with their Uncle John to try to save our own lives. They were obliged to stay back a few days to recruit their worn-out cattle. They divided the last bit of bacon, of which I had three slices. I had also a cupful of tea. This was the last division of all we had. No bread.

"We saddled our horses and set off, not knowing that we would ever see each other again. Captain Brown was too old and feeble to render any assistance or protection to me. I was obliged to ride ahead of him as a pilot, hoping to overtake four of five wagons that left camp the day before. Near sunset, we came up with the families that left camp that morning. They had nothing to eat and their cattle had given out.

"We all camped in an oak grove together for the night. In the morning, I divided my last morsel with them and left them to take care of themselves. I hurried Captain Brown to ride fast, so as to overtake another three wagons ahead. We passed beautiful valleys and over high mountains. We saw two Indians, at a distance, during the day.

"In the afternoon, Captain Brown complained of sickness and could only walk his horse, at a distance behind me. He had a swimming in his head and a pain in his stomach. In two or three hours he became delirious and fell from his horse. I was afraid to jump down from my horse to assist him, as it was one that a woman had never ridden before.

"He tried to rise up on his feet, but could not. I rode close to him and set the end of his cane, which I had in my hand, hard into the ground by him to pull up by. I then urged him to walk a little. He tottered alone a few yards and gave out. I then saw a little sunken spot a few steps from me.

"I led his horse down into that and with much difficulty got him once more raised onto his horse. I then requested him to hold fast to the saddle and the horse's mane and I would lead by the bridle. Two miles ahead was another mountain to climb over. As I reached the foot of it, he was able to take the bridle in his own hands, and we passed over safely into a large valley, a wide, extensive, solitary place, but no wagons in sight.

"The sun was now setting, the wind was blowing and the rain was drifting up on the side of the distant mountain. Poor me! I crossed the plain to where three mountain spurs met ravines meandering betwixt the points. Here the shades of night were gathering fast, and I could see the wagon tracks no farther.

"I alighted from my horse, flung off my saddle and saddlebag and tied the horse fast with a lasso rope to a tree. The captain asked what I was going to do. My answer was, 'I am going to camp for the night'.

"He gave a groan and fell to the ground. I gathered my wagon sheet that I had put under my saddle, flung it over a projecting limb of a tree and made me a fine tent. I then stripped the captain's horse and tied him, placed saddles, blankets, bridles, and so forth under the tent, then helped up the bewildered old gentleman and introduced him to his new lodging upon the naked ground.

"His senses were gone. I covered him as well as I could with blankets, and seated myself upon my feet behind him, fully expecting he would be a corpse before morning.

"Pause for a moment and consider my situation. Worse than alone in a savage wilderness, without food, without fire, cold and shivering, a sick old man to care for, wolves fighting and howling all around me. The darkness of night forbade the stars to shine upon me; all was solitary as death. But that same kind Providence that ever has been, was watching over me still. I committed my all to Him and felt no fear.

"As soon as light had dawned, I pulled down my tent, saddled the horses, and found the captain so as to stand on his own feet. Just at this moment, one of the emigrants that I was trying to overtake came to me. He was in search of venison.

"Half a mile beyond, were the wagons I was trying to catch up with, and we were soon there and ate plentifully of fresh venison. Within eight feet of where my tent was set, fresh tracks of two Indians were plainly to be seen, but I did not know that they were there. They killed and robbed a Mr. Newton, only a short distance off, but would not kill his wife, because she was a woman. The Indians killed another man on our cut-off. The rest of the emigrants escaped with their lives.

"We then traveled on and in a few days came to the foot of the Calipose Mountains. Here we were obliged to wait for more emigrants to help cut a road through.

"Here my children and my grandchildren came up with me. A joyful meeting. They had been near starving. Mr. Pringle tried to shoot a wolf, but he was too weak and trembling to hold his rifle steady. They all cried because they had nothing to eat. Just at this time, their son came to them with a supply, and all cried again."

Grandma Brown wrote: "Through all my suffering in crossing the plains, I not once sought relief by the shedding of tears, nor thought we should not live to reach the settlements. The same faith and hope that I ever had in the blessings of kind Providence strengthened in proportion to the trial I had to encounter . . . ."

LOREN MILLIMAN, Staff Writer, The Oregonian

To be continued

"God remains with us in these dark places and valleys, even when we feel out of control, lost, hungry, and angry." Robert J. Miller, *Grief Quest*

~ 193 ~

Strategy Obtains Release of Woman

In the spring of 1870, a caravan of pioneers trekked their way from Oklahoma to Oregon. Among them were Monroe Stayles, his wife, and their twelve-year-old daughter Inez.

The Stayles family camped in the Willamette Valley near Oregon City. Upon the slopes of the nearby hills were numerous Indian teepees. All of the Indians seemed friendly, but the Sayles soon found reason to worry because some of the Indians were constantly watching their daughter.

Inez was large, well developed for her age, and a very attractive girl, having inherited her smoldering dark eyes and raven-black hair from Spanish ancestry.

One day, a chief, in company with three other Indians, rode up to the Stayles camp. One of the Indians dismounted and informed Mr. Stayles that the chief desired his daughter, Inez. The chief offered many robes, horses and furs for her. Of course, Mr. Stayles refused to accept the offer.

A few days later when Mrs. Stayles went to the spring for water, she failed to return. Inez and her father, becoming worried, started out in search of her.

They had not gone far when they were met by an Indian who told them that some of his tribe had captured Mrs. Stayles and were holding her until the daughter would be delivered into the hands of their chief.

"If your daughter is not brought to the chief before sunrise, at sunrise your woman will be scalped and burned at the stake," said the messenger.

Realizing that it would be useless to try to rescue his wife by force, and even with the help of the few white settlers in the vicinity, because the Indians outnumbered them, Stayles quickly decided to resort to strategy.

The messenger was told to inform the chief that unless Mrs. Stayles was released, the "great spirit" would send his vengeance and disease upon his whole tribe.

The day came to its close, but Mrs. Stayles was not returned, and husband and daughter feared for her fate.

After darkness fell, Mr. Stayles took the fireworks which some of the children in the caravan had left over from their celebration of the last Independence Day on the trail. With these in a bag he approached the darkened Indian camps. When within about a quarter of a mile he set off several rockets which exploded and fell in a massive shower of brilliant colors over the Indian camps.

The Indians, believing that fire was falling from heaven, cowered in terror, and soon, Mrs. Stayles was released.

The following day the Stayles family resumed their journey, making their way to Southern Oregon.

JULIETTE FRAZIER, Cornelius, Oregon

~ 194 ~

White Man Smart; Also Smart Injun

In early 1880's in Oregon, my brother J.D. and I built a sawmill on the banks of the Long Tom River in Lane County six miles south of Smithfield. There was an Indian camp on one side of the mill and a white man named Kaiser lived across the road from us. One of the Indians named John had a pony and Kaiser had a cow.

One day, while the mill men were eating their mid-day lunch, the Indian came along (in the meantime, the white man's cow had died) and Kaiser said to the Indian, "John how will you trade your horse for my cow?"

The Indian said, "Me trade even my horse for your cow."

Kaizer said, "All right, it's a trade" and turned and said to my mill men, "Boys, you heard that the horse is mine and the cow is John's."

As the Indian started to walk away Kaizer said, "By the way, the cow is dead." The Indian stopped, turned and answered, "Huh, your horse dead, too."

An hour later we saw the Indian and his woman in Kaiser's pasture skinning the cow. For some time afterwards, when we would see Kaizer, we would ask when he was going to skin his horse, but he would name no date.

This Indian was an old chief that had been friendly to the whites. They did not send him, and a few others, to the reservations, but allowed them to live as they had been.

B. F. HOWARD, Shedd, Oregon

~ 195 ~

Death Extended as Matter of Kindness

Indians, like the peoples of any other race, vary accordingly. Whereas one tribe may possess all the traits of treachery and savage impulse, yet another tribe will be found with a reasonably high moral code of living. This story was told to me, and it serves as an interesting study of the many phases of Indian character.

An immigrant from Missouri had left the wagon train to do some trapping in the dangerous Blackfeet country. Against all advice, he became reckless in his wanderings and at length wound up a captive of the Blackfeet. The punishment meted out to him was a horrible death at the stake

As hot coals were placed over dry faggots and ignited, an arrow suddenly sped through the air and found its mark in the heart of the captive. A wandering member of another tribe, who perhaps knew the victim, had mercifully put an end to his suffering with a well-placed arrow from some hidden retreat.

JOHN LEACH, Portland, Oregon

'Grandma' Tabitha Moffatt Brown

Part 2

Concluding a Story of Great Pioneer Courage, Determination, and Humanitarian Generosity

BY LOREN MILLIMAN, Staff Writer,
The Oregonian, January 27, 1935

The last installment ended where Grandma Brown's party, now at the point of starvation, were working their way north in Southwest Oregon toward the headwaters of the Willamette River. Even with some of the members of their party dead from exhaustion and starvation, and with others killed by Indians, the wagon train slowly traveled their route, in a general way that follows the present Pacific Highway (I-5).

Many on the members of the party suffered from intense fear, but not Grandma Brown. She continues:

"Winter had set in. We were many days crossing the Calipose Mountains, able to travel only a mile of two each day. Trees along the route had to be cut and opened for us, and the mountain passes were covered with snow.

"With much difficulty we crossed over the headwaters of the Willamette, followed the river down a few days and gave up the idea of reaching the settlements before Spring returned. Provisions gave out, so Mr. Pringle set off on horseback looking for a settlement for relief, not knowing how long he'd be gone, or whether he'd get back at all.

"After a week or so, our scanty provisions were gone. We were again in a state of starvation. Many tears were shed during the day, by all but one. I had been through many trials, sufficient to teach me that tears could avail nothing for eternity. Through my suffering in crossing the Plains, I not once sought relief by the shedding of tears, nor thought we should not ever reach the settlements. The same amount of hope that I ever had, in the blessings of kind Providence, strengthened in relation to the trial I had to encounter.

"It was the only alternative or last resort, for at that present time, Mr. Pringle's eldest son had shot down one of his father's best young oxen and dressed it. It had not one ounce of fat about it. We then had something to eat, poor bones to pick, but without any salt.

"I must now digress a little. In the year 1843, my son, Orus Brown had traveled to what was then known as West Tualatin Plains, and settled on land of which later became the town site of the city of Forest Grove. He had built a small cabin and barn of logs. He also split a large quantity of fence rails, L. C. Brown of Hillsboro recalls. He then started back to Missouri to get me and the rest of our family. He sold his property to Rev. Harvey Clark, who came to Oregon in 1841 as an independent missionary to the Indians. Rev. Mr. Clark offered five hundred bushels of wheat, which had not yet been grown, for the land.

"Land was cheap, but the labor Orus had performed was worth the wheat, so he agreed to sell. Although Orus worked hard, he was always 'poor as a crow' because he had such a large family. When he returned to Oregon, he returned without a penny. He did receive all of the wheat he had been promised for the land."

Confusion in the handling of land claims in Washington County had caused the official recordings to be lacking the names of those who were living on the claim at the time, so the land on which Forest Grove has sprung up is known as the Clark Donation Land Claim, although Orus Brown had first settled on it.

Grandma Brown continues, speaking of Orus's trip back to Missouri:

"When within four or five hundred miles of their destination, he and the three men with him were taken by the Pawnee Indians and robbed. When allowed to leave the Pawnee camp, Orus had been given his gun and ammunition because he won the admiration of the Indians by helping them instead of pleading for his life as some of the others in the party had to do. On foot they started on. They traveled across the plains for several days without sighting any game.

"Finally Orus shot a skunk. They did not build a fire to cook the skunk meat for fear of attracting the Indians again, so they cut chunks off the odoriferous animal and sat down to eat. When Rev. Mr. Clark suggested that they give thanks, Orus replied, "No! I'll be damned if anybody is going to thank the Lord for this raw meat!"

Grandma Brown's letter continues:

"In 1865, when we all started for Oregon, Orus was appointed pilot of a wagon train, having crossed the plains twice before. His wagon train was six days ahead of ours and had taken the old emigrant route. They reached the settlements in September."

Orus Brown's family reached Forest Grove on October 7, after camping for several days to rest up at Oregon City, then one day somewhere near the present town of Tigard and another day on the Hill Farm in part of what is now Hillsboro.

Indians from the Jason Lee Mission hunting in Southern Oregon encountered the wagon train in which his mother was traveling. The Indians learned of the desperate condition of Mrs. Brown and her party and carried word to Orus. His action then is explained by Grandma Brown:

"Orus heard of the suffering emigrants at the south and set off, in haste, with four pack horses and provisions for our relief. He met Mr. Pringle, turned him about, and in a few days they were in our camp. Before they arrived, we had all retired to rest in our tents, hoping to forget our troubles, until daylight should remind us again of our sad fate. In the gloomy stillness of the night, footsteps of horses were heard rushing toward our tents. Directly, a 'Halloo!' It was the well-known voices of Orus Brown and Virgil Pringle. Who can realize the joy?

"Orus, by his persuasive perseverance, encouraged us to more effort to reach the settlements. Five miles from where we had camped, we fell in with a company of half-breed Frenchmen and Indians with pack horses. We hired six of them and pushed ahead again. Our provisions were becoming short. We were once more on allowance, until we reached the first settlers. There our hardest struggles were ended.

"On Christmas Day, at 2 o'clock p.m., I entered the house of a Methodist minister, the first home I had set my foot in for nine months. He soon requested me to take the whole charge of his house and family through the winter. His wife was as ignorant and useless as a heathen goddess. My services compensated for my own board and Captain Brown's through the winter.

"For two or three weeks of my journey down the Willamette River, I had felt something in the end of my glove finger, which I supposed to be a button. On examination, at my new home in Salem, I found it to be a six-and-a-quarter cent piece. This was the whole of my cash capital to commence business in Oregon.

"'With it, I purchased three needles. I traded off some of my old clothes to the Indian women for buckskins, and worked them into gloves for the Oregon ladies and gentlemen, which cleared me upwards of $30 extra of boarding.

"In May, 1847, I left Salem, which is now our seat of government, for Oregon City, thirty miles down the Willamette. I went in an open boat in company with my Methodist minister and family. From there, down the Columbia River to the Pacific Ocean.

"Here I spent the summer at a settlement south of the bay. At this time, there were but ten families residing there. I boarded with a

Mr. Pray and lady, missionaries from Ballston, New York, a very genteel family. I spent the summer in visiting and bathing in the ocean.

"In October, I started in an open boat up the river for Salem again, with the wind and tide against us. We were thirteen days in reaching Oregon City. Here I was within twenty miles of the Tualatin Plains, Orus Brown's location. It would not do for a mother to pass by.

"I luckily found a man with an empty wagon going out, who lived neighbor to Orus. I gave him two dollars for my passage, calculating to spend two weeks only with Orus and his family, and to reach Salem before the winter rains set in.

"We went to a Presbyterian meeting on Sunday. After the meeting, Orus gave me an introduction to Mr. and Mrs. Clark, missionaries from New York, who came here in 1840. They invited me home with them to spend a few days.

"Winter set in. The Clarks pressed me hard to spend the winter with them. I accepted the invitation. Our intimacy ever since has been more like a mother and children, than that of strangers. They are the same age as my own children, and look to me for advice and counsel equally as much.

"In October, 1847, came news from the suffering emigrants of much sickness and death on the plains, and many poor orphan children left to be cared for by strangers.

"I said to Mr. Clark, 'Why has Providence frowned on me and left me poor in this world? Had he blessed me with riches, as he has many others, I know right well what I would do.' 'What would you do?' was his question. 'I would establish myself in a comfortable house and receive all poor children and be a mother to them.'

"He fixed his keen eye upon me, and asked if I was candid in what I said. 'Yes, I am.' 'If so', he replied, 'I will try with you, and see what effort we can make'."

Mrs. Clark had been conducting a school for children in their log house, so the idea of a school was suggested to the right man. He had been working on the idea of establishing a permanent educational institution at Forest Grove. When he heard of Grandma Brown's plans, he donated 200 acres of his land as a foundation fund. Later still, he contributed another large tract to be used to assist in paying the teachers.

"Mr. Clark would take an agency, and try to get assistance to establish a school in the plain. I should go into the old log meeting house, and receive all the children, rich and poor. Those parents that were able were to pay one dollar per week for board, tuition, washing, and all.

"I agreed to labor one year for nothing. Mr. Clark and others agreed to assist as far as they were able in furnishing provisions, providing there was not a sufficiency of cash coming in to sustain the poor. The time fixed was March, 1848.

"The last Saturday night in April, after visiting my children in Salem, I arrived at the Tualatin Plains again. I found everything prepared for me to go into the old meeting house and 'cluck up' my 'chickens' the next Monday morning.

"The neighbors had collected what broken knives and forks, tin pans and dishes they could part with for the Oregon pioneer to commence housekeeping. I had a well-educated lady from the East, a missionary's wife, for a teacher. My family increased rapidly"

Mrs. Jane Kinney Smith, who came to Oregon at the age of ten with a pioneer Yamhill County family later recorded her impression of the school.

"It was set in a natural park amid clumps of oak trees and occasional groups of firs. A small swale ran through the park. Meat for the boarders was furnished regularly by a pioneer named Black. Grandma Brown had a fine kitchen garden, and she set a neat, tasty table with a white tablecloth—a rare article in those days."

Spoon holders made of cardboard, covered with fancy calico, also caught the eye of Jane Smith when she arrived, early in the summer of 1848.

"On Sundays, Grandma Brown wore a black dress and bonnet, but week-days a large striped delaine with flowers in the stripes. At home, she wore caps which she trimmed with pillow lace that she had made herself. She also embroidered her own collars and taught the girls in the boarding school to embroider and sew."

Word of the Whitman massacre reached the scattered frontiersmen, and they took hurried council of the best means of defending themselves. They decided to build a stockade on a farm two miles east of the little log church which was then serving as the school.

Taking her cane, Grandma Brown limped down the street, confronted some of the men and boys and persuaded them that they could, and should, fortify the academy. They got busy and dug a trench on what is now Pacific University campus. Watch was kept day and night, but the feared Indian attack did not materialize.

Indians were friendly with Grandma Brown while she gave reason for the friendliness. When one of their children was sick, they brought it to her. She took it into her home and nursed it until it was well.

"In the summer, they put me up a boarding house. I now had thirty boarders, of both sexes, and of all ages from four-years-old to twenty-one. I managed them and did all my work, except washing. That part was done by the scholars.

"In the spring of 1849, we called for trustees. Had eight appointed. They voted me the whole charge of the boarding house free of rent. I was to provide for myself. The price of board was established at $2.00 per week. Whatever I made over and above my expenses was my own.

"In 1851, I had forty in my family at $2.50 per week. I mixed, with my own hands, 3,423 pounds of flour in less than five months. Mr. Clark, for the establishment of the school, gave over to the trustees a quarter section of land for a town plot. A large and handsome building is upon the spot of ground we selected at the first starting."

The "large and handsome building" is still used at Pacific University and is known as the "Chem Shack." It is the oldest building west of the Rocky Mountains used continuously for educational purposes.

Men came from all over the Tualatin Valley, bringing their families with them, to erect the two-story frame building. It was a gala time for the whole community as the families camped on the grounds. The women cooked the meals while the men hewed the timbers. The substantial frame has preserved it longer than most pioneer structures.

"It has been under town incorporation for two years, and at the last session of the legislature, a charter was granted for a university, to be called Pacific University, with a limitation of $50,000. The president and professor are already here from Vermont. The teacher and his lady in the academy are from New York.

"You must excuse my troubling you with such lengthy narrative. I have endeavored to give general outlines of what I have done. You must be your own judges, whether I have been doing good or evil. I have labored hard for myself, the public and the rising generation.

"But I now have quit hard work, and live at my ease. I am independent as to worldly concerns. I own a very nicely finished white frame house on a lot in town, within a short distance from the public buildings that I let out for $100 per year.

"I have eight other town lots, with out-buildings, worth $150 each. I have eight cows and a number of young cattle. The cows I let out for their milk and one-half the increase. I have rising $1,100 cash due me, $400 of it I have donated to the university, besides $100 I gave to the academy three years ago. This much I have accumulated by my own industry, independent of my children, since I drew a six-and-a-quarter cent coin from my gloved finger.

"Now I must give you a short description of the beautiful scenery of this delightful and healthful country.

"Grass is green here all winter, and the cattle get their living without being fed. Snow seldom lies on the ground longer than a few days.

"Large improvements extend out into the plain in every direction. You may see at all times, large bands of cattle, horses, and people passing in every direction morning and evening. We have a cool refreshing breeze from the sea. The nights are cool and pleasant. We sleep under almost as much clothing in summer as in winter. I wish you could see this beautiful country.

"We have no prevalent diseases. Most of the deaths that occur here are emigrants, whose systems were diseased before leaving the states. It is very seldom that we hear of a child's dying that was born in Oregon.

"I have not time nor space to give you the Oregon prices current. Everything in the farming line has been very high, and merchandise very low, but at this time, all is low.

"Horses, last spring, were valued at from $200 to $300. American cows, $100. Last spring I could have taken $800 for my eight. Now I could not get more than $60 per head.

"Adieu for the present. TABITHA BROWN."

Harvey Scott, the first graduate of Pacific University, and later famous as the Editor of *The Oregonian*, always insisted that Grandma Brown was wholly responsible for the school's being. Members of the class of 1867 provided a marker in the form of a petrified stump which stands on the site of the first log cabin where Grandma Brown started her boarding school.

Cholera on the plains caused Grandma Brown's group of orphans to increase rapidly. The early pioneers on the way to Oregon had a comparatively easy time of it because there was plenty of grass for their oxen although the trail wasn't well marked and there were no stores of supplies along the route.

"The later trains of slowly toiling oxen found grass was scarce, although stores with supplies for human beings had been set up. But cholera infested the camping places.

Gold in California was another reason why "Tabby" Brown, as she was known to her family, found her flock of "chickens" increasing phenomenally. As the '49-ers rushed off to the southern gold fields, their children were left to others to care for or sent to the school until they returned.

In the sunset of her years, Grandma Brown encouraged and cheered up Sidney Harper Marsh, who at twenty-eight became the first President of Pacific University. Lack of accommodations forced him to live in the unfinished second story of what is now the Chem Shack, then the principal building on the campus. He had to climb to his rooms by ladder and make his bed on trestles standing on joists of the unfloored rooms. He was the son of a president of the University of Vermont and unused to the hardships of a pioneer.

On many occasions, when he was on the point of giving up and returning to the East where conditions were more advanced, he would talk to Grandma Brown. Although the discouragements seemed overwhelming to him, the good soul would cheer him up. She built in him a grim determination to "stay it out" than to return to the comforts of the East.

Practically all her life, Grandma Brown lived with, or near, her son Orus, but she grew too old and feeble to care for herself, so she moved to Salem where her daughter, Mrs. Pherne Pringle, lived.

She died there May 4, 1858,. She is buried at Salem.

LOREN MILLIMAN, Staff Writer, *The Oregonian*

~ 196 ~

Vagrants Frightened When 'Corpse' Speaks

A very few old Oregon City pioneers still remember this Halloween incident.

A not too scrupulous physician, who had located in Portland, engaged the services of a couple of vagrants to exhume the body of a man who was scheduled to be buried on his farm on the outskirts of Oregon City.

"You will follow the funeral today, and locate the grave, and then tomorrow, after dark, you will hire a team and light wagon. Take the body, rebury the coffin, and bring the corpse to my establishment for dissection. I will pay you well and stand all expenses, and here is ten dollars to carry on with."

The two Irishmen followed their instructions to the letter. They exhumed the body, and propped it up between them on the seat, well wrapped in a heavy overcoat and slouch hat, pulled down.

"Say Moike" said one, "sure 'tis Halloween and I feel a bit queer. Let's stop at the Last Chance Saloon and get something to hearten us up like!" "Shure, but what about our passenger? Guess he's not goin' nowhere." They tied up the horses and went in.

Just then a man came out of a nearby stable and spoke to the supposed driver. "Say, mister, will you give me a lift if you are going to Portland? I am broke and must get there tonight." He repeated his plea, laying his hand upon the man's cold, stiff arm. He immediately "caught on," thinking it all a Halloween prank. Quickly, he took down the body and placed it in a straw stall in the stable. Donning the overcoat and hat, he sat up stiffly in the driver's seat, replacing the cold corpse and waited motionless.

Presently the men, somewhat the worse for their libations, clambered in on either side of the supposed "corpse", cast off the lines, and shouting "Gerrrupowish!" were on their way. As they bounced along, Pat spoke to the driver: "Say, Moike, if I didn't know this feller was dead I'd say he feels kinda warm."

In a sepulchral tone the "corpse" spoke: "If you had been in hell for the last twenty four hours, you would be warm too."

With a wild yell they fell out on opposite sides of the wagon and began running for their lives. One was brought back gibbering with fright; the other was caught about a mile away, floundering in the light snow, half dead with cold and almost crazed with fear.

The driver went on to town, put up the team at a livery stable to be called for, and went his merry way. I never learned what the doctor did to straighten out this tangle when the body was later found hidden in the horse stall.

MINERVA THESSING OATFIELD, Milwaukie, Oregon

~ 197 ~

Sweetbriar Tells of Charming Romance

On February 15, 1852, Seattle's first families, the Dennys and the Borens drove their stakes in the soil which now lies under the pavements and buildings in the downtown section of the city.

Among the land claimants was David Denny, who filed his claim in his father's name because he was a year under the legal age of 21.

David was destined to be the city's first bridegroom. The bride was Louisa Boren. The courtship, which had begun in Illinois and continued as the two families migrated across the plains, blossomed into real love during the summer of 1852.

During that summer, other emigrants staked land claims as well. A settlement grew up which was first called "Duwamps" and then later in the summer was changed to "Seattle" in honor of an Indian chief.

David worked hard clearing his claim and making plans for his cabin by day. At night he courted Louisa. Early in 1853, the little log cabin, located approximately at the foot of the present Denny Way, was completed. It lacked windows and the floor was dirt, but on January 23, 1853, Seattle's first wedding was solemnized.

Louisa planted some sweetbriar seeds, which soon grew in such abundance that young Mrs. Denny was known in the settlement as the "sweetbriar bride." The plant spread so rapidly that it finally outlived the young couple, and it was not until 1930 that the ruthless jaws of a steam shovel, on Denny Way, uprooted the last traces of that bride of long ago.

JACK OSBORNE, Portland, Oregon

~ 198 ~

Was This Pioneer Settler Chagrined?

My father, J. W. Salisbury, was one of the first settlers on Big Butter Creek, between Pendleton and Heppner, in Eastern Oregon. He fought in the early Indian wars and in consequence didn't have a very high regard for the noble Indian.

The Indians were great thieves and beggars and they used to pester my father to death.

One day, a tiny little eighty or ninety pound Indian woman came to my father, asking for a sack of potatoes that leaned against the cellar wall.

My father was a large man, six feet tall, weighing about 190 pounds. He knew the sack of potatoes would weigh about 100 pounds. So, with a twinkle in his eye, he told her she could have them, if she could carry them.

Imagine his embarrassment when that little woman, grumbling, maneuvered the sack onto her back and waddled away.

MADGE M. HEADLEY, La Center, Washington

~ 199 ~

Brief Ceremony—but It Worked

Daniel Waldo, an early Justice of the Peace in the Willamette Valley, had the proverbial "heart of gold," his friends agreed, but no one could deny that he was a very profane man.

His wife was quite unable to break him of the habit of swearing, especially when he became excited, and it seems likely that the poor woman eventually abandoned the attempt.

It happened one day that while a Mrs. Jesse Looney, a neighbor, was visiting the Waldos, a young couple rode up on horseback, asked Waldo if he was the Justice of the Peace and, when informed that he was, stated that they wished to be married.

Waldo escorted them to the parlor, asked them to join hands and then cleared his throat nervously while he groped for the appropriate words. Finding none that exactly suited him, he suddenly blurted: "I now pronounce you man and wife."

The abruptness of the ceremony did not seem to satisfy anyone present. Even Waldo realized that the essential air of sanctity was lacking. Catching the eye of his wife and Mrs. Looney, Waldo hastened to tie the marital knot a little tighter by adding, "By God."

With the proper inflection of course, the words would have added just the proper note of holiness, but the habit of a lifetime was too difficult to break and Waldo pronounced them with the inflection of a blasphemous oath.

No great harm was done however, for the couple went on their way, happily married for many years.

HERBERT RUBENTHWAITE, Portland, Oregon

~ 200 ~

White Man Regrets Ardent Flirtation

This is a yarn of the good old days when my father was a young man of nineteen. After completing the mathematical calculation, I place the date in the fall of 1883. Daily mail services and fresh fruit were unknown luxuries in Curry County, Oregon, at that time.

Gold Beach was a mining town, and since transportation was limited to the chance visits of an occasional freight wagon hauling mining equipment, such luxuries as watermelons and cantaloupes were practically unknown until a wise old Indian, who had a farm up the Rogue River, discovered that the white miners, at the mouth of the river, would pay big money for these delicacies.

The old warrior also owned a huge canoe, and every fall he made trips down the river with the canoe loaded to the gunwales with melons. They sold like hot cakes and he did a land-office business. One day he paddled down the river with his wife, his daughter and the load of melons in the canoe. It was late in the afternoon when they landed on a gravel bar above the town. The old chief decided it was too late to do any trading, so they camped on the river bank for the night.

All would have went well with the melon expedition had not a half dozen white men happened by. I sadly admit our Father was one of the party. The canoe load of melons caught their eyes and they went into a huddle to elect a purchasing agent.

Then, one of the party caught sight of the Indian maiden. The huddle lasted five minutes, and then five white men approached the canoe, where the old chief and his woman were guarding their merchandise. The Indian girl was at the campfire a good hundred yards away. She looked up with a broad grin as the sixth white man slipped quietly up the bank and approached her with a Don Juan smile.

The old chief had a difficult time making a sale to the five white men who wanted melons. They argued and dickered for half an hour before they would buy, and instead of leaving they sat down on the gravel bar and calmly ate their melons.

The old chief and his wife stood guard over the canoe. They knew white men. Suddenly the woman pointed to the campfire and said a few words in her native tongue. The sixth white man was seated at the campfire with their daughter! What was more to the point he was unquestionably holding her on his lap.

The old chief reached into the canoe and instead of a watermelon he produced a Winchester. "White men stand back." He ordered. They stood back and the big rifle thundered. The Romeo at the camp leaped to his feet with a wild yell as the bullet sent the embers of the campfire flying. He bolted up the gravel bar with the speed of a frightened deer as the old chief worked the lever of his rifle and sent gravel flying about the feet of the frightened white man.

A small creek emptied into the river at the end of the bar. It was a swimming show for any man who wanted to cross that point, for it was a good twelve feet wide, but the fleeing Don Juan cleared it with one tremendous bound. He disappeared into the brush and the old chief lowered his gun. He turned to the five white men who were rolling on the sand bar, helpless with laughter.

"Damn fine jump," the smiling chief commented. Dad swears there was a twinkle in his eye.

JACK WOODRUFF, Bandon, Oregon

Columbia River "Medicine Rock"

L. G. Richards, Staff Writer, *The Oregonian*

Is it fish, fowl or fantasy? Is it altar, art work, petroglyph, medicine rock, sacrificial stone, or merely some surviving sample of a rock age comic strip? Whatever it is, the stone that sits so smugly on the banks of the Columbia River is shrouded deep in mystery.

The "Sacrificial Stone" is a mighty lava boulder on the Washington bank of the river at Fisher' Landing, ten miles east of Vancouver, Washington on the Evergreen Highway. It has the sinister shape of a sarcophagus or an altar of ancient times. It is also locally known as the "Medicine Rock".

It's length is more than nine feet, its width six feet, its weight many tons. Deep carved in the six-foot end of this astonishing stone is a figure unlike anything recorded in the local annals of archeology or the halls of history. It is a mocking mixture of the mysterious and the comic. It makes you laugh or it makes you shiver. Maybe both.

No picture can quite do it justice. It has the head and the neck of a sort of man, with great round eyes carved deep in the rock and a natural beak of rock emphasized for a nose or proboscis. The lines throughout are deep and crude in design, if not in workmanship.

It has two hands, or maybe they're claws or flippers with five fingers carefully carved. It has two plain legs like the legs of a pair of red woolen underwear. So far it has the semblance of a human figure, however puckerish and caricatured.

But at the sides of the "body" are parallel curved lines that might be intended to represent ribs, or the legs of bugs, or just something the artist added to bring gray hair to the beards of archeologists who might subsequently dig up the masterpiece.

Further to confuse the issue of the right side at the hip line the unknown chiseler added a short fin, flapper, leg or claw resembling the upper arms, but shorter. Apparently a similar excess appendage, now cracked away from the main stone structure, once adorned the left side.

Most inexplicable of all in the center of the figure is a bowl or hollow about one foot in diameter and seven inches deep carved in the center of the rock just almost big enough to hold two quarts of blood from a human sacrificial body or perhaps a half gallon of whiskey. Such a feature is found in no other artifacts of this or any other area.

Although it looks like something you see in a drop of dirty water under a microscope, or the scribbling of some Stone Age student who gets tired of dissecting dinosaurs and drew a picture of the professor when he wasn't looking.

The popular tradition is that the early Indians, or a race earlier than the Indians, once offered human sacrifices on this stone to some great god or other, or merely to appease the elements to assure an abundance of fish and other food.

It is argued that the receptacle in the rock was so placed as to catch the blood that would flow from the victim pierced in the neck or heart by the sacrificial knife—and obsidian knives have been found nearby, although they are no more "sacrificial" than stone knives found elsewhere.

There is no record of human sacrifices among any of the Coast or Columbia Indians or their predecessors, however, except the occasional slaughter of slaves to be buried with their masters.

Self-identified scientists who have seen the figures have called it "The Great Bear of the North," or a turtle or other totem of some early Indian tribe. Others, these the commonsense unimaginative citizens, have guessed that the whole business is but the idle nonsense of idle Indian hands as they squatted about the communal mortar in the center of the rock. The depression in the rock, however, is not the size or shape of the typical mortar and shows none of the signs of such use.

W.K. Peery of Washougal, Washington, a thorough student of the culture of the Indians of this immediate area, hazards the guess that this may have served as a "medicine rock" for some shaman of the early

Indians, a secret place where he came to commune with the spirits that served him and to mix his mysterious medicinal concoctions.

In support of this hypothesis he notes that the feet of the figure point directly at the mirage-like outline of worshiped Mount Hood in the distance as if the eyes of the figure were fixed.

The Columbia Indian of historic times, however, did not mix any physical "medicines" or charms so far as known, according to Professor Verne Ray of the Anthropology Department of the University of Washington. Neither did they sacrifice human or other victims in any religious rites.

Neither did they carve totems, except in wood, and that practice was limited to the Coast tribes of Alaska.

The face of the figure, however, in the Indian school of carving, might have represented a bird, probably an eagle judging by the beak.

The body might have been that of a bear or a human or a combination of all three, intended to symbolize the virtues of each. Or it might have no significance, except as an exercise in response to the "art urge."

Professor Ray would estimate the age of the 'object d'art' in hundreds rather than thousands of years. How many hundreds no one knows. Amateur geologists estimate the age of the lava boulder on which the figure is carved as more than 1,000, but probably less than 5,000 years.

The fact that the Indians of 100 years ago had not even a legend concerning the stone is not significant, Professor Ray believes.

Unfortunately, the public cannot be allowed to draw its own conclusions as to the history or meaning of this 'object d'art'. The mighty stone nestles intimately in the backyard of Mr. and Mrs. H. W. Westgate's home at Fisher's Landing, surrounded by garden tools, clothes lines, woodsheds and a small greenhouse.

Mr. Westgate's hobby is the growing of dahlias which annually take prizes in the Portland dahlia shows and the location of the stone makes it impossible to permit the public to view it, the Westgates state quite firmly.

L. G. Richards, Staff Writer, *The Oregonian*

~ 201 ~

Indian Woman Asks for Gift of Child

My grandparents, William Wade Watson and Mary Ann Watson, successfully made the trip across the plains in 1858. They first settled near Olympia, Washington.

Grandfather was one of the pioneer preachers in the Campbellite Church; later called the Christian Church. He was a "circuit rider" among the scattered white settlers and neighboring tribes of Indians. He learned to speak to the Indians in the Chinook jargon and made many friends among them.

He made no distinction between white people and Indians, inviting persons of both races to visit his home. Among those who came was an elderly Indian woman who was childless. Either death had taken her children or she had failed to have a child. Grandmother could never learn which it was. In either case she was somewhat demented about her "disgrace", as it was considered, among the Indians.

The Indian woman was extremely interested in Grandmother's six children. The youngest, Perry, was less than a year old. One day she was so bold as to ask Grandmother for the baby.

"Are there no babies in your tribe that have no mother?" asked Grandmother.

"Ah-h-h, none," the Indian woman answered, sadly.

Grandmother then told her of all the trouble she had been put through bringing Perry across the plains when he was only six-months old. Surely she could not part with him after such a trying experience.

The Indian woman went away greatly disappointed. In about a week she returned heavily laden with a bundle of blankets and trinkets, possibly everything she owned. She threw them down on the kitchen floor and eagerly begged grandmother to trade the baby for her possessions. Of course Grandmother was very sympathetic, but would not trade her baby for anything.

The Indian woman took her belongings and unhappily went away into the forest, never to be seen again.

MRS. IMOGENE HUMPHREY, Salem, Oregon

~ 202 ~

Folks Shocked When Woman Rides Horse

During an uprising of the Nez Perce Indians, along about 1878, my father was captain of a fort being built near Anatone, Washington. The settlers were working frantically to get the huge logs in place to form a corral, inside of which the cattle were to be placed.

The fort was never attacked, but we experienced one incident, which I have never forgotten, as in those days it was a surprising sight, indeed, to see a woman ride astride a pony.

One-half mile from the fort was the new home of a Mr. and Mrs. Coop. Mr. Coop worked on the fort, often leaving his wife at home with her two small children. Outside the cabin door a pony was tied, saddled, and ready for emergencies.

One day, Mrs. Coop thought she saw a band of Indians approaching. So she jumped astride her pony and headed for the fort, after placing one child in front and one behind her. Kicking the pony in the ribs and yelling at the top of her voice, "Indians are coming," she charged into view, to the consternation of the prim settlers.

The small children were herded inside the fort and the women stood guard with loaded guns, while the men tried desperately to finish the stockade before the attack. Two scouts were sent out. They soon returned with good news. It was only a band of wild horses.

MRS. FRANK MOSSMAN, Portland, Oregon

~ 203 ~

Old Yellow Pooch Faithful to Boots

My grandfather, the late W. C. Stillwell, was born in Belle Plains, Iowa, in the year 1845. When he was nine-years-old, he left for Oregon, going via the Santa Fe Trail.

He had an old yellow dog that guarded everything Grandfather owned. Grandfather's boots were worn beyond repair so his mother decided to discard them one night where they camped along a river on the trail.

When they left in the morning, the dog was not around, but had apparently gone hunting for rabbits. The wagon train went on, thinking he would catch up with them. The dog returned to the old camping ground and seeing the old boots there, stood guard over them, as he had always done before.

As Grandfather's wagon train went on, they began to worry about the dog. One day as the wagon train was camped, a mule team caught up with them. The family asked if they had seen the dog. The team driver reported that he had seen an old scrawny yellow dog guarding over a pair of worn out boots. When anyone tried to go near them, he would snarl and bark.

The dog was never seen again.

WARREN TUNISON, Portland, Oregon

~ 204 ~

Danish Folk Learn to Love Country

In the early 1880's, my Danish grandparents left their orderly, comfortable way of living in their native country, and came to live on an Oregon homestead.

Their three boys (the youngest became my father), had immigrated to America before their parents and had built a log cabin where their three claims joined together. This was a few miles south of Crown Point on the Columbia River Highway.

There was no wilder country in Oregon fifty five years ago. The forests were dense and dark, the narrow roads steep, winding and often impassable in wet or snowy weather.

One of the incidents they told came near to discouraging them. They had raised two fine hogs for their winter's meat. When the work of butchering and salting down the meat was completed, the big barrel was covered with a slab of wood and placed in the cellar which had been dugout in the side-hill below the house.

Everyone had gone to bed when suddenly a terrific scrambling and squealing began in the cellar. Grandpa grabbed his gun and went out to investigate.

By the stench he immediately knew a skunk was there. He didn't need his gun, however, for Mr. Polecat has gotten the heavy lid off the pork barrel, fell in and drowned in the brine. None of the precious meat was salvageable and had to be buried.

Several years later the sons sold the farms and moved to Portland. They thought the old folks would be pleased at the prospect of leaving the wild hill country. However, they had by this time, fallen too much in love with the life on the mountain and moved to a neighboring farm; part of which was later donated as the site for Vista House, a viewpoint structure overlooking the beautiful Columbia River Gorge, near Corbett, Oregon.

MRS. FRED ANDERSON, Portland, Oregon

~ 205 ~

Lucky Strike Len Given Phony Cigar

In the early days of the old west, there was a character in a small frontier town that was known as Lucky Strike Len. He was notoriously famous for his never-ceasing stock of tales, all of them fictitious, and concerning the number of finds he had made in the gold fields.

Now and then, Len did find someone gullible enough to grubstake him. At such time, he would leave town with a gallon jug under his arm and disappear into the hills. When he came into town again, it was always with a hard-luck story that he had run out of provisions.

If Lucky Strike Len was famous for his tall tales, he was equally famous for his unkempt appearance. It was said that Len had not taken a bath since he was two weeks old. His face was adorned with a rank growth of uncombed beard that made his features unrecognizable.

One of Lucky Strike Len's victims swore vengeance. As Len prepared to take to the hills on one of his gold prospecting sprees, this party gave Len a homemade loaded cigar. Len set out from town, but two hours later a very dejected figure rode through the town. It was Lucky Strike Len astride his old burro with his whiskers burned and charred completely on one side of his face.

The guilty party was forced to hide out for several days. It was months before Lucky Strike Len regained his former unkempt appearance.

JOHN MORELAND, Portland, Oregon

~ 206 ~

Father Defends His River Toll Bridge

In 1852, my father, Jacob Hunsaker, built the first toll bridge across the Clackamas River in Oregon. Unable himself to be on duty constantly, he hired a man to collect tolls but found it difficult to keep a reliable and honest man, so Mother and the older children took the job.

It was in 1854 that the Klamath Indians came visiting the Clackamas and Molalla tribes, hoping to enlist their help in exterminating the whites. The Klamaths were much more warlike than the valley Indians and resented their hunting grounds being taken for pasture and their rivers mined for gold and fish.

The Indians were camped near Oregon City, feasting and fighting. Games and horse races were their entertainment. The road from Oregon City straight across Father's bridge was found to be an ideal race course. Therefore, Father built a gate at the south bridge entrance.

One morning, Jake, who was just nine-years-old, was left in charge. Curt, age seven, and I, age five years, stayed with him for company. Jake could count money and make change, so managed very well.

We were playing near the bridge when we saw a small band of Indians coming, whipping and racing their ponies. The closed gate halted them. The foremost, a Klamath, ordered Jake to open the gate, but Jake did not move to do it. The Indian pulled out a knife and said he would kill us if we did not open the gate. I said, "Jake, he will kill us if you don't open it." Jake replied, "He will kill us anyway, so I won't open the gate."

We three stood close together expecting to die right there. Then we saw father coming, with an ax in his hand.

He laid the ax down, walked to the Indian with the knife, pulled him off his horse and hurled him off the bridge and into the water below. He turned, grabbed another, sending him after the first. Father turned for the third, but there was no third, not an Indian left on the bridge.

A shout of approval went up from the Clackamas and Molalla Indians who had ridden up to see the action. They cried "Hias skookum Hunsaker—hias close tillicum—hias tyee Hunsaker." These words saying he was a good friend.

Father then came to us children, telling us not to be afraid, that there was no further danger. Then he went among the Indians, talking with them as though nothing unusual had occurred. The Clackamas Indians were very friendly to Father who hired them to work and fed them when hungry.

Before Father's coming to our rescue, I had said my childish prayers. When he came, I considered it a direct answer to my petitions.

MRS. SARAH HUNSAKER TOMPKINS, Cutler City, Oregon

~ 207 ~

Telephone Lad Feels Wrath of Subscriber

Portland, Oregon, in 1870, had but twelve telephones and the company decided to furnish the dozen subscribers with free service in an effort to build up a better business. That the effort was successful may be seen from the fact that in 1882 there were 190 subscribers, who paid $5 a month and 5 cents for each call.

The telephone, however, was not yet firmly entrenched in the business world. The founder of one of the city's large department stores offered a bet to J. H. Thatcher, general agent for the telephone company, that his store would never install a telephone. The "toy," he charged, was impractical because people would not buy goods which they could not see. He would rather use the money to hire a new messenger boy and be saved a lot of bother.

Incidentally, he was not entirely wrong in saying that the possession of a telephone entailed considerable "bother." The few persons owning phones in those years often found themselves carrying messages to all their neighbors who didn't have a phone. A most amusing reversal of conditions from the present day was the fact that *The Oregonian* newspaper used to call telephone subscribers to ask for the location of fires or runaway-horse accidents

Still, the telephone business grew by leaps and bounds. By 1883 there were over seven hundred subscribers. Boys were employed as operators. Hiring girls was out of the question because they might hear "profanity" going over the wires.

One day, General Agent Thatcher returned to the exchange to find one of his young male operators lying on the floor, his coat torn. The lad was crying, while an angry citizen stood over him, shaking his first. "What's going on here?" Thatcher asked.

"I'm teaching this young man some manners," the man, who happened to be a new subscriber, answered. "I tried to talk to my wife on our telephone and the lad impudently told me that my line was busy. A good thrashing will teach him not to be rude to his elders."

It was not recorded what action the telephone company took, if any, in the matter.

P. D. WEBSTER, Portland, Oregon

"Northwest Empire Builders"

BEN HOLLADAY

An Empire Builder Deserted by His Friends

By HENRY E. REED: A Portland newspaperman who knew Ben Holladay well. March 17, 1935

One sunny afternoon in June, 1887, I stood at the entrance of old St. Vincent Hospital, facing Couch Lake. A man, very ill, was carried on a stretcher into the building. He spoke feebly to me, but so emaciated was he since I had last seen him about eight months before that I did not recognize him. About two weeks later there was an imposing funeral at the Catholic Cathedral on Southwest Third Avenue and Southwest Stark Street. The hospital patient had died and his body was wheeled away for burial. This was the end of the colorful career of Ben Holladay, once king of the overland mail stages, master of railroad transportation in Oregon, and political dictator of this state.

Many mourned Holladay. He had spent money freely in Oregon and had friends galore while his power and gold lasted. He was charitable, and for this trait he was highly esteemed. Of the many that had been his associates, two remained faithful to him and to his widow and two half-orphaned children, General Rufus Ingalls and George W. Weidler.

Less than four hundred feet from the cathedral, on Southwest Fourth Avenue, lived one of Ben Holladay's bitterest enemies. He was his cantankerous brother Joe, whom Ben in the 1860s had saved, by influence and the expenditure of $25,000, from the consequences of a murder in Salt Lake City. Joe did not visit the hospital where his brother was dying. Nor did he attend the funeral.

Holladay had other enemies besides his brother Joe. Chief of these was Joseph Gaston, early railroad promoter and author of a voluminous history of Portland. Gaston is responsible for the unfavorable opinion of Holladay which persists to this day. Ben came into the Oregon railroad picture in 1867. The story is a long one but only the high points, with a glimpse of the historical background can be touched upon here.

The covered wagon pioneers came railroad-minded to Oregon. There were railroad projects and railroad talk as far back as 1845. William R. Kilborn built a mule-power, wooden-rail line between Bonneville, Oregon and Cascade Locks in 1855. On May 10, 1862, a steam locomotive, Oregon's first, ran on the rails which had been overlaid with iron strips.

W. W. Chapman obtained pledges for $100,000 in one week for a railroad from Portland to Lafayette in 1850. He was countering a proposed line from St. Helens to Lafayette. Thenceforth for some years, the question was whether Portland or St. Helens would be the northern terminus of a railroad.

When Holladay cast his fortunes with Oregon, there were two railroad companies claiming the name Oregon Central. One was the East Side Company, backed mainly by Salem men, and the other was Gaston's West Side Company.

The prize, when all the good things had been put into the package, was a Congressional Land Grant of supposedly great value and vast operating profits. Gaston and an engineer associated with him had estimated that a railroad from Marysville, California to Portland, costing $30,000,000 would earn, net, $5,600,000 per year. It was estimated also, that the land grant lands, when sold, would pay off bond issues. Holladay and his financial backers in California, England and Germany swallowed the estimates whole. He wrote to a friend in Missouri that he expected to clean up $15,000,000 as his share of the profits.

Both Oregon Central Railroads began building southward from Portland and East Portland one day apart in April 1868. The land grant was to go to the one which completed the first twenty miles of railroad track by December 25, 1860.

Holladay, with ample finances, but in the state of conditions which would have discouraged many another man, finished first, The east side company reached the goal two days early, on December 23, 1860, and ran a train over the road the day before Christmas. It was not much of a railroad as railroads now go, but it was a noteworthy achievement in the history of Oregon.

The land grant proved to be a bauble. The twenty miles cost to build and equip, nearly $70,000. Up to 1875, the Oregon & California Railroad Company had patented or was entitled to claim 64,500 acres, worth a little over only $16,000. The settlers had taken the most valuable lands.

To put events in their proper sequence, it should be said that the East Side Oregon Central Company was found by court decision to be an illegal corporation. It looked for a while as if Holladay was holding a big empty sack. A way out of the difficulty pointed to a legal opinion by William M. Evarts, the Under-Secretary of State of the United States. For his service, Mr. Evarts was paid a fee of $25,000.

Holladay, acting upon Evarts advice incorporated the Oregon & California Railroad Company with $20,000,000 in capital in March, 1870, and acquired the assets of the East Side Company, estimated to be worth between $800,000 and $1,000,000.

Gaston's West Side Oregon Central Company had been fought to a standstill. Holladay took it over through his Willamette Valley Railroad Company, and in the summer of 1870, he was the master of the railroad empire in Oregon. Gaston's project cost Holladay somewhere between $50,000 and $70,000. With Holladay in the saddle, and no one to oppose him in any way, he was a cause of fear. Gaston's plan called for railroads from Portland to McMinnville and from Forest Grove to Astoria. It was thought that the master would cross his west side lines to the east side at Oswego to the benefit of East Portland and leave Portland out in the cold. He proposed that if Portland would pay him $100,000 gold, he would build the Gaston lines. The money was cheerfully, and promptly raised. It was a plain business proposition, a good investment for Portland, and not a holdup, as some have said.

Before he was unhorsed by his German bondholders, Holladay ran trains to Roseburg, 198 miles, December 3, 1871; to Hillsboro, 20 miles, December 18, 1871 and to St. Joseph, 27½ miles beyond Hillsboro, November 2, 1872. All told, he built 245½ miles of railroad. Considering that the territory which the lines were to serve did not at any time while Holladay was boss have as large a population as 75,000, or about one-fourth as many people as Portland had in 1930. Holladay can at least be credited with having been supremely confident of the future of the Willamette, Umpqua and Rogue River Valleys.

Thirteen days after the failure of Jay Cooke & Company, the financiers of the Northern Pacific Railroad, in the fall of 1873, Oregon & California Railroad defaulted on their bond interest payment and Holladay's mastery came to a quick end. By 1875, he was definitely out. He did not have a chance to survive the great depression of 1873-1879.

Holladay gave Oregon its first railroad system and Portland its first street cars. He built Clarendon Hotel on the west side, the Holladay House on the east side and a hotel near Seaside, Clatsop County, Oregon. Holladay's Addition was platted to be a center of population on the east side. A large sawmill on the west side was another enterprise. His steamships ran to California and he was the first to develop the great railroad terminals north of Northwest Glisan Street.

In person, Holladay was tall and powerfully framed, keen eyed, with a countenance that bespoke a man ready for fight or play, at any time.

He was neither shifty-eyed nor personally selfish, as some of his critics have said. He had had a limited education and what he knew he had gained in the university of hard knocks.

He was haughty and dictatorial but withal very companionable. His creed was that the end was justified by the means. He could win men by personal magnetism or money, and these failing; he would use the steam roller. He had a fondness for getting the best of every bargain. He loved pomp and show, which caused people to regard him as a nabob. (very rich)

He was active in politics in the interest of his enterprises. He won United States Senator George H. Williams over to his side in an issue with Gaston. The people resented this by electing a democratic legislature. Holladay influenced the legislature to elect his man, James K. Kelly to succeed Williams. United States Senator Henry W. Corbett displeased him by standing with Gaston. Holladay defeated him with John H. Mitchell. Many minor officials bowed to him. A mayor, who might be useful some time, was presented a ring worth $4,000.

In entertaining his friends, Holladay was in truth, a prince. The choicest foods, wines, liquors, and cigars were always provided. There was an abundance of good things for the legislature of 1868 when the land grant action of 1866 was reversed. Gala parties were staged in the hotel near Seaside. Holladay's private car, "The President" was frequently stocked for fishing and hunting trips down the Willamette Valley.

Holladay, a blood relative of a Virginia family named Hughes, was born in Kentucky in October, 1819. When he was eighteen-years-old, his family moved to Liberty, Missouri, near the rendezvous of the overland Oregonians. During the persecution of the Mormons in Far West, Missouri in 1838, Holladay was an orderly for Brigadier-General Alexander W. Doniphan of the State Militia. Doniphan prevented the summary execution of seven of the Mormon leaders. Holladay was kind to the Mormons after they surrendered to the militia and was helpful to them.

For the next twenty-one years, Holladay was a resident of Weston, Missouri. He was a druggist, a dealer in real estate, and a trader in the old Southwest where Sublette and others had operated. He early earned a reputation as a man who could do things. This he proved when the war of Mexico began. As a contractor of the army of the west centered at Fort Leavenworth, he provisioned the American forces. His promptness in furnishing supplies was a factor in the capture of Santa Fe and El Paso, and in the driving of the Mexicans across the Rio Grande River. When the Mexican war ended, Holladay started across the plains with goods to sell in the newly discovered California gold fields. He carried a letter from General Doniphan to Brigham Young, commending him for his kindness to the Mormon people at Far West in 1838. Brigham Young opened the way for Holladay's trade with the Mormons. He told his people that Holladay was the first Gentile trader to the Mormons.

In 1859, Holladay moved to New York City and became a man of finance. His Pacific Coast ventures had made him a fortune and he lived in grand style. He had a city house and a country home with seven hundred or more acres, called Ophir Farm near White Plains. This place cost him $750,000 and as much as $7,000 a month to maintain. At one time, he owned a very fine home in Washington, D. C., so that he could be near congress and the government officials. He entertained lavishly wherever he lived.

On one point Holladay never lost his perspective. He was opposed to the marriage of his two daughters to foreign noblemen, but the first Mrs. Holladay prevailed in this matter. With the dwindling of the Holladay fortune, the New York, White Plains, and Washington, D. C. homes passed to other owners. When Ophir Farm was lost, the bodies of his first wife and the seven children born to her were laid to rest in the chapel of the mansion. They remained there until 1919, when Mrs. Whitelaw Reid, the owner of the property, had them removed at her expense to a plot in St. Mary's Catholic Cemetery, Port Chester, New York.

Holladay claimed that the United States Government owed him $500,000 for the destruction of property on his stage routes by Indians during the Civil War. He was once offered $100,000 in settlement, but he answered that if the government could not pay its just debts, it could keep the money. He went to Washington in the fall of 1856, in the last effort to have his claim paid. Failing, he returned to Portland, Oregon to die.

His estate was appraised at a little over $1,100,000. In administration of it, covering over thirteen years, it shrank about one-half.

A short distance west of the main gate of Mount Calvary Cemetery, there is a stone monument with moss on it. Under it are the bodies of Ben Holladay and his second wife, Linda Campbell, the twenty-five-year old girl whom Holladay, when he was fifty-five, married in 1874. Below the hills to the south and west is the beautiful Tualatin Valley, through which Holladay in 1871 built his railroad to Hillsboro and caused Portland to rejoice that it was at last, in fact and in truth, a railroad terminus.

Ben Holladay must be measured by the standards of the time in which he lived, and not by the standards of this age of streamlined trains, automobiles, airplanes, paved roads, radios, electric power, telephones, and all the other modern conveniences of life. He came to an Oregon dependent for transportation upon river steamers, canoes, bateaux, stage coaches and vehicles drawn by horses over roads that were not much better than trails.

He taught the people to live in fairly good hotels, to take recreation at the seashore, and to travel by ship and trains. Moreover, he introduced them to the high life. Up to his coming, with the exception of the pony engine which steamed out of Bonneville in 1862, the whistle of a railroad locomotive had not been heard before in Oregon.

Mistakes he made, to be sure. The capacity of the country to support railroads was much overestimated. Others made similar mistakes. Henry Villard, the successor of Holladay, and the first to realize in a practical sense, the value of the Columbia River water-level route--over-calculated, also. Hardly had Portland's plaudits for

Villard's success been stilled in 1883, than Villard fell. There were plenty to kick at him when he was down, as there were at Holladay. Villard came back, but Holladay stayed down. In Holladay's case, one need not shed many tears for the bondholders who let him have money at 40 percent discount and seven percent annual interest.

The allegation that Holladay played a sharp game of politics may be answered by the question, "Since when have business and politics not been mixed in Oregon, or Chicago, or anywhere else?" If Holladay spread himself to win the good will of the legislature of 1868, nothing that he did, there and then, approached the legislative holdup of 1897, when the House of Representatives even failed to organize themselves.

In the contest with Gaston, Holladay outsmarted his rival at every turn. Longer experienced in business and commanding larger resources, he won out. The prize was the control of a great state through its transportation. It was a prize worthy of the effort of any group of men in the 1860's and 1870's. It is what men do, and not who they are, or what they are, that counts. Measured by what he accomplished, and disregarding personal foibles and the conflicts and struggles of men, Ben Holladay was among the great men of the Old West, and is entitled to be enrolled among the "Empire Builders" of Oregon.

HENRY E. REED, Printed in *The Oregonian*, March 17, 1935

~ 208 ~

Three Panthers Frighten Man into Full Retreat

In the year of 1882, Martin Friend, a young man twenty-two years-of-age, was hunting deer on a mountainside below Camas Valley, Washington.

On hearing a disturbance, not far from him, he jumped upon a log which lay across a deep, but narrow, gully. To his amazement, he saw two very large panthers on the other end of the log, faced off at each other, lashing their tails and snarling. They apparently were paying no attention to him. He was afraid to shoot, as he carried only an old muzzle-loading rifle and could only get off one shot. The other cougar would likely attack him before he could reload.

While debating what best to do, he heard a slight rustling in the shrubbery near his end of the log. He was struck with horror to see another panther step up on the log, thus trapping him between them. Even though their interest seemed not to be on him, he didn't like the odds being in the middle of a feline squabble.

In his fright, he tossed his rifle and jumped about fifteen feet down the steep hill and lit running. Martin didn't stop running until he was about a half mile away. Early next day, he and a friend returned to the log with their hunting dogs, but the dogs wisely refused to take up the scent.

After much searching, he finally found his old muzzle-loader, about twenty feet from the log, hanging in a tree.

BESSIE MARTINDALE, Camas Valley, Washington

~ 209 ~

Hearse Prized by Pleased Indians

My grandfather ran an undertaking establishment in Springwell, a small frontier village. His funeral coach was a horse-drawn vehicle. The driver rode in a jump seat in front, while the coffin reposed within the coach body, the walls of which were transparent glass.

Grandfather decided to close out his business, but was in a quandary as to how to dispose of the coach. He parked it in front of his house with a "For Sale" sign on it. Several days later an Indian showed up and offered to buy the vehicle. Much puzzled as to what use the Indian would make of the funeral wagon, Grandfather closed the deal.

Several days later, a strange spectacle rode into town. Seated proudly upon the driver's seat was the Indian who had purchased the funeral coach. Inside, behind the glass walls, was his family, seated on the floor, well aware of the notice the townsfolk were giving them, and satisfied that they were creating a big impression.

EDNA CRABTREE, Portland, Oregon

~ 210 ~

Twin Santa Clauses Visit Eager Children

With the spirit of Christmas once in the air, readers of this page might be interested in the story of a pioneer Santa Claus. This is the story of how St. Nicholas visited the children of the struggling village of Seattle, Washington, many years ago in 1854.

The little community was only a few years old, and it had just experienced a disastrous Indian war which had sorely affected the courage of its founders. With the coming of Christmas, the settlers were attempting to forget the recent slaughter as they sang the old carols of "peace on earth".

In order to make it a real Christmas for the children, two men, Ira Woodin and George Frye decided that Santa Claus must pay the town a visit. Starting to carry out their plans, they bought out the stores' stocks of oranges, hard candy, wooden lockets and other trinkets.

Santa Claus' visit was intended to be a surprise, but the men's secret leaked out and parents began telling their children of the expected visit of the corpulent red-nosed gentleman with the white whiskers and bright coat. Instead of coming down a chimney, however, it was explained that he would emerge from the dense woods, which bordered the settlement.

Frye and Woodin met at the appointed spot, but neither one had succeeded in securing the necessary red suit in which to play the Kris Kringle role. To make matters worse, neither one was willing to allow the other to have the honor. If either one possessed a suit, of course, the problem automatically would have been solved

The compromise finally reached was rather surprising and somewhat frightening to the children. Out of the woods strode, not one, but two Santa Clauses, side by side, and each was dressed, not in a Santa suit, but in an Indian blanket.

The youngsters quickly forgot their surprise, however, when they discovered that the twin Santa Clauses, in the queer disguises, really were carrying genuine Christmas good things in their packs.

ESTER HALPIN, Portland, Oregon

~ 211 ~

Jokester Almost Sends Militiamen to Battle

In the olden days, a good practical joker was just about as popular, and as well liked, as the town mayor, or in some cases, perhaps hated as much as a horse thief, depending on who was the subject of the joke. Perhaps no one of these laugh provokers ever stumbled upon the means of causing as much mirth as did the one, who in the early 1880's, victimized Company H of La Grande, Oregon.

Early one Sunday morning a telegram was received from Salem, duly signed by the Adjutant-General instructing the soldiers to go, at once, to Portland to protect the Oregon Coast from a raid by Germany and also to quell uprisings on the part of the Indians, who were on the warpath in that vicinity.

The excitement which followed was tremendous. Company H had the name of being the best drilled company in the regiment and the men were more than glad for the chance to win laurels on the field of battle.

The company, which was soon fully equipped and armed in full attire, began proudly parading up and down the main streets of La Grande. Along toward noon, the boys retired to the hotel and partook of their "last dinner" at home.

The final hour finally came. The crowd which had assembled at the station was the largest seen in that city for some time. Fathers slapped their sons on the back and bid them a fond farewell. Wives, mothers and sweethearts, with tears welling in their eyes and lumps in their throats, gave their loved ones a long hug and a last kiss, thinking that they perhaps would never see them again.

At that moment the west-bound train pulled into the station--and right there is where the jokester reaped his reward.

The scene immediately surrounding the soldiers became, suddenly, like a mad house. Chaos spread quickly through the crowd. The boarding lines changed from silence and stateliness to disorder, laughter and utter pandemonium. All because of a telegram which arrived just before the solemn Company H was about to board the train, which read:

"Company H, Oregon National Guard, will proceed immediately to Hot Lake--and take a bath."

BOSS WOMAK, Wallowa, Oregon

~ 212 ~

White Man's Bicycle Astonishes Indian

Grandfather operated a blacksmith shop in a small western town on the early frontier. His workshop was the center of attraction for the whole village. Among those who came daily to watch him at his labors was an Indian who went by the name of "Long Feather."

It might have been suspected that this old fellow came to warm himself by the open forge on cold days, rather than to view the ordinary processes of manufacturing, which are distasteful to the average Indian. Wrapping himself in a blanket, he would sit cross-legged by the fire, and smoke a long wooden-bowled pipe.

One day, Grandfather came across a design for making a bicycle, a thing which had never been seen in that remote town. The plan was all that Grandfather needed; his skill would supply the rest. After several weeks the vehicle was finished and he wheeled it out of the shop for a trial ride.

Old "Long Feather," from his post by the fire, viewed the spectacle with considerable interest before he was moved to speak. Then he exclaimed, "Hmph, white man plenty smart--walk sitting down."

HERBERT KEITH, Portland, Oregon

~ 213 ~

All Ends Well for Very Capable Liar

This episode, of which I am writing, concerns one of the early settlers of Scroggins Valley and an Indian who made his living by tanning hides. The whites always saved them for him until he came around on his yearly visits.

The settler, S. E. Wilcox, had killed a large bear having an exceptionally fine coat of fur. Wishing to have the pelt properly cured and tanned he placed it in the hands of this old Indian with the instructions that he wanted to be sure of having the same skin returned to him. The Indian took the raw skin over his arm and said, "Sure, Wilcox. Me do good job for you."

Many days went by, until one afternoon the Indian came riding up with a bear skin in his arms. The skin had been beautifully tanned. Mr. Wilcox was about to pay the Indian for his work and praise him for his skill when he noticed that the bullet hole which had been in the head of his bear skin was not present in this finished product.

Pointing his finger at the spot where the hole should have been, he told the Indian that he was trying to "cheat white man" by bringing back a different hide. The Indian thoughtfully cast his eyes away for a moment. Then drawing himself up to his full height, he shook his finger in the man's face saying, "Shame, shame, Wilcox. You think I lie?"

"Well, then," said Wilcox, "maybe you will tell me just why this skin doesn't have the bullet hole in it, like it did when I gave it to you."

"Well," said the Indian, "that easy. My woman, she momick and momick and momick that skin (Momick was the Indian word meaning "to work.") She keep momicking and momicking that hole toward edge, with her teeth, till finally she momick it right out through side of skin. That why white man no findum bullet hole."

Mr. Wilcox, who was my great-grandfather, thought the lie was such a good one that he paid the Indian his fee and accepted the skin--which was nearly as good as the original anyway. The Indian happily galloped off, down the creek, as fast as his small horse could carry him.

SANFORD MATTESON, Gaston, Oregon

~ 214 ~

Wolves Chew Pants of Sleeping Pioneer

My grandfather was among the pioneers who crossed the plains in the days of the early west. The following amusing adventure he never tired of telling, although at the time it could have hardly been so funny to Grandfather. But years later, it was always with a hearty laugh that he told the incident.

The wagon train was upon the threshold of the Oregon Country. The emigrants were all tired and weary, so the train halted for the afternoon. Curious to become acquainted with this beautiful new land, Grandfather set out, alone, on a scouting expedition. He left camp late in the afternoon and traveled some distance. The country was interesting, so by nightfall, he had decided to make camp and return to the wagons the next morning. He wore the common garb of the day, a combination pair of heavy buckskin pants and coat. He placed his trousers a short distance from his blankets and turned in.

Towards morning, he awoke with a start. There was something moving at the outer edge of his camp. He sat upright. Through sleep blurred eyes he caught sight of two gray wolves running off, one of them with a leg of his buckskin pants dangling from its jaws. The leg had been chewed and torn off several inches above the knee.

A comical sight rode into camp that morning; grandfather astride his horse, his pant leg missing high above the knee.

HERBERT KEITH, Portland, Oregon

~ 215 ~

Hog Goes West in Most Unusual Way

In April, 1851, the Powell train consisting of my great-grandfather, John A. Powell, captain of the train. His two brothers, Alfred and Noah, together with their families, ranging from babies to young married men and women, all traveled from Illinois to Oregon. Accompanying them was S. Hamilton, who once related the following incident, which was also verified by my grandmother and others.

"About the tenth of May, we crossed the Missouri River, about where the city of Omaha, Nebraska now stands. There had been a hog, weighing about 100 pounds that had followed us for several days before reaching the Canesville Camp. When we came to cross the river, the barge was small, so we had to swim the cattle across."

"The hog was on hand, as usual, and went into the river with them. Some trouble was experienced in getting the cattle to leave the shore, but while they were swimming around, a cow came into proper position for the hog to climb upon her back. Standing on her back, the pig rode across the river, then slid off as the cow climbed up the bank. All got ashore safely amid many cheers."

"Soon afterwards, the hog evidently wandered a little too far--disappearing in the vicinity of one of the settlements along the river."

W. L. ARANT, Forest Grove, Oregon

"When Oregon Went Berserk"

EPISODE 1 OF 6

An Account of Ten Spectacular Years (1855-1865) When the Northwest Was Host to War, Greed and Death

By JOHN W. KELLY, Staff Writer, *The Oregonian*, September 13, 1936

Introduction

In a decade, the Oregon Country experienced its most thrilling era. More sensations and excitements were crowded into this period than all the years prior, or since. It's span was from 1855 to 1865, approximately, with preliminaries preceding the opening date and a tailing off after the later date.

Savage warfare, gold rushes, organized crime and vengeance dealing vigilantes came in rapid sequence. It is a chapter of the history of the Oregon Country that has totally been overlooked, yet it carried more color, more drama, story, and picturesqueness than a present-day resident realizes.

Sudden death by arrow, or gun, or rope, punctuated the era. Bad men, red and white, murdered without compunction. Crime was organized with all the symbols of a secret society until an outraged citizens group, known as the Vigilantes, took the law into its own hands.

In those days, the old Oregon Country was wild and wicked, far from the antithesis of the peaceful, respectable, law-abiding humdrum immigrants. Fortunes were made quickly, and lost quickly, through greed and vice. Gold flowed through Portland in unbelievable quantities, destined for the San Francisco mint. Navigation on the Columbia and Willamette Rivers received its greatest impetus during those years. Great numbers of wagon trains and stage coaches rolled in over the trails.

Into Oregon swarmed the rough elements of humanity; fugitives from justice, killers, highwaymen, horse thieves and criminals of every description. Law-abiding, honest men rarely made the morning news. The decade of daring deeds, when trouble reigned, had its beginning when Oregon was still a territory. Most came after the American Civil War had ended.

These were stirring times, delivering enough melodrama to furnish material for a hundred historical novels. While many of the events were played out in the Willamette and Rogue River Valleys and along the coastal region, the proverbial stage was set from the Cascades west through Eastern and Central Oregon and the adjacent segments of the northern Oregon Territory, now Washington and Idaho.

EPISODE 1

No White Man's Life Was Safe

For months, signal fires flamed menacingly from the crest of the Coast Range to the western slopes of the Rocky Mountains. Indians were acting impertinently, but the preliminary signs of impending disaster caused small alarm at the time.

Secretly the land was to be washed in blood, and all the terrible horrors and barbarities of Indian warfare were to be unleashed upon the few thousand white people who were in the region from California to British Columbia and from the Pacific Ocean to the Rocky Mountains.

Kamiakin, "hias tyee" (supreme leader) of the Yakimas, plotted extermination of all white people. By the time he was ready to strike, there was scarcely a neutral tribe. The tribes, large and small, were almost without exception, involved in the conspiracy for wholesale slaughter.

It was no sudden uprising. Kamiakin made his preparations with care, sent his missionaries throughout the country and armed the tribes with weapons and ammunition. For many years, Indians on the coast of Western Oregon were well stocked with munitions through the efforts of the Klickitats. Other tribes only had enough ammunition for a year.

Kamiakin prepared for a five-year war, believing that long before that, the last paleface would be killed and scalped and the country once more in their possession.

For a period of more than two years, the whites were in constant danger of losing their lives. Indians spied on all of the settlements. The whites did not realize they were living on a volcano until the redmen struck. Before the Indians were crushed, hundreds of lives were taken—the exact number will never be known—the atrocities of Indian warfare had been called into the play.

Men were butchered and mutilated, women captured, children and babies slaughtered. The word "mercy" was totally forgotten. White men soon became as ferocious as their red foemen. Over the great Pacific Northwest, mostly primeval wilderness, no white man's life was safe. Stealthy warriors prowled the forests and death stalked day and night.

Kamiakin had a well-defined program. Indians were to rub out wandering prospectors and miners, wagoners and drovers, they were to seize Fort Vancouver and Fort Steilacoom, obtaining the munitions stored at those places, then moving against the settlements, killing and burning and sparing neither sex nor age.

This ambitious plan was crowned with partial success, but a few decisive defeats enabled the whites to gain the upper hand. By accident, the sloop-of-war *Decatur* was on the beach and fired their big guns when the Indians attacked Seattle, then a sawmill village, disrupting the plan with its superior firepower.

Scarcely 335 regular army troops were in the region, but by happenstance, troops arrived at the Cascades on the Columbia River just in time to prevent the hostiles from sweeping over the trail around Mount Hood with plans to sack and burn the cluster of houses known as Portland, the village at Willamette Falls (Oregon City), and other scattered settlements up the Willamette Valley.

Every able-bodied man took arms against the enemy, many losing their scalps. Until toward the end of the conflict, however, there was built up antagonism between the regular army troops and the Oregon volunteers. In those days, regular army officers were sympathetic with the Indians and had not yet seen the atrocities, learned the character of the warring foe, or heard of Kamiakin's planned program to kill all whites in the region including the army personnel.

Previous to the uprising, many government treaties were made with various tribes. Joel Palmer, Superintendent of Indians, with headquarters at Dayton, Oregon, and Governor I. I. Stevens of Washington Territory, negotiated with the natives but Kamiakin and his lieutenants believed they were being robbed of their lands by these treaties. Palmer established the Grande Ronde Reservation and began herding Umpquas and others to the location, thereby arousing the resentment of settlers. The Territorial Legislature passed a resolution demanding Palmer's removal.

Klickitats were insinuating themselves into tribes, spreading the doctrine of extermination. Warriors from the Klickitats arranged for the consolidation of tribes to attack Seattle and Fort Steilacoom; they even penetrated south into the Klamath Country until Palmer finally ordered them back to their own land in Washington.

Kamiakin's method of whipping reluctant tribes into the confederation was simple. His dictum was, "Join or be killed, or if not killed, enslaved." Few Indians could resist that threat, and when all was in readiness, Kamiakin had the greatest Indian army that was ever assembled on the Pacific Coast of America.

A few isolated murders of miners by Shastas and Coquilles occurred and the Yakimas wiped out a whole encampment of miners. These events were the curtain-raisers to the bloody drama. In June, 1856, the hostiles were on the warpath, their activities being largely between the Jacksonville and Illinois Rivers, on Applegate Creek and various creeks where prospectors were looking for gold. Then came attacks on the Klamath River with ten miners murdered.

In August, an Indian at the mouth of the Rogue River shot a white man and the soldiers from Port Orford quickly captured the Indian. While they were taking him to the fort, settler friends of the wounded white man laid in ambush and fired on the prisoner in anger. The soldiers returned the fire, killing two of the whites. This heightened the ill feelings between the settlers and the regulars which spread over the Pacific Northwest for the duration of the war.

In September, teamsters were killed crossing the Siskiyous. And, there were other murders, which the whites balanced with an attack on an Indian camp on Butte Creek on the Rogue River, resulting in twenty-three dead Indians.

Twenty-seven white men and women were killed on October 9, among them two school teachers on the road to Crescent City; also the crew of a pack train at Jewett's Ferry and miners on Grave Creek. An express was dispatched to the Governor petitioning a proclamation for volunteers. Port Orford troops were forced to retreat from their post at the great bend of the Rogue River. Settlers were threatened and terrified at Althouse, Phoenix Mills, Deer Creek, and Galice Creek.

At Skull Bar, on the Rogue, volunteers, miners, Chinese and Indian women were besieged in their cabins, which the Indians destroyed with flaming arrows. A few days later, settlers on Cow Creek were wiped out.

Houses on Jump-Off Joe Creek were burned. Raiding proceeded on the south side of the Umpqua River. Christmas eve witnessed a battle on the north branch of Little Butte Creek and the new year saw a battle in the snow in the Applegate country. There was also the battle of Hungry Hill, with more loss of life.

Volunteers were in the field in snow and rain, never camping more than four days in one spot in three months. While fortifications were being made at Empire City, and the hostiles were on the rampage in Southern Oregon, the gun and scalping knife were given play on the Washington side of the Columbia River.

Sub-Indian Agent, A. J. Bolen, left The Dalles to have a powwow with Kamiakin. Qualchin, son of Owhi, a brother of Kamiakin, killed Bolen a few miles north of the Columbia, burned and buried the agent and his horse. Major Haller of the regulars, left The Dalles to investigate; encountered 1,500 Indians sixty miles from The Dalles--and retreated. A company from Fort Steilacoom crossed the Natchez Pass in Washington, looked and also retreated.

Soon came the attack on Seattle, which was frustrated by the sailors and marines on the *Decatur* and *Jefferson Davis*, both American Navy ships. This saved Fort Steilacoom.

Out of the north, from British Columbia, came a fleet of war canoes bent on ravaging the settlements. These invaders were beaten back, but later on, they made a second attempt, in which shells from the American gunboats destroyed part of the fleet of canoes and killed several painted warriors. Volunteer companies patrolled the roads in the vicinity of Olympia, but the White River tribe, and other tribes, still managed to murder settlers, burn houses and kill a few regular soldiers.

Major Raines took the field with all the regular troops on the Columbia and refused to co-operate with the four volunteer companies under J. W. Nesmith. After scouting it out, Raines returned to Vancouver, while Nesmith took his volunteers to the Walla Walla country.

Commanding all the Federal troops was General Wool, who had a contempt for the volunteers and civilians generally. He declared that Governor Curry of Oregon Territory should not have called for volunteers. He believed that the whites were in the wrong for taking the Indian's land and said there was no cause for alarm—his army would solve the problem.

And then the general asked the Federal Government to send him, at least, one regiment. General Wool was icebound at Vancouver for three weeks, unable to communicate with The Dalles or San Francisco. He had ordered horses, ammunition and supplies from San Francisco, but the Columbia was closed with ice. Not until Wool was relieved of command did the regular army officers recognize the wisdom of the tactics of the brave Oregon Volunteers.

The strategy of the volunteers was to keep the Indians on the move all winter and destroy their caches of food whenever possible. In after years, this method of fighting Indians was adopted by the regular army, as winter campaigns wore down the resistance of the warriors, who had been accustomed to being unmolested during the inclement season.

East of the Cascades there were no settlers to destroy, so loss of life was confined to soldiers and Indians. The shooting, burning, and torturing, however, continued with little abatement west of the Cascades, where Indians could always find a miner of two or some settler's cabin, and the relative mildness of the climate enabled the hostiles to appear and disappear like phantoms.

Tragedy came with the celebration of Washington's birthday at Gold Beach, where a stronghold had been erected. In the evening, a message came from the Mackanotius tribe on the south side of the Rogue River to Ben Wright, Indian Agent, that Enos, a renegade half-breed, was in their camp and they wanted him arrested. By this ruse, Wright was lured to his own cabin, where he was killed with a tomahawk. The captain of the volunteers shared his fate. The heart of

Wright was cut out, cooked and eaten by the Indians. His scalp was recovered on the Siletz River years later.

Years earlier, Wright had lured a group of Modocs to a feast under pretense of "burying the hatchet" for the massacre of a wagon train of emigrants in the Klamath country at Bloody Point. From the feast a single Indian escaped—Enos. He was active with the hostiles along the Rogue River the year previous to Wright's murder. Enos, who was a guide with Fremont in 1843, was caught and hanged for a crime at Port Orford in 1857.

In a dozen hours, the Indians killed twenty-six men and women, burned sixty houses on the Rogue River below Big Bend, and white women were taken captive. Attacks were made at seven different points.

Refugees fled to a fortified house at Gold Beach, or Whalehead, and then began a siege of many weeks. The siege of Miners' Fort at Gold Beach dragged on until the thirty-first day, when, headed by fife and drum, two companies of regulars came marching up the beach from Crescent City, California. Three attempts by water to rescue the beleaguered 180 men, women and children of Gold Beach were failures, with Indians capturing one crew of six and hacking them to death.

Pistol River and Chetco River were scenes of engagements between soldiers and savages. In the valleys, the Indians made raids, picking off defenseless settlers at every opportunity, and each scalp was another step toward the objective of the natives—extermination of all whites.

The first part of the uprising witnessed the antagonism between the regular troops and the Oregon Volunteers. General Wool issued orders that none of his subordinates should recognize volunteers in the field. Despite this ill feeling, the volunteers hunted the enemy in Western and Eastern Oregon, performing service which logically belonged to the Federal troops and they occasionally extricated the regulars from tight spots.

Month after month the trail of blood spread. For a thousand miles north and south the Indians took lives wantonly and destroyed property at every opportunity. No settlement had more than a few hundred souls, and when a man volunteered for the field of battle, he weakened the defenses of his own family. A hard decision to make.

One handicap was the shortage of weapons and ammunition. Volunteers had to equip themselves, and there was an insufficient amount of supplies. Some volunteers were armed only with pistols. On the other hand, the redskins had stores of munitions and expected to take the forts at Vancouver and Steilacoom for more supplies. Because of the attitude of the regular army officers, the volunteers were denied adequate supplies from either of the army posts.

East of the Cascades, Kamiakin received reports from runners, and watched the progress of his campaign with satisfaction. He had accomplished what other chiefs had attempted in vain—a consolidation of all the tribes over an area greater than many countries of Europe. Snake Indians disposed of wagon trains on the Old Oregon Trail; the tribes in Northern California and in Oregon were co-operating whole-heartedly to rid the land of whites; the warriors on Puget Sound were killing settlers, and Kamiakin was patiently waiting to deliver several swift, telling blows which would enable hordes of wild Indians to eradicate all signs of the white man in the Oregon Territory.

At the end of the first year, the Indians had the best of it; Indian losses were heavy, but the whites had suffered even more.

Those whites who could, moved into the larger settlements, to Empire City and Port Orford, to Jacksonville, Roseburg, Dayton and Willamette Falls (Oregon City). In all of these settlements, each larger than Portland, no one went to sleep at night with positive knowledge that the Indians would not attack and burn the collection of houses before morning. The handful of settlers east of the Cascades concentrated at The Dalles, where always there were a few soldiers held in readiness to take the field.

Deep snows failed to stop the movements of the Oregon Volunteers in the Eastern Oregon terrain. Poorly equipped as they were, the volunteers rode far and wide, while the regulars were in warm barracks at The Dalles, Vancouver and Steilacoom.

Winter campaigning was not to the liking of Kamiakin; he had not foreseen this strategy by the citizen soldiers; it was one of the unpleasant phases of warfare.

Personally, Kamiakin preferred dealing with the officers of the regular army; they were not versed in the Indian character as were the settlers who had lived among the tribes.

Unknown to this war chief, developments were coming which would result in such punishment of his followers that he himself would flee the country, as Sitting Bull was to do years later following the Custer massacre, and his confederacy of tribes be broken forever.

To be continued ...

~ 216 ~

Minister of Gospel Shocked by Greeting

The names of the two principal characters in this little episode are unknown to the writer, but one was a minister of the gospel--the other was an Indian. The year was 1845, the place was the pioneer post of Fort Hall.

The good minister was traveling with a caravan in which were included W. H. Rector, his wife and six children. The next morning after their arrival at Fort Hall, the preacher went for a walk around the grounds and proceeded towards one of the buildings. In the doorway there stood an Indian. When he saw the white man approaching, the brave raised his hand and shouted, "Ho! Haw! God damn you!"

To quote the words of Mr. Rector, as he tells it in his journal, "The old minister reeled back as if he had been shot at."

When the preacher complained of the Indian's "incivility" to Captain James Grant, Hudson's Bay Company employee, then in charge of Fort Hall, Captain Grant laughed heartily. "Why, that fellow was one of the friendliest Indians in the country. He says that to everyone."

In a special effort to be polite, he had attempted to address the white man in his own tongue. He had used the unfortunate phrase because it happened to be the only English greeting at his command.

HARRY FOWLER, Portland, Oregon

~ 217 ~

Three "Brave" Wolves Scare Missionaries

A party of wandering missionaries had camped for the night in the Oregon woods. They ate heavily of their food supplies "for fear of being scalped by an Indian before they'd had time to enjoy it."

After supper, they all turned in for the night. Their remaining supply of meat was placed under pillows, to keep it from the wolves, which even then, would sometimes pull it out and make away with it.

One of the party was a droll Englishman who spoke cockney English. In the middle of the night, the Englishman awoke. By the flickering firelight he saw three wolves, seated by the fire. He stared at the scene and then remarked,

"Hi'll be 'anged hif the wolves aven't grown so bold and saucy they come to the fire to warm themselves."

Investigation disclosed the wolves toppled over when they were touched. A practical joker in the party had killed them earlier … then propped them upright around the fire while the men slept.

ALLEN REICHER, Portland, Oregon

~ 218 ~

Wedding Party Has a Change of Scene

One of my earliest recollections in 1865 was seeing a group of merry people coming down the flower-covered hills to the Mohawk Valley near Eugene, Oregon. Ministers being scarce, my father, Judge Thomas Lister, often performed wedding ceremonies. Upon arriving, this wedding party found, to their consternation that their marriage license was from another, nearby county. Then, to my surprise, I saw Father and the whole jolly party going down the road and into the sweet-scented orchard on the other side of our property. Father, thankfully, had remembered that the invisible line ran there, dividing the two counties. And so, Mr. and Mrs. William Guilliford became man and wife beneath the blossoming apple trees--legally in the right county.

FLORENCE LISTER HOLBROOK, Portland, Oregon

~ 219 ~

Gourd Proves Handy for Darning Socks

Grandmother became fussed indeed, when she lost her darning ball, crossing the plains in 1864. There were six children, ranging in ages from sixteen years to six months. The older ones walked a great deal of the distance. Grandfather walked sometimes, then letting James, fifteen, do the driving. Walking certainly wore out a lot of stockings. There was a pile of stockings to be mended every day. Also after each night's encampment there was a fresh collection of rents in shirts, jackets and pants. The loss of a darning ball was really quite a serious affair.

How could one darn over one's fingers while jolting along in a covered wagon? There was not only the continuous jolting, but the unexpected jerk and the accompanying swaying from side to side when a wagon wheel went down into a chuck hole. But the darning must be done. Mary Ann Watson was not the woman who would allow her family to reach Oregon looking like a band of ragamuffins.

They had not gone far on their journey from Bethel, Missouri when the darning ball came up missing. They were still in the middle states. Grandmother kept a constant watch for something to answer the purpose of the ball but nothing turned up. When her fingers had so many needle pricks in the ends of them that they were painfully sore, she tried a stone, but it was awkward and cumbersome.

One day in passing a clump of gourd vines that grow in abundance in Nebraska, and other middle states, she saw a round, cream-colored gourd lying on the ground. It was thoroughly ripe and dry, making it light weight and tough skinned. Just what she desperately needed,.

"Stop, Father! I want that gourd!" she said to Grandfather.

But Grandfather was not stopping for any old gourd. Mercy, no! His was the third wagon in the train. Why lose his place in line and have to drop back and be a dust-eating tail-ender? The idea of stopping for a silly gourd was unacceptable!

"James! James!" she called to her son, walking several yards away. "Get me that gourd! That round, ripe one!"

James was quick and active. He captured the gourd and brought it to Grandmother in the wagon. The gourd worked perfectly and made the whole trip to Oregon. It was full of needle marks when it arrived, but it was very precious.

Grandmother put it away as her most valuable keepsake. As time went on, it became for her, the symbol of that trip across the plains. She kept it and cherished it carefully.

The third generation now has the gourd, and is keeping it remarkably well. It is seventy one years old at the present time--in 1935.

MRS. IMOGENE HUMPHREY, Salem, Oregon

~ 220 ~

Magic Fire Glass Impresses Indians

My grandfather left Westport, Missouri in the early 18'70's in a wagon train bound for Oregon. Arriving here, he settled in the Willamette Valley and set to work constructing a house, after first putting up a makeshift corral to hold his three horses.

There was a band of Indians who rode by his place occasionally, sometimes stopping to sit,. in silence, and watch him at his work. After a few such visits, he discovered that he was missing several small articles, and although certain that the visiting Indians had made off with them, to avoid trouble, he made no mention of the fact.

One morning, however, he awoke to find the corral empty and his three horses gone. Shortly thereafter, several Indians appeared, and after a grunted greeting and several minutes' silence, one of them asked him what had happened to his horses.

He was virtually certain that they knew more concerning the whereabouts of the animals than he, but he merely replied, "Some really bad Indians have stolen them."

They asked him if he was going after them, and he replied that there was no hurry, that he had ways of finding where the horses had gone.

But, if they were not returned soon the thieves would be very sorry they took them.

He had been filling his pipe as he talked. He carried a small sunglass in his pocket, which he used to light his pipe.

When his pipe was packed with tobacco, he took this glass out and held it cupped in his hand. Soon he had the tobacco burning--without using a match.

Evidently this was the first time the Indians had ever witnessed such a demonstration, as they watched in wonder as clouds of smoke arose from the pipe.

They did not linger long after that, and the next morning the three horses were back in the corral. The "Man Who Make Fire From Clouds" was never bothered by horse thieves again. They also seemed to speed up every time they passed his farm.

KENNETH M. DAY, Portland, Oregon

~ 221 ~

Coatless Man Gets Dinner After Delay

Persons of the older generation in Marion County, Oregon, may remember Charlie Benson, often known to a host of acquaintances as "Little Charlie." He died in 1902, at the advanced age of eighty-seven.

Benson came to Oregon in 1848 by wagon train. Years later, when steel had been laid to the Pacific, Benson decided that he would visit his old home in Illinois.

He had done well in the West and as he boarded the train, he had $700 in currency in his pocket. His attire however, didn't bespeak prosperity. He was coatless and waist coatless. His blue shirt was light weight--but he was wearing his "Sunday-go-to-meetin" trousers. Benson believed that it was better for one's health to dress lightly.

His wife had prepared a huge lunch which he carried in a shoe box, but it's a long way to Illinois and somewhere east of the mountains, his food supply ran out. Trains, at that time, did not yet pull dining cars, but stops were made at road restaurants along the way.

Dinner time came at last. The train made the scheduled stop and the passengers poured into the eating place--that is, all except Benson. A veneer of eastern "culture" was just starting to spread over the West, and Benson, for the first time in his life, found the entrance to the business blocked because of his lack of a coat.

"I'm no tramp," he protested, and showed his precious $700 to the man who stood barring the doorway. Benson's own credulity knew no bounds when he discovered that even his proven ability to pay for his meal did not furnish an entry.

When the train started again, Benson confronted the conductor, as that official came down the aisle, and explained his plight to him. The conductor was sympathetic and agreed that a man should not be allowed to starve to death merely because he lacked a coat and the "proper" attire.

Sending a telegram ahead, he ordered a full meal for a "man without a coat." When the train reached that point, the conductor held the train long enough for Benson to dine. Schedules apparently did not mean as much in those early days of railroading, as the train was held up for more than thirty minutes while Benson, still coatless, dined in solitude—while a train full of confused passengers watched impatiently.

E. RALSTON, Portland, Oregon

~ 222 ~

Wandering Indian Aids Suffering Child

This story was found in some old letters and papers in an old abandoned homestead shack near the present Salmon River Cutoff to the Oregon Coast. It could have been entitled, *Indian Medicine Man.*

The story is one of trail after trial. It was an adventure of a homesteader with a wife and two small children trying to wrestle a living to survive in a cabin in the woods.

In the summer, a garden, berries, fish and venison were suffice, but as winter came the needs became greater. The man was forced to leave home to seek employment, leaving his wife and two little ones to do the best they could. Plenty of wood was prepared, a little fern and hay was put away for the only cow, but severe hardship was knocking at their door.

Winter came on early that year and it began to snow, and it snowed hard. The snow was drifting and the wind was howling down the mountain canyons. The only way out was by way of an old, poorly marked Indian trail to Phil Sheridan's Fort and the Grand Ronde Indian Agency. It was a hazardous adventure to go out crossing over fallen logs, rocks and swollen streams.

During the storm, one of the children became sick with a cold, which went into pneumonia. The nearest doctor was miles away at the government school in Grand Ronde. To get word was impossible; to take both children out for medical help was out of the question.

One Sunday evening as the woman was meditating what she needed to do, a knock came at the door. Rather a repeated "thud" instead of a knock. The woman alone was shocked as never before. She had heard the panthers howl and the wildcats whine, but this thud on the door gave her the greatest fright of all.

Grabbing the gun that her husband had loaded and left for defense, she slowly opened the door.

To her surprise, there stood a large Indian man. He assured her, "You need not gun, me good man." Reluctantly she let him in to warm by the fire.

The Indian, in his broken language, tried to tell her, "Big storm coming, no flour; want trade fish for flour." The woman asked what he meant by "storm," whereupon he pointed in the direction of the ocean and said, "Come soon; know not when."

The woman packed flour and bread and made the exchange for dried, smoked salmon.

She did not tell him she was alone, as she feared him, but she did tell him about her sick child. His eyes sparkled and he said, "You smart woman, me tell you fix mud." He told, in his crude way, how to heat mud, put it over the ailing child's chest, and cover it with deer skin.

He went off in the blinding snow eating on the bread she had given him. She quickly prepared and applied the remedy he had prescribed. The next morning the sick child was better and appeared to be on the road to recovery.

Where this primitive man came from, and where he went after his visit, has been a mystery to the appreciative family ever since. The saved little boy often insists that he owes his life to this mysterious "Indian medicine man".

K. APPLEWHITE, Neskowin, Oregon

~ 223 ~

Aunt Polly Resents Mr. Nude Indian

In the year 1849, my great aunt, Polly Leabo, left her home in Kansas and came to Oregon with her husband and children.

The wagon train made camp on the banks of the Rogue River, in Southern Oregon, and, as game and fish were plentiful, they spent several days there.

On the evening of which I write, the men were later than usual returning from their hunt. Aunt Polly was busy cooking juicy venison steaks, the children, close around her, eagerly waiting for their evening meal.

Out of the dusk a figure appeared. Slowly it walked toward the fire and squatted down beside Aunt Polly. He was an Indian and entirely nude. Nudist colonies, with their benefits to health, were unheard of in those days. Why, the very thought of nudity was intolerable.

Polly was angered more than she was scared, but what could she do? She continued frying her steak, using a large butcher knife to turn it and lift it out onto the platter. Every time she would place a steak on the platter, the Indian would reach out, grab the meat and eat it.

Polly finally had had enough! As the Indian reached for the next steak, she brought down the knife across his wrist with all her strength. The Indian jumped up howling with pain and disappeared into the forest.

When the men returned and Mr. Leabo was told of the incident, he said, "Why, Polly! Whatever possessed you to do that? He will get his entire tribe and return and massacre all of us."

"Massacre or no massacre," said the little woman, "I'm not going to endure the sight of any naked Indian, squatting down, eating our food."

The Indian had evidently learned his lesson, as the whites were not molested and continued their journey on into the beautiful valley of the Willamette River.

LILLIAN LEWIS CUTSFORTH, Estacada, Oregon

~ 224 ~

Chinese Disappear in the Black of Night

Years ago, in Oregon City, Oregon, a large crew of Chinese were imported to work in the factory there. Many white men were thrown out of work, and feelings ran high against the yellow men. The "Chiny House," a large hotel-like building where they stayed, was a very unpopular place.

My mother, then a small girl, lived right across the street from this building. One night the family went to bed with the noise of the chattering Chinese ringing in their ears, but when they arose the next morning, all was quiet in the "Chiny-House." Not one Chinaman was visible, nor did any appear.

White help was rehired at the factory, and several days later, word leaked out as to what had befallen the Chinese.

A committee of men, still unidentified, chartered a river steamer in Portland. In the dead of night it came up the Willamette River to Oregon City and docked.

The men quietly routed the Chinese from their beds, loaded them on the boat and told them Oregon City was going to be a very unhealthy place for them to return to.

The river steamer was likely only chartered to transport the Chinese back to Portland, only a few miles downstream. There they were forced to re-establish themselves in a very unfriendly social atmosphere--in the dead of a very dark night.

MARJORIE HEDRICK, Lake Oswego, Oregon

~ 225 ~

Distressed Mothers Find Babes Mixed

If any Portlanders are not truly the children of the supposed parents who raised them, it may be that they were on the steamboat "Jennie Clark" the night Tom Mountain played his famous joke.

The Columbia and Willamette Rivers, like the Mississippi, once knew days when river traffic was heavy with stern-wheelers belching smoke and whistling "round the bend."

When not hauling freight and passengers, the boats were often sent up or down the rivers on "grand excursions." The "Jennie Clark," with Captain John Ainsworth at the wheel, set out, one evening, on one of those pleasure trips. As many of the excursionists had brought their children, Tom Mountain, an employee of the Oregon Steamship & Navigation Company, was appointed to, reluctantly, "baby-sit" the youngsters.

As the parents danced the old-time steps a mischievous idea occurred to Tom. Undressing the children one by one of their outer clothing, he mixed the outfits, as completely as possible, and then redressed each child in a different outfit taken from the general pile.

When the dance was over, it was a confused and dismayed group of parents that claimed their children. As far as is known, every child was restored to its rightful owner--but the same could not be said for all the frilly dresses and ribbons.

HERBERT RUBENTHWAITE, Portland, Oregon

Prehistoric Indians of the West

Introduction

Following is the first of three articles tracing the possible migrations of early human tribes of the Columbia River district, particularly as regards movements to the south into Mexico, and further, getting right into the heart of the land of the Maya.

Mr. John W. Kelly published a previous article in the December, 18, 1934 issue of *The Oregonian* citing evidence to the effect that the Columbia River was a center of migration for pre-historic tribes.

"It is a noticeable fact that Indian tribes speaking dialects of the same stock language have usually been found in territorial continuity, however extended their common area. The same has, in the main, been true of all tribes of mankind linguistically united. It requires special advantages in the means of subsistence to render any area an initial point of migration through the gradual development of a surplus population.

These natural centers were few in number in North America. There are but three. First among them is the valley of the Columbia, the most extraordinary region on the face of the earth in variety and amount of subsistence it afforded, prior to cultivation of maize and other plants.

It can be shown with a great deal of probability that the valley of the Columbia was the seed land of the Ganowanian family, from which issued, in past ages, successive streams of migrating bands, until both divisions of the continent were occupied. And, further, that both divisions continued to be replenished from this source down to the epoch of European discovery. These conclusions may be deducted from physical causes, from the linguistic relations of the Indian tribes."

Lewis H. Morgan, Author of "Ancient Society"

Prehistoric Indians of the West

Part 1 of 3

By JOHN W. KELLY, Staff Writer, *The Oregonian*

From the Columbia River in Oregon, the Shoshonean linguistic family has been traced to Central America and South America. Out of the loins of this family may possibly, if not probably, have sprung the Maya people, who had attained a high place in the arts when Europe was a wilderness inhabited by wild tribes. There are reasons for the opinion that the builders of Chichen-Itza and the nomadic aborigines classified as Shoshoneans were akin.

What is set down in this and the two subsequent articles of this series is based upon the opinions of men of science, documented from government reports and papers of scientific societies. Apparently while much has been published regarding the Mayas, and concerning the linguistic families, no attempt has been made heretofore to show the connection between the two and the Oregon Country.

This research was prompted by Dr. Walter Hough, head curator of the American National Museum, who made the observation that the Shoshonean linguistic family had produced the highest and the lowest types in the western hemisphere; that of the Maya Indians and the Digger Indians were related.

With this statement as inspiration, the writer has accumulated a mass of material from public documents, and the reader may draw his own conclusion as to whether Dr. Hough's deduction is correct.

Today all of the Indian tribes of North America have been classified into linguistic families.

There are 55 such families, according to J. W. Powell in the report of the Bureau of American Ethnology, 1891. To the white trapper and early fur trader or explorer of the past 200 years the Indians were identified by various names and regarded as distinct tribes. But ethnologists discovered that many of these tribes are actually members of a particular linguistic family.

Having made this discovery, the scientists began the patient task of tracing the area of each linguistic group.

It is from this careful and slow investigation that the scientists have been successful in checking the zones of these families and satisfying themselves of the relative position, extent, and migration route of the families. Many of the results have been astonishing as revealed in the language charts of government authorities.

The linguistic map of the American Indian discloses how geographic barriers, such as rivers and mountain ranges have separated one family from another and shaped the character, culture, and living conditions of each.

On either side of a range of mountains, not particularly high and easily scaled, lived tribes as widely different in customs as the French and Germans of modern days.

Bit by bit the language students followed the trail of each of the 55 linguistic families as carefully and as painstakingly as the Indians tracked the spoor of their quarry and the researches of these men have mapped the Shoshonean from Oregon to the land of the Maya.

East, west and south of the Shoshoneans were other linguistic families, but the Shoshoneans preserved their identity from other families much as the gulf stream retains its own individuality.

Sharing present-day Oregon with the Shoshonean were 11 other families, listed by the Bureau of American Ethnology as Chinookan, Shahaptian, Waiilatpuan, Kalapooian, Athapascan, Salishan, Yakenan, Kusan, Takilma, Lutoamian and Shastan. These, with the Shoshonean, represent 12 of the 55 linguistic families.

Of all the many families, however, the scientists trace only the Shoshonean into Mexico and beyond. Many of the coast families were quite restricted to their area. Others, such as the Athapascan—to which 53 tribes belong—swept across the continent from West Coast to East Coast, being the same stock as the extinct Mound Builders in Ohio and several southern states.

The Shoshoneans did not cross the Cascade Mountains to the Pacific Ocean, 200 miles to the west. Nor did they extend toward the east very far. Undoubtedly a few individuals made such journeys, but they were casual adventurers. An outpost or two were located at the Big Bend of the Columbia, now in the state of Washington.

Apparently the Shoshoneans were children of the sun, for they selected as their habitat the hot, sandy interior of Eastern Oregon, avoiding the gentle mists of the Willamette Valley between the Cascades and the coast. They dwelt in a land of barren rocks and juniper, of sage brush and greasewood, of pine forests—assuming that the thousands of years which have elapsed, the country occupied by the Shoshoneans has not materially changed.

The dense forests of Douglas Fir with their luxuriant ferns and tangled underbrush were avoided by these people.

Mostly their country was waste—dry lake beds, deserts and precious water holes—it is today, but may have been different then. And in this land were occasional large, shallow lakes, such as Harney, Malheur, Silver Lake, Christmas Lake and the bitter water of Lake Abert and Alkali Lake. North of Harney and Malheur Lakes were the Blue Mountains, covered with forests of pine. That region was studiously avoided.

From the Columbia, in the vicinity of The Dalles, Oregon, the Shoshoneans migrated south, keeping east of the Cascades in Oregon and the Sierra Nevada Mountains in California. The southern part of Idaho is topographically and climatically identical with southeastern Oregon. The Shoshoneans also inhabited that portion of Idaho.

Nevada is a continuation of the same character of country, and over Nevada spread these people. They gave a sparse population to what is now Utah, for that state's topography is a piece with southwestern Oregon, southern Idaho and Nevada.

The southern movement continued, and next the Shoshoneans crossed into Arizona, reaching first the northwestern part. In time, they were settled around Four Corners, the region where the states of Utah, Arizona, Colorado and New Mexico meet. The restless spirit urged them on and ever southward. They worked their way into Mexico.

"Under various names the great race of Shoshones is found scattered over the boundless wilderness from Texas to the Columbia River." – Brownell's *Indian Races*, pp. 537-8.

"The great Snake nation may be divided into the Shirrydikes, or dog-eaters; the Wararereekas, or fish-eaters, and the Banattees, or robbers. But as a nation all go by the general appellation of Shoshones or Snakes."-Simpson's *Route to California.*

From a report of the Bureau of American Ethnology, 1885-6, on *Linguistic Families of America North of Mexico*, the continued southern drift from the start on the banks of the Columbia River is shown thus:

"Over the wide expanse of territory the Shoshoneans split into a number of major divisions, each composed of numerous bands speaking a great number of related dialects. On linguistic ground, as determined by Kroeber, it is convenient to classify the Shoshonean family as follows:

1. **Hopi**. 2. **Plateau Shoshonean**, (A) Ute-Chemehueir; Kawaiisu, Paiute, Panamint, Ute and some of the Bannack. (B) Shoshoni-Comanche-Gosiute, (C) Mono-Paviotso and Shoshoneans of Eastern Oregon. 3. **Kern River Shoshoneans**. 4. **Southern California Shoshoneans**. (A) Serrano. (B) Gabrieleno. (C) Louiseno-Kawii; Agua Caliente; Juaneno; Kawia and Louiseno.

"The genetic relationship of the Shoshonean languages with those of the Pima and Sonoran group and the Nahuatl or Aztec group in Mexico were investigated by Buschman in the middle of the last century. Kroeber, Brinton and Chamberlain maintain the Shoshonean group is only part of a larger family which they have designated Uto-Aztekan."

In *Ancient Civilizations of Mexico*, Spinden says: "The language having the greatest geographical extension within the area under consideration is the Nahuan, now consolidated with the Piman and Shoshoneans in a great stock called Uto-Aztecan."

Another ethnologist, writing on the marvelous Shoshonean ramifications, declares the "Nahua (language kin of Shoshoneans) were in southern Guatemala, Honduras, Nicaragua, Panama and Salvador."

That is getting right into the heart of the country where the Maya people left their monuments. Continuing, says the same writer, the

Toltecs, held by some to be of kindred stock with Nahua, pushed south into Central America, and their descendants were known as Maya-Quiche, Aztecs followed the Toltecs into the valley of Mexico, but that has nothing to do with the trail of the Shoshoneans from the Columbia River, in Oregon.

Spinden, a recognized researcher and authority, put it this way: "The wide geographical distribution of Uto-Aztecan languages has an undeniable historical significance. The numerous tribes represent a very wide range of culture, albeit nearly all are dwellers of arid or semi-arid regions.

"Some, like the Paiute, are miserable 'diggers,' willing to eat anything that will support life; others, like the Comanche, are war-like raiders; more progressive tribes, like the Hopi, have adopted agriculture and developed interesting arts and customs; while the highest members of the group are among the most civilized nations of the new world.

It seems clear that language can be used as a basis of classification over a much greater stretch of time than can other social habits summed up as 'culture.' Particular phases of art, religion and government develop and disappear but the grouping of sounds used to express ideas remains as proof that peoples now far apart geographically were once close together. The peculiar distribution of the Uto-Aztecan languages may indicate a general southward movement of the stock."

Source of the primitive Shoshonean pioneers has not been discovered. This particular strain, presumably, immigrated to North America, as did the Kitchen Midden people and those more daring explorers, the Algonquin and Athapascan, who by slow degrees pushed toward the east until they arrived at the Atlantic seaboard. Or the Shoshoneans may have evolved from the nomads who found and first captured salmon at Celilo Falls on the Columbia River.

A considerable number of rugged tribesmen, bound together by some common cause which may have been born of necessity, after many generations, developed a group which the ethnologists have designated as Shoshonean.

Rough, hardy pioneers of the Pacific Coast settled that region ages before the days of the covered wagon; ages before the principle of the wheel was discovered. These dark-skinned pioneers came in dribbles across prehistoric Berinia, a narrow strip of dry land connecting Northeast Asia and the Americas near the Arctic Circle; an area too dry for glaciers, but moist enough for hardy grasses and herbs, mammoths, and other giants of the Ice Age. Today only a shallow body of water separates Russia and Alaska and is known as the Bering Strait.

There was no prehistoric migration of caravans nor any considerable number engaged in the adventure at one time. Infiltration came slowly and there may have been considerable periods when there were no arrivals. Gradually, however, more and more crossed to the North American side.

First of the pioneers, probably, were those ancient people known to ethnologists as the Kitchen Middens. They found sheltered nooks along the beaches and at the mouth of rivers emptying into the Pacific Ocean.

Their food came from the sea, principally shellfish easily procured from rocks and sands.

For centuries the Kitchen Midden people dwelt at the edge of the surf, ate their simple food and tossed the shells aside. The long period they lived there is attested by the shell mounds extending from Alaska southward along the Pacific. Much has been written of these people in Oregon. The Kitchen Midden people were not the ancestors of the Shoshoneans. The Shoshoneans came much later.

These later arrivals, more curious than the coast dwellers, turned inland from the mouth of the Columbia and followed it east where it cut through the Cascade Mountains. Other large rivers were followed inland as well, but the area around the future city of The Dalles provided the most abundant food supply.

After many centuries, North America was slowly populated. Always more invasions came from Asia, reinforcing the waves of bands which were trickling thinly over the landscape.

How many of these waves slowly arrived into this section of the continent will never be known. Surprisingly, all this occurred before there were civilizations in India or Egypt.

Whether dinosaur, wooly mammoths or the three-toed horses were still roaming the swamps and shallows of lakes or lurking in the jungles may never be determined. Some undiscovered cave or future road-cut may give us the answer when we least expect it.

Restlessly the ancient pioneers explored such regions as provided sustenance with the least effort. Eventually families, or groups, or tribes--the one developing the other--found areas which appealed to them and this region became their range. They resented the presence of others not of their family or tribe who were coming to share the food supply.

This congregation of several tribes was a natural evolution, and it was equally natural that each should develop its own method of expression, thereby giving birth to distinct tongues or languages.

Here and there small knots of Shoshoneans found some spot irresistible, camped, made settlements and lived out there days there. Wanderlust forced others to continue looking for an ideal new home by searching for it to the south.

From the Columbia River down to Mexico the Shoshoneans wandered, but always remained in a country bathed in burning sands, lava beds, rattlesnakes and lizards.

In such manner sprang up tribes of various kinds of Utes, but instead of these tribes being dissimilar, they are part of the remarkable Shoshonean family. Their local name may have deceived early white men, but the scientists demonstrated beyond a doubt the linguistic relationship of widely scattered tribes to the main stem.

Modern science, in its methodical way, discovered a kinship which the tribes themselves did not realize, and the work of the language students has been supplemented by evidence literally dug up from the past by the archeologists in their hunt for artifacts.

Continued residence in certain localities had an influence on and shaped the habits of the Shoshonean groups. It caused them to adapt their mode of living to the nature of the countryside. In certain areas they were huntsman, in others they tilled the soil and raised crops. The Shoshoneans were, perhaps the first agriculturalists on the continent of North America.

They were the pioneer irrigationists, and these prehistoric farmers discovered that the soil which appeared so bleak and uninviting required only the baptism of water to produce abundant food.

The Shoshoneans were so convinced that, with the perpetual sunshine, bountiful crops were assured on watered land. So they built irrigation canals and ditches--which would be a great reclamation project in these days with modern machinery. The Shoshoneans, however, turned irrigationists only after some had left Oregon and had arrived in Arizona.

Why did the ancient peoples of the Columbia turn south instead of another direction? Here is what one scientist says in *Ancient Society, part 2:*

"The great expanse of the central prairies which spread continuously more than 1500 miles from north to south and more than 1000 miles from east to west interposed a natural barrier to a free communication between the Pacific and the Atlantic sides of the continent of North America.

"It seems probable, therefore, that an original family commencing its spread from the valley of the Columbia and migrating under the influence of physical causes would reach Patagonia sooner than they would Florida.

The known facts point so strongly to this region as the original home of the prehistoric Indian family that a moderate amount of additional evidence will render the hypotheses conclusive."

To be continued ...

~ 226 ~

Indian Attack Foiled by White's Quick Wit

In the fall of 1845, Dr. Whitman was informed by friendly Nez Perce Indians that the Walla Walla's were planning to massacre the members of a large train of immigrants, who were, at the time, near the spot where Lewiston, Idaho now stands.

The kindly doctor started at once with a few Nez Perce Indians to meet the train and pilot them to their destination, the Willamette Valley in Oregon.

After Dr. Whitman joined the train his Nez Perce spies reported that the Walla Walla tribe and the Cayuses were gathering and were planning an immediate attack. Young warriors came to the white men's camp prepared to smoke the pipe of peace, but it was evident that they were fully armed and were only taking this method of throwing the immigrants off guard.

The Walla Walla chief stayed in camp during the late afternoon. As dusk fell, the signal fires were gleaming from every hill, and Dr. Whitman knew that a signal from the chief would bring forth the merciless horde.

The chief suddenly demanded that my great-grandmother's baby brother be given to him as a hostage. Seeing that trouble was imminent, Dr. Whitman, by a quick movement pointed his rifle at the chief and commanded great-grandfather to hold him at the point of the gun. Benjamin Walden did as directed, and the chief made no move.

Dr. Whitman said sternly, "Make a move and my man will shoot you like a dog. The command had its desired effect. The vigil lasted until morning, when a group of Nez Perce Indians arrived to give further protection for the remainder of the journey.

Sarah Walden described the night as "a night of terror to all, when no one slept except the younger children."

The kind old Nez Perce chief shook hands with Dr. Whitman that morning, and then addressed himself to the sullen chief, "The Great White Spirit watched the white man, and the Indians should know better than try to kill him."

A cup of good coffee was brought to the Walla Walla chief before he was released. He drank it and ate the proffered food, but refused to talk to the friendly chief. He then walked in dignified silence to his grazing pony and rode away.

MISS VELLEDA OHMART, Salem, Oregon

~ 227 ~

Whites Fare Badly During Stage Raid

During the year of 1866, my uncle was running a stage station at La Grande, Oregon, and my father was a stage driver on the run between Baker, Oregon and Walla Walla, Washington.

It was early in the spring. The roads were in very bad condition from the mud and melting snows, and although a change of horses was made at each station, the horses soon became exhausted, and travel was slow. As the stage, piloted by my father, was nearing Thorn Hollow, on the Old Oregon Trail, a group of Indians hidden in the brush, near the road, gave chase.

Because their horses were fresh, the stage was very soon overtaken. The Indians surrounded the stage, killed one of the passengers, wounded father in the leg, and another man in the hand. The survivors were able to escape in the underbrush, where they remained during the night.

As soon as darkness came, the Indians build a huge bonfire, scalped the man they had killed, dressed themselves in some of the clothing found in the baggage of the passengers, among which were linen dusters, and what was known as bee-hive hats.

Placing the scalp on a pole, they proceeded to dance around the fire and chant their war songs until daylight came. My father and his companions watched from their hiding place, but, as they had made their escape without their guns, they were helpless.

When morning came, the Indians mounted their horses, taking the stage horses and the baggage of the passengers, and rode away. One of the chiefs carried an open umbrella over him which he had found in the stage.

As soon as they were out of sight the passengers started for Pendleton, Oregon, with Father and the other wounded man. Father had become weak from loss of blood, and it was necessary to carry him on a crude stretcher made from poles.

Soon after reaching the road, a settler came along with a team and wagon and took them into Pendleton, where Father and the other wounded man were given medical attention.

The doctor was unable to remove the bullet from Father's leg, and although he lived to be seventy years-of-age, he carried the lead to his grave.

MRS. J. E. JONES, Milton-Freewater, Oregon

~228~

Clerk Pays Twice for Indian Maiden

More than a century ago, when Spokane, Washington was a fur trading post, one of the young clerks at the fort, fell in love with an Indian girl of the Spokane tribe.

Whatever may be our ideas of mixed marriages today the practice was common at that time when there were so few white girls in the whole Oregon Territory. Consequently the young white man did not hesitate to ask for her hand in marriage. The girl's father was dead, so the terms of marriage were settled with her mother and brother.

Since the girl was one of the prettiest in the tribe, it was decided that she was worth an extra amount of blankets and kettles. The price was paid and preparations were made for the wedding.

The prospective bride was bathed and scoured until she was free of paint and bear's grease, and a calico dress was substituted for her fringed leather jacket. Arrayed in her newly acquired finery, the bridegroom found her even more fair, and he congratulated himself on his good fortune.

Then, as in an old-fashioned melodrama, the villain, in the person of a young Indian, rode into the courtyard, heavily armed and with several followers. He almost wrecked their happiness.

"Why have you stolen my wife?" he demanded savagely. In vain did the bridegroom protest that he knew nothing of the previous marriage. He explained he had paid for his bride with blankets and kettles in the best of faith and family approval.

While the subject of the controversy ran away and hid in panic, the outraged Indian 'husband' scorned all offers of settlement.

Nothing short of dire revenge on his faithless wife would give him satisfaction.

At last, however, a happy compromise was reached. For a gun, a hundred rounds of ammunition, two kettles, three blankets, a spur, a dagger and several pounds of smoking tobacco, he would renounce all claim to his wicked young wife.

The incident sounds suspiciously like what is termed in the underworld today as "the old badger game," but according to historical records, the white man paid the articles demanded and, at last, he had clear title to his lovely Indian bride.

PHILLIP STARR, Portland, Oregon

~229~

One of Joe Meek's Noted Tales Retold

Joe Meek is one of the best remembered "mountain men" of Oregon. He settled in the Willamette Valley in time to be made the first United States Marshal for Oregon. More than 65 years ago, Mrs. Frances Fuller Victor took down from Meek's own lips, many stories of his trapping adventures and wove them into her book, *The River of the West.*

She tells us that "from something humorous in Joe Meek's personality or some wonderful 'luck' to which he was born, or both, most of his adventures with bears, as with men, were of a humorous complexion. This enabled him, not only to have a story to tell, but one at which his companions were certain to laugh. This one which happened during the Fall hunt in 1830 we will let him tell for himself."

"The first fall on the Yellerstone, Hawkins and myself were coming up the river in search of camp, when we discovered a very large 'bar' on the opposite bank. We shot across and thought we had killed him, for he laid quite still.

"As we wanted to take some trophy of our victory to camp, we tied our mules and left our guns, clothes and everything except our knives and belts and swum over to whar the bar war.

"But instead of being dead, as we expected, he sprung up, as we came near him, and took after us.

"Then you ought to have seen two naked men run! It war a race for life, and a close one, too. But we made the river first. The bank war about fifteen feet high above the water and the river ten or twelve feet deep, but we didn't halt.

"Overboard we went, the bar after us, and in the stream about as quick as we war. The current war very strong and the bar war about halfway between Hawkins and me.

"Hawkins was tryin' to swim down-stream faster than the current war carrying the bar, and I war tryin' to hold back. You can recon that I swam! Every moment I felt myself being washed into the yawning jaws of that mighty beast, whose head war up the stream and his eyes on me. But the current war too strong for him and swept him along as fast as it did me.

"All this time, not a long one, we war lookin' for some place to land where the bar could not overtake us. Hawkins war the first to make the shore, unknown to the bar, whose head war still upstream. Hawkins set up such a whoopin' and yellin' that the bar landed too, but on the opposite side.

"I made haste to follow Hawkins, who had landed on the side of the river we started from, either by design or good luck. We then traveled back a mile or more to whar our mules war left--a bar on one side of the river--and two bares on the other!"

ROBERT MOULTON GATKE, Salem, Oregon

~ 230 ~

Lewelling Developed Many Fine Cherries

The world owes a real debt of gratitude to Seth Lewelling, who came across the plains in 1850 with his wagons loaded down with fruit tree saplings with which he started, and developed the Lewelling Nursery, located just a few miles south of Portland and a few miles north of Oregon City.

There he grew a great many cherry seedlings and pollinated many blossoms in his search for improved varieties. His painstaking efforts went not without some failure and some tribulations.

The story is told of the extreme care needed to save the pits of cherries, and how on one occasion a prominent lady visitor was embarrassed through not understanding the experimental procedure.

Mr. Lewelling practiced bagging of the blossoms to prevent contamination after being cross-pollinized. After the bags had been removed, he tagged the branches by means of blue and red strings to indicate the fruits to be saved so that the seeds could be planted later.

The lady visitor was sampling cherries from the trees, and on spying the brightly colored strings, concluded that these would be the tastiest cherries to eat. Seth Lewelling stood by watching the event, and finally, holding out his hand, said, "Madam, may I have the seeds?"

The lady was said later to have expressed her indignation at the unintended insult, and told others that she considered Seth Lewelling a stingy miser because he would not let her have but a few cherries to take home--and he even asked for the pits.

At any rate, he contributed the finest sweet cherries to the world, notable among which are named the Black Republican, Bing, Lincoln, and the Willamette Seedling.

The story of the naming of the Black Republican variety was told recently by a living relative of Seth Lewelling, Mrs. Herman F. Ledding of Milwaukie, Oregon.

At the time he was experimenting, the Oregon Country was overwhelmingly Democratic. Many of the early settlers had come from the southern states and were in sympathy with slavery.

Seth Lewelling was an abolitionist, and was severely condemned by his neighbors and was spoken of as a "black Republican." The cognomen was first taken lightly, but later Mr. Lewelling decided to perpetuate the name, and by naming one of his new sweet, dark red cherry varieties, he said, "I will make them relish the name Black Republican."

And he did. Today, this favorite sweet cherry is enjoyed by hundreds of thousands of people, but without any thought of stigma attached to it--as it was the day it was named.

The Bing cherry variety was also originated and named by Seth Lewelling. The name was selected in honor of a Chinese foreman who worked for Mr. Lewelling. He had been employed in their household for more than 35 years. Seth was very fond of Bing and preferred his company and friendship above many others. In appreciation of his loyalty and friendship, one of the finest, bright red, sweet cherries ever produced was named in honor of Bing.

The variety named Willamette Seedling was developed from the wild cherry trees that grew along the foothills west of the Cascade Range at an unincorporated area about six miles east of Sandy, Oregon called Cherryville.

The Lewelling Nursery was established near the banks of the Willamette River, near Milwaukie.

The cherries originated in Oregon by the Lewelling family have brought wealth and happiness to many people on the Pacific Coast as well as around the world.

WILLIS P. DURUZ, School of Agriculture, Oregon State College, Corvallis, Oregon

~ 231 ~

Ponies Offered in Trade for Bride

In 1852, Julia Parker, a young bride of seventeen--tall, black-haired, brown-eyed and beautiful--and her husband, together with a small company of brave pioneers, left Cincinnati, Ohio, by wagon train, for that new, unexplored country in the far west--Oregon.

They traveled practically the entire distance of two thousand miles on foot, walking beside the wagons--sometimes barefooted, their shoes worn from the long journey. They followed the Old Oregon Trail, later made famous by history.

At one point along the way, the wagon train was surrounded, in broad daylight, by a band of Indians. The chief fell in love with Julia Parker on sight and offered to trade several Indian ponies for her. But her husband refused. And he offered more ponies, and still more. Still Mr. Parker refused, trying to convince the chief no amount of ponies, or anything, could purchase his loving bride.

Finally the Indians left, only to return that same night, under cover of darkness, to try to steal her. There was a fierce encounter, during which two members of the wagon train, sadly, were killed, Many Indians gave up their lives as well before they finally rode away. The little band of whites cautiously proceeded on their way, finally settling in Albany, Oregon.

Among Julia Parker's descendants are many who are tall, black-haired and brown eyed--just like the brave pioneer bride.

BERYL LeLONG, Eugene, Oregon

~ 232 ~

Heroism Displayed by Brave Woman

Here's a tale of feminine heroism relayed to the writer by an eye witness, Charles Brunzell, one of a family of that name, long prominent in the affairs of Southern Idaho and Eastern Oregon. Brunzell came in with the gold rush in the early 1860s. Ruby City, War Eagle City, and later Silver City, were the new mining camps of that hectic period.

Twenty thousand people were busy placer and lode mining for gold in and around these camps. The miners were killing the deer and other game. The Indians were resentful and continually on the warpath. The Central Pacific Railroad was not yet completed, so supplies all came from Umatilla Landing by ox and mule teams, and by horse pack trains.

"It was 1865," said Charley, "I was coming out of the mines with a four-mule team, near Monday's Ferry. A miner was riding with me. Behind us, a short distance, was a Mr. and Mrs. Cox driving a two-horse team and wagon. They were from the Reynolds Creek settlement.

"As I came to the top of Signboard Hill, I heard a volley of shots and looking around saw a band of warriors closing in on the Cox's wagon. The horses were in a dead run and the woman held the reins.

"I put the blacksnake to my mules and we went down the steep slope of Signboard Hill at full speed. Two hundred yards from the foot of the hill, one of my mules fell. I set the brakes, jumped out, unhooked the mules, got astraddle one of them and was on my way. Out of the corner of my eye, I glimpsed at my companion running toward a deep gully with a six-shooter in one hand and a hatchet in the other. He escaped, undetected.

"The Cox team was running away, but the cool-headed woman kept them in the road and brought herself and the dead body of her husband, who had been killed at the first fire back at Monday's Ferry. The cavalry had heard the firing and came on the gallop. The Indians halted on top of Signboard Hill, fired a few shots at us, turned and rode swiftly away.

"When Mr. Cox was killed he would have pitched forward, out of the wagon, but his wife caught him and jerked him back so that he fell into the wagon-box behind her. She held the reins with the other hand and by her coolness and daring, saved herself from unspeakable torture--and the body of her husband from mutilation at the hands of the relentless warriors."

JAMES R. KEITH, Grants Pass, Oregon

~ 233 ~

Boy Falls Victim to Attack of Cougar

In 1869, my family landed in Cowlitz County, Washington. It was in Rose Valley, then Shanghai Valley, and our home was located about two miles southeast of Carrolls.

At that time, there were lots of wild animals in the woods, bear and cougar being numerous. While there were instances of cougars having stalked human beings, there were no tragedies, from this cause, in Shanghai. This probably was owing to the fact that children were never allowed out after dark, except when accompanied by older people.

But in the late 1870s, a tragedy occurred on Mount Pleasant, on a ridge beginning at Carrolls and running for several miles parallel to Shanghai. In

1867 or 1868, there was a terrible forest fire which destroyed most of the big timber on Mount Pleasant. It then grew up with thick brush.

One afternoon, a daughter of one of the settlers, Myra Graves, who was about fifteen years old, was walking along a road that was not much more than a trail. She was accompanied by a half-brother, about five years old. A large cougar suddenly sprang out of the brush, seized the boy by the head and started back through the brush with him.

Myra picked up a club and beat off the brute, but not until the boy was badly lacerated, the head wounds causing his death. A hunt immediately was started by the settlers and after a few days the animal was found and killed.

Some skeptical doubt was expressed as to Myra's defense story of the boy. But the fact that the cougar did abandon the unconscious boy, after tasting blood, was considered ample proof of the correctness of her story.

J. L. LYSONS, Snohomish, Washington

~ 234 ~

Dire Tragedy Claims Bridal Party Lives

Early in February, 1843, Cornelius Rogers decided to leave his post in the Presbyterian Missions of Eastern Oregon and set out to renew his missionary work in the Willamette Valley. He was accompanied by his wife, a bride of three weeks, and her younger sister. Their destination was the Willamette Falls, the present site of Oregon City.

As they were preparing to leave, a man by the name of Raymond arrived from Clatsop, Oregon for the purpose of obtaining supplies which were to be transported in a large canoe belonging to the mission. The

Rogers and their party decided to embark for the falls in the supply canoe. No hint did they have of the terrible fate that awaited them.

The Willamette River, swollen with winter rains and snow melt-off from the Cascade Mountains, was running high and with great force. Arriving at the rapids below the falls, the passengers unloaded and departed the canoe which was then portaged around the falls where it was lowered, by means of a rope, to a point near a loading dock where the Rogers, and others in the party, again climbed into it to continue their trip up the river .

Four Indians also joined them, while Raymond stayed on shore, and with the assistance of three half-breeds held the line on the canoe as it drifted to the proper landing. Unfortunately, it went past the landing a short distance and drifted alongside a log sometimes used as an emergency landing.

One of the party stepped out on shore with one foot and made an attempt to hold the canoe with the other. But the buoyant canoe was easily set in motion by the slightest movement and the main current caught the bow of the boat carrying it into midstream.

The river was rushing onwards toward the cataract with seething, pitched force. Hopelessly, those on shore endeavored to hold their grip on the rope, but as the tugging lime hauled them into the water, they were forced to let go in order to save themselves. Two of the Indians aboard, sensing the immediate danger, sprang into the water and swam to shore.

Meanwhile, the canoe, now wildly out of control, sped like an arrow toward the falls. A cry of terror and blood curdling screams went up from the doomed passengers.

Over the cataract shot the craft, crashing on the rocks below, then disappearing beneath the boiling waters. Five whites and two Indians descended to the river below, never to be seen alive again. Later, only two bodies were recovered from the water--Cornelius Rogers being one.

KEITH SOESBE, Portland, Oregon

~ 235 ~

Bad-Man Example Brings Gun Reform

My father, the late J. L. Dumas, educator and citizen, told me of his reasons for discarding the wearing of a revolver when he was a tenderfoot in the early 1880s. "I taught school for one term at the wild and wooly little settlement of Marengo, on the Tucannon River, about 20 miles from Dayton, Oregon. By reason of my 'education' I was called on to act as coroner, doctor, and even in the capacity of priest. I was constantly armed, gun holstered, except to annoy an occasional jack rabbit, and I found it was really quite a nuisance, and unnecessary for a school teacher to carry a gun.

"Finally occurred the incident which caused me to unstrap holster and gun and put them away in the bureau drawer. I was in Dayton, the county seat, on a busy Saturday afternoon. In those days, when the weather was good and no farm work was pressing, every buggy, hack and wagon team, with dozens and dozens of saddle horses, was tied to the hitching racks near the courthouse and on all the side streets and alleys. Groups of farmers were knotted on the wide wooden sidewalks--or sitting on the benches in front of the stores.

"Down the street came riding one of those tough guys, such as we see nowadays in movie westerns. Wooly chaps, spurs, sombrero, tobacco label on a string hanging out of the breast pocket of his flashy shirt, and on each hip a holster and gun. He threw his reins over a post in true Buck Jones fashion and swaggered toward the swinging doors of the local saloon. But before he got there, and old fellow sitting on the bench accosted him."

"Boy, com'ere", said he in a mild tone. "What is yu afeered of?"

"By God, I ain't askeerd of nothin", blustered the would-be bad man.

"Oh, yes yu are, my boy, or yu wouldn't be a wearin' all them guns. Like as not, yu've got a big, sharp frog sticker hanged sommers on yu. Just who or what is yu askeered of?"

"His mild ridicule was the signal for a wave of biting remarks from the crowd, and before long, the he-man with the heavy artillery had been joshed so bad he rode out of town. He couldn't fight words with guns.

"I imagine that when I put away my six-shooter that night, I was only one of many who had decided that heavy armament is a pretty sure indication of either fear--or braggadocio."

LOUIS F. DUMAS, Dayton, Oregon

"Northwest Empire Builders"

GEORGE H. WILLIAMS

A Statesman of a Bitter Era

By DAVID W. HAZEN, Staff Writer,
The Oregonian. March 24, 1935

George Henry Williams lives in history as Oregon's greatest statesman. There are many disputed questions in the story of this state, but no one debates the premiership of this leader.

He came here from Iowa in 1853 as Chief Justice of the Territory of Oregon. His first important decision freed the slaves, a decision that did much towards making Oregon a free state.

Judge Williams was Chairman of the Judicial Committee of the Oregon Constitutional Convention, and had a notable part in the writing of that great document. He was a leader in forming the Union Party here at the outbreak of the American Civil War. He was a United States Senator from 1865 to 1871. He was a member of the Joint High Commission that framed and signed the Treaty of Washington, one of diplomacy's most glorious chapters.

Soon after he was appointed Attorney General in President Grant's cabinet, and there played an outstanding role in the tragedy of southern reconstruction. He originated the 14th Amendment to the Constitution of the United States. Williams was appointed Chief Justice of the

Supreme Court by Grant, but such a bitter personal fight was made on the ex-Senator that he asked the President to withdraw his name.

Returning to Oregon and resuming the practice of law, Judge Williams continued to be active in party ranks. He was Mayor of Portland from 1902 to 1905. When death recently closed the judge's eyes in eternal sleep, Harvey W. Scott, Editor of The Oregonian, wrote this tribute:

"His greatness, like all true greatness, was rooted in his unconsciousness of it. All the mistakes he ever made were due to the simplicity and trustfulness of his nature. Himself without guile, he never imagined it, even to his latest day, in others. If this was a limitation, it was a fault that leaned to virtue's side."

George H. Williams served on the bench in Iowa. He was elected a judge in 1847, when only twenty-four years old, having been born March 26, 1823, at New Lebanon, New York. In 1852, he was one of the Iowa Presidential electors. The following year, President Pierce, wanting to do something for the Hawkeye political worker, appointed Judge Williams with the title of Chief Justice of Oregon Territory to succeed O. C. Pratt, who was named to the far-away post by President Polk.

Pratt had been one of the stalwarts in the democratic party here, but he lost much of his influence by a bit of sharp practice. He bought a drove of common Spanish cattle from a man named Durham, then turned around and sold them for a very high price by making the buyer believe the critters were fine-blooded Durham stock. When this trick was discovered, the judge's power began to wane. The Senate rejected Pratt's renomination.

The ex-jurist then tried to succeed Joseph Lane as the territory's delegate to Congress, but was politically slaughtered. J. W. Nesmith, when writing to M. P. Deady about the contest, said, "Pratt's sun of Austerlitz has gone down amid the gloom of Waterloo—no man was ever let down so fast."

Had Judge Pratt continued on the bench, it is very unlikely that the young jurist from Iowa would ever have resided in Oregon. Most Iowans, traveling west, linger in California. Judge Williams came to Oregon as an uncompromising Democrat, but he said the appointment was made without his knowledge or consent.

He was considered an outsider, an alien, by members of the party already in the territory. They were trying to have the National Administration adopt their motto, "Oregon Jobs for Oregonians on the Spot."

George H. Williams was such a wonderful man that he soon won over the leaders who had been growling about his appointment. But within a few weeks he gave the southern faction of the party here a blow between the eyes. From it, the faction never fully recovered. It was the most momentous decision ever given from an Oregon bench, for it settled at once, and for all time, the question of slavery in this territory.

It was in 1853 that he awarded freedom to all negro bondsmen here on the grounds that slavery did not, and could not, exist in Oregon. The decision was accepted as final. The case was bought before Justice Williams by attorneys for a slave named Robbin, and his family, who sued for liberty by writ of habeas corpus.

These slaves were brought to this section in a coffle owned by Nathaniel Ford, who came out from Missouri and settled on a Polk County homestead. Years afterward, in speaking of this decision, Judge Williams said:

"Among the first cases I was called upon to decide when I came to Oregon in 1853, was an application by a colored family in Polk County to be liberated upon habeas corpus from their Missouri owner, who had brought and held them here as slaves.

"They were held upon the claim that the Constitution of the United States protected slave property in the territories. But it was my judgment that the law, made by the pioneers upon the subject, was not inconsistent with the spirit of the Constitution and was the law of the land. The petitioners were set free. And, so far as I know, this was the last attempt at slave-holding in Oregon.

"When the State Government was formed, strenuous efforts were put forth to make Oregon a slave state, but inspired by the example and sentiments of the early pioneers, we decided to go into the Union as a free state."

When the growing storm over slavery became the paramount political issue throughout the nation, Judge Williams wrote a forceful statement in favor of Oregon becoming a free state. He had lost caste with the southern wing of his party when he freed Robbin. Now he was out in the cold, in total zero weather in so far as the Democratic Party in Oregon was concerned.

The Salem Statesman, then an outstanding newspaper of the party in power, said in March, 1857, "Had our climate, productions and markets unquestionably favored slave labor, Oregon would have knocked for admission into the Union as a slave state."

This same newspaper on July 28, 1857, printed Judge Williams' famous "Free State Letter." I took up the entire front page of the Statesman. Although a true Democrat, the jurist has always opposed the spread of slavery into the new states. He pointed out that "isolated, as Oregon is, by thousands of miles from other slave states, and from all the supports of slavery, an effort to maintain the institution here would be almost as impotent as the command of the vain Canute to the waves of the ocean."

And then the writer of the historic letter asked, "Can Oregon, at present and in the future, by making its great claims upon the government, afford to throw away the friendship of the North—the overruling power of the nation—for the sake of slavery?" But he didn't have any quarrel with the owners of slaves in the southern commonwealths. George Williams was never of the John Brown cult. In his Salem Statesman article, the judge is careful to make this plain. He says:

"Whatever may be inferred from my arguments against slavery in Oregon, I disclaim all sympathy with the abolitional agitators of the North, and deprecate and denounce all sectional organizations on the subject."

But he realized the seriousness of the situation, and at the beginning of his letter, Judge Williams declared, "Conscious that this slavery discussion has shaken the pillars of the republic, has rent the most powerful church of the nation in twain, has appeared upon the plains of Kansas with fierce strife and bloodshed, I address myself to it, feeling somewhat as I would to approach a cloud charged with lightning and whirlwind."

The letter caused a sensation. It wrecked the writer's political hopes as a Democrat. He was to reach great heights in statescraft, but, as a member of the Union and later the Republican parties. He had hoped to be one of the first United States Senators from Oregon when the territory was admitted. But upon the publication of the "Free State Letter," he realized that his "hopes vanished like the pictures of a morning dream."

Just the same, he became a candidate for the high office, running as a Douglas Democrat. In canvassing Linn County, he challenged his opponent, Delazon Smith, to a verbal battle. They made their trips about the settlements together, fighting each other in bitter speeches each day, but usually sleeping in the same bed every night. Inns were very few, spare rooms in private homes likewise. Of course, Smith won.

In 1862, Judge Williams took an active part in the Union movement that swept the young commonwealth. At the Union State Convention, held at Eugene in April, he was the new party. In December, 1863, the "Union League of America for the State of Oregon" was organized in Portland. It was formed to fight the Copperhead movement that was growing in the Northwest. Two weeks after the first council was started here, Multnomah Council No.2 was installed with G. H. Williams as President.

The campaign of 1864 opened early and violently. The Union cause was not prospering on the battlefronts. One of the first important political meetings in Oregon that year was held in Lafayette on February 23. Williams made a stirring address. Lincoln's policies were strongly indorsed. Throughout the campaign, Judge Williams was the chief speaker for the administration. Again the Unionists won.

And again Williams was a candidate for the Senate. "The third time's to charm," an old saying goes. Harding had been elected only to fill out the unexpired term of E. D. Baker, slain in battle. Harding had not measured up to the Republican ideals, so was out of the running. The ex-Chief Justice and T. H. Pearne, called the "Holy Cobbler," were the chief candidates. Williams was elected by the legislature on the third ballot. He was named as a Unionist, not as a Republican. But he never returned to the Democratic Party.

Senator Williams' term in the Senate was marked by such bitterness that it has been termed by one great historian, Claude G. Bowers, "*The Tragic Era.*" In the battle against President Johnson, the Oregon Senate played a most prominent role.

He was one of the Senate's six members on the famous Joint Committee on Reconstruction, sometimes called the Committee of Fifteen. This group led the terrific fight made on the President. And it was Senator Williams who introduced the measure that was to lead to the impeachment of Andrew Johnson.

On the first Monday in December, 1866, Williams presented to the Senate a very important bill "to regulate the tenure of civil offices." This bill was intended "to deprive the President of the power of removing Federal officers." The measure was in fact a declaration of war against the Chief Executive and became a law over his veto.

At the impeachment trial, Senator Williams voted "guilty." Throughout that long, strange contest, this Oregonian was one of Johnson's bitterest and most clever foemen.

The Democrats having gained control of the Oregon Legislature in 1870, Judge Williams was not re-elected. But President Grant appointed him a member of the Joint High Commission to pass on the questions of dispute with Great Britain, including the Alabama claims. The Commission met in Washington, where the treaty was signed May 8, 1871. This treaty of Washington is considered one of the four most important treaties made by the United States in the 19th century.

In writing of the peaceful settlement of war-breeding disputes, James G. Blain in his "*Twenty Years of Congress*" stated, "The gentlemen constituting the Joint High Commission were well known in their respective countries, and enjoyed the fullest measure of public confidence, thus insuring, in advance, the acceptance of whatever settlement they might agree upon."

Sometime later, President Grant appointed Williams Attorney General. The soldiers were still stationed in the late Confederate states. Carpet-baggers were holding many of the public offices. There was much hatred, an orgy of bloodshed. The Attorney General had to uphold the laws passed by Congress, passed in revengeful mood. Again it was a time that tried men's souls. George H. Williams was to make a few new enemies, who were to defeat him in his hope to gain the highest office in the land, that of President of the United States..

But, according to historian Bowers, it was the smart, elegant wife of the Attorney General who kept him from becoming Chief Justice of the United States Supreme Court. The Oregon statesman was appointed to the position by Grant. But we must return to Bowers. In writing of Mrs. Williams, he says in his book, "*The Tragic Era*."

"But she has the weakness of ambition too, and breezy westerner though she is, she has aroused the deadly ire of Senators by announcing that, as a cabinet lady, their wives must call on her first. Alas, the memory of that blunder is to send her to her bed one day, when her husband's nomination for the Supreme Court will fail of confirmation."

Grant doubtless could have pushed Williams' appointment over. He only needed a few more votes, and there are ways for gaining these. But the nominee was weary of the nasty, nauseating fight made against him and insisted that his name be withdrawn.

"Bitter as the blow was to Grant, it was more bitter to Williams, and still more bitter to Mrs. Williams, consumed with pride and ambition, and within two months, she was to take to her bed, crushed and heart-broken," writes Mr. Bowers.

One of the queer things brought up against the Attorney General was that he and his wife rode about Washington in a government-owned landaulet. The rig had been furnished to the Department of Justice, the same as carriages were assigned to other departments of the Government. But there was so little on which to base the attack on Williams that this was seized by his enemies, and added to, until it became a grand issue. He was called by opposition newspapers, "Landaulet" Williams.

The Judge was a delegate to the Republican National Convention in 1880, when a determined effort was made to nominate Grant for a third term. But while the ex-cabinet member continued to be interested in politics throughout his long and useful life, he devoted most of his time to the practice of law upon his return to Portland from Washington. During his years in the Senate, he did much towards aiding legislation for railroad development in Oregon. In 1870, Senator Williams succeeded in getting the Post Office Department to put in a daily mail service from Portland to Corvallis.

The route ran by way of Hillsboro, Forest Grove, North Yamhill, Lafayette, McMinnville, Amity, Dallas, Monmouth, Independence and Buena Vista. Contractor J. C. Carr used four-horse coaches between Portland and McMinnville, and two-horse coaches pulled from McMinnville to Corvallis.

Judge Williams was one of the early promoters of the woolen mills at Salem and for a time was President of the company. He took an active part in the development of Portland, and also was one of three who laid out the townsite of Albina in the early 1870s. He made a notable address at the laying of the cornerstone of the Portland Chamber of Commerce building on January 1, 1892.

From July 1, 1902 to June 30, 1905, Judge Williams was Mayor of Portland.

His sunset years were happily spent, enjoying the company of friends, in writing and in reading favorite classics and histories. On Saturday, April 2, 1910, he attended a matinee to see Robert Mantell in "Romeo and Juliet." Sunday he spent at home reading and chatting with a few callers.

The next morning, he did not answer the call. He was sleeping the sleep of the ages.

DAVID W. HAZEN, Staff Writer, *The Oregonian*, March 24, 1935

~ 236 ~

Marriage of Princess Brings Peace Pact

An Indian princess, the daughter of Chief "Sly Horse," and his wife, "Running Fawn," of a Washougal tribe living on the Columbia River, won the heart of Richard Ough, one of Dr. McLoughlin's men at Fort Vancouver, Washington. Their romantic courtship and marriage resulted in a pact of peace with the tribe.

Many years ago, I heard the story from the lips of a grandson of this union, whose mother had died when he was quite a small child. He had spent his boyhood with his Indian grandmother under the very shadow of Angel's Rest, the well-known landmark just east of Bridal Veil Falls on the Oregon side of the river.

The story as related to me, and as told by herself to a reporter in 1910 (the year before she passed on at Washougal at the age of 105) is substantially as follows:

When Dr. McLoughlin was establishing the Hudson's Bay Fur Company trading post at Vancouver, Washington in 1822, he and some of his men visited the Indians at their fishing grounds near Celilo Falls, seeking to peaceably trade with them. They came upon the Indians while the chief and his daughter were out on the river, she paddling their canoe and her father fishing.

The girl was then 18 years old. Richard Ough and she fell in love--at first sight. Ough was a commanding figure, like the doctor, six feet two inches in height and weighing 240 pounds.

The Indians retreated upon the appearance of the whites and considered killing the newcomers. When Ough indicated that he would like to make overtures to the girl, Dr. McLoughlin, anxious to avoid and trouble, said to him, "No!. Do you want to lose your scalp?"

About a month later, while the girl and her father were again out fishing, much to their surprise, Ough reappeared, this time approaching in a canoe--alone. His bravery, in daring to come unarmed and alone into the camp of a hostile tribe won the admiration of the chief.

For eight days, Ough remained in camp, pressing his suit for the girl's hand. The chief finally gave his consent upon extracting a promise that Ough would settle down and build his bride a house at Vancouver. Ough promptly did so and shortly a hundred canoes bought the chief and his men to celebrate the marriage. The couple were married by Dr. McLoughlin, who said (again to quote the aged Betsy Ough) "Now all be brothers—you must live in peace and never fight each other." Then chief say, "As long as Richard and Betsy live in house on river, red man and white man no fight."

They lived in their new home for eight years. Among the stories related of the good times they sometimes had at the company post, is one of Dr. McLoughlin's being prevailed upon, by bantering friends, to compete with the Indian bride in an endurance jig dance, in which the agile girl easily out-did him.

Many too, are the stories told of the generosity of this pioneer couple in helping newly arriving starving immigrants. On one occasion, there came to them a struggling family of four, and man and his wife with two baby girls--all half-starved. At the time, the Oughs had scarcely enough food for themselves, to say nothing of feeding others. The need of this destitute family was so evident that when the parents felt they must proceed on their way, it seemed to the Oughs that the babies could not possibly survive without help. So they gave their only milk cow to the departing strangers. That cow saved their lives, and Betsy had the satisfaction, in later years, of meeting the two girls--then grown to womanhood. Perhaps this is why a common name given to a family milk cow is "Betsy."

THEODORE BURKHART, Portland, Oregon

~ 237 ~

He Got His Harem, But What a Harem!

In the early days, before the white man's law penetrated the wilds of the Northwest, the Indians of the Pacific Coast had a unique and very effective method of performing marriage rites.

They would dig large caves in hillsides and into these the tribe would congregate once a year for the wedding dance. One such dance was located on what later became the Grand Ronde Reservation in the near vicinity of what is now New Grand Ronde.

Pierre was a husky Indian lad, large and wise beyond his years. He loved to slip quietly into the cave and silently watch as "Chamato Jack" built and lit the peculiarly constructed fire in the center of the dugout, around which those seeking matrimonial venture would later dance.

No detail escaped his adolescent eye. Watching with interest as the women assembled and stoically encircled the blaze. His interest quickened when the men glided in and formed a large circle around the women. The men then commenced their wild, fantastic dance, accompanied by the weird music of tom-toms and the eerie light of the flame playing upon their immobile features.

This festival lasted three days and as many nights. Pierre's curiosity enjoyed the maximum degree of satisfaction when the first male placed a wooden chip on a maiden's shoulder. He rejoiced when the chip remained, for he knew the wooer had won his suit, and felt keen disappointment when the chip was shaken off, as that meant the brave was looked upon with disfavor by the chosen woman.

Wooing, rejecting, accepting--on went the dance until each male had chosen and carried away his "bride" for the ensuing year--mayhap at the next meeting he would return to make another selection.

The over-watchful observant, Pierre, noted at the termination of these gala affairs, there were always a goodly number of unclaimed, would-be brides. When he reached maturity and was finally invited to join the circle, Pierre laid his plans well.

He came gorgeously arrayed in heavily beaded and fringed attire--but minus his wooing chip. His dancing was wilder, faster, leaps higher and mightier than any other participant.

When the dance ended and the braves with their women departed to their winter quarters, Pierre surveyed his harem. In the pale light of the dying embers by which "Chamato Jack" still squatted, stood seven women.

With a silent command to his possessions, and a sly glance to "Chamato Jack," he turned and passed into the night--swaggering just a little.

Leading the way to a ramshackle barn not far distant, he lined up the weaker sex and with the aid of sulfur matches, peered into their faces, seeking the most comely. After seven matches lighted up seven ancient and withered countenances, he stood staring blankly into darkness--until the fire of the last match, burning cruelly into his fingers, brought reality back.

A great understanding descended upon him. Alas and alack! There was no Venus among them. Pierre bolted.

The next autumn the wedding dance was attended by a more subdued, but much wiser Pierre. "Chamato Jack" couldn't suppress a knowing glance and a subtle smile as Pierre stepped into the cave.

In the bosom of his none-too-clean buckskin shirt, reposing against his young sweating body was a brand-new, pungent cedar chip.

MAY WHITEAKER, Monmouth, Oregon

~ 238 ~

Indians Kept at Bay by Dog's Resistance

A family named Contner lived in a log cabin about twenty miles east of Portland, Oregon in 1853. The father worked at his trade in Portland and regularly, on a Saturday morning, trudged home with his week's earnings.

One evening during his absence, six Cayuse braves and three Indian women camped near the cabin. They had driven a band of ponies across the Cascade Mountains a few days before and were returning. They had been successful in selling and trading them, and were well supplied with flour, clothing, blankets and a beverage they liked.

They were quiet and well behaved and frequently passed through the yard for water, but as the night advanced they grew noisy.

The mother became alarmed, knowing they were drinking alcohol. The children were all in bed asleep. Their little white dog, Carlo, was at the gate barking, for the cabin was enclosed by a fence. The pioneer mother roused her children, threw the cabin door wide open, and had all six of them gather around her.

She told them that the Indians were drinking, that Carlo might be able to keep them out of the yard, but if he couldn't, they must try to escape and hide in the woods, fearing they all might be killed. The children were frightened, but not one cried. They had great confidence in Carlo and they believed he could keep the Indians away.

It was a fine moonlight night and the pioneer woman and her children could see very plainly all that transpired. Presently an Indian woman came, staggering up the path to the gate. She screamed, in Chinook, "Chuck, chuck, nika hias tika chuck," which means, "Water, water. I want water badly."

She tried to open the gate, but the little dog jumped at her viciously and barked excitedly. She drew back, afraid, and made no further attempts to enter, but she hung onto the gate for more than an hour and screamed at the top of her voice for water.

Three Indian men came to her aid and tried to drive the little dog away, but he barked and snapped at them so viciously they also became frightened. All four finally staggered back to their camp.

After they had gone, the children crept back into bed and slept, while their mother sat at the door and watched until morning. Not long after sunrise, four Indian men, somewhat sobered, and a woman came to the cabin gate and asked for "fire water."

"I have none," replied the mother. Slowly they turned and walked away, very disappointed.

Carlo, still guarding at the gate, heard her voice and ran into the cabin barking and wagging his tail. The children hugged him and cried, "Carlo, Carlo, you saved our lives last night."

He guarded and played with the children only a few weeks longer. When the salmon came up into the mountain streams, he ate some of the raw meat, sickened with salmon poisoning, and died.

The grief-stricken family buried Carlo and marked his grave lovingly--with white stones.

MRS. ANNIE K. BORBRIDGE, Pasadena, California

~ 239 ~

Rogue River Settlers Take Terrible Revenge

During the early spring months of 1855, the Indians of the lower Rogue River country, puzzled and angry over the encroachments of the early settlers and miners, went on the warpath in an effort to kill all the whites.

After a few skirmishes and minor engagements, the federal troops and local volunteers forced the To-To-Tin tribe to surrender. They were sent to the Siletz and Grand Ronde Reservations, while the white men settled like a cloud of locusts on beaches and creek beds in a mad search for gold.

My grandfather was mining at Ellensburg (now Gold Beach, Oregon), when the following incident happened in the summer of 1856.

The To-To-Tins' surrender wasn't exactly unanimous, for a few were overlooked when the tribe was deported. Others left the reservation, driven by nostalgia that afflicts all mankind regardless of race or color. The settlers clamored for their removal and finally the Indian agent deputized Captain William Tichenor of Port Orford to collect them in a group and take them to the Siletz Reservation.

Tichenor managed to round up the remnant of the tribe, and under the white man's guarantee of safety, nineteen warriors crossed the Rogue River for the last time, bound for the reservation. There was only a narrow trail up the coast at the time and the Indians were on foot, beaten and dejected, following Tichenor over the rolling foothills where their ancestors had walked, centuries before the first white man ever saw the coast of North America.

Four miles from the river, the trail dipped into a narrow valley flanked by low hazel brush. West of the trail was a forest of pine with a tiny clearing a few hundred yards from the trail. Horrible things had happened there when the To-To-Tins had surprised the Geiasal family during the first night of hostilities.

The blackened pines where the cabin had burned were almost abreast of the marching Indians when a long line of white men rose from the hazel brush. There was no warning. A ragged, murderous volley and the To-To-Tins went down as if scythed. One brave, at the end of the line escaped the first volley.

Doubling in his tracks, he turned and fled down the trail with the speed of a crazed horse, while the white men reloaded their muskets in frantic haste, lest one red "varmint" escape from the trap they had set.

Over the ridge the Indian fled with bullets singing past his ears. Then, the trail made a sharp turn and he ran full into the arms of my grandfather and his partner who were arriving a bit late on the scene of this "battle." They shot him down like a trapped coyote as he leaped into the brush.

These Indians were absolutely unarmed. They surrendered in good faith to white men who guaranteed their safety. Captain Tichenor was not to blame for the slaughter, as he was ignorant of the plot to ambush the tribe's remnant.

Pioneer residents try to justify the killings by pointing to the murder of John Geiasal and his sons by the same Indians. I have often wondered what historians would have written if the situation had been reversed and nineteen white men had been murdered, from ambush, by an Indian tribe after they had surrendered in good faith.

My only comment is that when Indians killed white men, it was always a massacre, but when unarmed Indians were shot down like dogs from ambush, the pioneer historian speaks of "justified execution."

JACK C. WOODRUFF, Langlois, Oregon

~ 240 ~

Correspondence Bride Has Great Adventure

In 1876, my Mother, Kathleen Forreststall, came over from Ireland, having received $300 from her sister who was married to a soldier at Fort Klamath in Southern Oregon. The money was borrowed from another soldier that wanted an Irish bride.

On the ship over, were quite a few Germans playing accordions and singing. The drinking water was so salty, she lived on beer and crackers. Coming over on the ship, was a girl roommate, and Mother showed her the money she had sewed in her corset.

They came around by Panama, and Mother bought a whole limb, covered with ripe bananas, for ten cents. Everything was fine until she arrived in Portland, but when it came time to catch the stage for Fort Klamath, she discovered her money was missing. She had to wait several days until she received stage fare from her sister.

When she got to Fort Klamath she took care of her sister's baby and took him out walking daily. One day while the baby was sleeping, a group of Indian women were standing around outside talking and laughing and making so much noise it disturbed the baby and her, so Mother went out and hollered. "Klaut-a-wa, Klaut-a-wa." Which means, "Go away." It made the Indian women so mad they almost scalped her. Her sister had to rush out and save her.

Mother did become engaged to the soldier boy who had paid her way over from the old country and was almost married to him by Father Blanchet. But, her soldier sweetheart had to make a trip to Walla Walla, Washington.

She promised him she wouldn't go to dances in his absence, but she was young and liked pleasure and she went anyway. Someone saw her and told him--and their engagement was quickly broken.

Two or three years later, she married my Dad.

MRS. E. Bello, Salem, Oregon

~ 241 ~

Who Killed Umtux? Still Moot Question

Twenty five miles northeast of Portland lay a thriving little community with the largest rural high school in the state of Washington and the largest co-operative cheese factory under one roof. They call it Battle Ground. Because no battle was ever fought there. And thereby hangs a tale, as the traveler remarked when he saw his first dog.

When the Indians of the Oregon Country rose up and massacred the settlers in the Indian War of 1855, and 1856, the site of Battle Ground was part of the hunting grounds of the aggressive Coweleskie (Cowlitz) Indians, who were part horse Indian and part canoe Indian, allies both of the river Indians and the Yakimas of the eastern Washington plains.

Because of this alliance, the commander at Fort Vancouver thought it best to keep a close guard on the Coweleskies, lest they join their allies in war.

Accordingly, they were moved into a "concentration camp" just outside the stockade of the fort, where their sullen resentment added to the tension of the little colony of settlers who huddled about the fort under the protection of a company of volunteers while General (then

Lieutenant) Phillip Sheridan and his regulars were attempting the rescue of the white settlement at the Cascades.

One morning, the colony awoke to find the whole Indian camp gone. Vanished like the morning mist. The volunteers immediately started in pursuit, lest the Indians go on the war path and slaughter the settlers in the back country.

About fifteen miles northeast of the fort, near the east fork of the Lewis River, they overtook the sullen tribe. Not wishing to precipitate a new war that would endanger the defenseless settlers already scattered over the countryside, the captain of the volunteers began a pow-wow with Chief Umtux and his Indians, which, after several days, resulted in a treaty of peace.

That night, the two camps slept peacefully, drawn up in military lines, with a strip of No-Man's-Land between them.

Who shot Chief Umtux? To this day that remains as much a mystery as the famous riddle of the death of Cock Robin. In the morning the body of the revered chief of the tribe was found halfway between the lines of the two camps, dead of a bullet wound. The battle rage of the Indians rose with the rising sun. War seemed inevitable.

Thus the two hostile camps faced each other for hours. The commander dared not add this tribe to the many that already endangered the lives of the settlers.

Finally a fearless volunteer was found who boldly advanced between the lines to the Indian camp to resume the pow-wow. Immediately, he was surrounded by hostile savages, but with the wit and eloquence of a statesman, he finally soothed the Indians and patched up another peace. The Indians, however, imposed one strange condition upon their surrender.

The volunteers were to march away and leave them alone with their sorrow for twenty four hours, after which they would deliver themselves to their captors. This looked like a piece of Indian treachery, but the commander was compelled to accept.

During that silent night, the Indian tribe stole away and delivered the body of its respected chief to the arms of the Unknown, with what uncanny rites no one shall know. For the Indians kept their secret. No one ever knew where the fallen chief was buried or how, although the itch of curiosity impelled many then as now to search for the site of his grave, whether in some tall tree or in some stone tepee.

Thus the name of "battleless" Battle Ground.

L. GOSS, Portland, Oregon

~ 242 ~

Free Trader Gets Hand of Princess

When the young Simon Plomondon, who was pledged to the priesthood, but had taken no obligatory vows, arrived on the beautiful Cowlitz River plains, he put aside his priestly intentions and promptly fell in love with the charming daughter of a Cowlitz Indian chieftain.

Since young Simon was a free trader, he was at liberty to conduct his affairs according to his own ideas, and when he chose the daughter of Scha-nee-wah, a tribal ceremony of considerable pretense took place.

The couple were made to kneel with their faces toward the sun and repeat the tribal marriage vows, which were to endure as long as breath remained in their bodies At the close of this ritual, the Indian chief pronounced a blessing upon them, in the name of the sun god, and gave them the charge that they should go to their teepee and both of them place their heads upon one pillow.

This marriage was later ratified, according to church rites, when the Catholic fathers, Blanchet and Demers came to Cowlitz Prairie in 1838 and established a mission at that place.

Turning to the church records for further information, four baptisms are found of children born to this union. They are: Sophie, Simon Jr., Therese and Maryanne.

A notation following Maryanne's record closes the chapter of the Indian princess with this comment: "Daughter of Simon Piomondon and Cowlitz woman, dead."

Simon made two other marriages, but none of them appear as romantic as the first.; He became an influential man on the prairie and during the Indian trouble of 1865, he was Indian agent at the Cowlitz. His grandson, J. B. Sareault of Cowlitz Prairie, Washington, has many of the original letters and documents which belonged to his grandfather.

He recalls that his grandfather, Simon Plomondon, was a man of powerful physique and stood six feet one, erect as a poplar tree and sturdy as an oak. Mr. Sareault also recalls that his great grandfather, Chief Scha-nee-wah, was at least two fingers taller than Simon, also a man of commanding figure and proud bearing. Simon's wife, the princess, was the chief's third daughter. She died at the birth of her third daughter.

The descendants of this prominent, early day settler, still live in the Cowlitz vicinity and adjacent districts. They are identified in a prominent way with the present day affairs of the community and are lawyers, bankers and agriculturalists. It is to them that recognition must be given for the information regarding that historic character who founded the family of Plomondon in Cowlitz District.

M. LEONA NICHOLS, Portland, Oregon

~ 243 ~

Indian Angry When White Bride Refused

In 1845, the Daniel Bailey family, consisting of the father, mother, five daughters, and a son, started west from Clay County, Missouri, and after several months on the plains, landed in Oregon.

The family settled on a donation land claim in the Chehalem Valley, Yamhill County, Oregon. A daughter at the age of seventeen married the late Francis Large. They lived in Yamhill County for a number of years, and then moved to Forest Grove, Oregon, where they resided for over forty years.

An Indian was struck with the beauty of another daughter who was eighteen at the time. He asked her father what he would take for her. The father, as a joke, answered that she was an extra fine girl and he wouldn't take less that twenty-five head of horses for her. The Indian, however, took the joke seriously, returning the next day with the twenty-five horses and demanding the girl.

But the father refused. The Indian persisted in taking the girl as he had made the bargain for the white wife. Another man pointed a gun at the Indian who finally departed sulkily, but followed the wagon train for several days before giving up.

Another incident to the family took place at Fort Boise, Idaho, where the Baileys were persuaded, along with others, to follow Stephen Meek's advice to take a shorter and easier route from there into Oregon. The Baileys and others, joined with Meek and his Indian wife. But were soon lost for several days, and had to live on berries and grasshoppers. They were also without clean water to drink.

The upset men in the crowd decided one evening to hang Meek the next morning. At midnight, Daniel Bailey got the rope that was to be used in the hanging, woke up the Meeks, gave them the rope, told them of the plan and advised them to beat it. They did so and finally landed in Washington County, west of Portland, Oregon.

An Indian guide was then put in charge of the group who led them out safely to The Dalles, Oregon.

MRS. ANNIE L. BILLINGER, Forest Grove, Oregon

~ 244 ~

Bonneville Causes West's First Strike

Captain Bonneville, in 1832, unwittingly brought on probably the first strike and boycott west of the Rockies.

Captain Bonneville of the United States Army, on furlough, started with one hundred men across the Rockies to the Oregon Country. When he arrived at the Walla Walla Valley on the Columbia River, he traded with the Walla Walla, Cayuse and Nez Perce Indians. The Captain paid higher prices for furs and gave more presents than did Peter Pambrun of the Hudson's Bay Fur Company, who was in charge at Fort Walla Walla.

Upon Captain Bonneville's departure, the chiefs assembled at the fort and insisted on a change of the tariff, in their favor.

Mr. Pambrun, who had long dealt with the Indians, and had been a favorite with them for years, refused to change his prices, whereupon the Indians seized him, stamped violently upon his breast, beat him severely, kidnapped him and held him a prisoner until they gained, to a considerable extent, their objective.

Upon his release, Pambrun retaliated by boycotting all the Indians who had taken part in the outrage. They were unable to sell their goods to the company for a long time--at any price.

Years after the actual boycott had been lifted, its influence was still felt. The Prince, once a strong chieftain of the Cayuses, who was stripped of his authority because of his part in the strike, twelve years later, had not regained his prominence, but still occupied only an insignificant position in his tribe.

TOM WINBOURNE, Scappoose, Oregon

~ 245 ~

Redskins Demand White Man's Dance

Rising 155 feet above the Sweetwater River, Independence Rock spreads over twenty seven acres on the plains and looks down on the Old Oregon Trail. Over a century ago, some hunters celebrated the Fourth of July at that point and gave the elevation its name.

Asa Lovejoy, a young lawyer, who helped to write the Constitution of Oregon, had a thrilling time at the rock in 1842. If the Indians who captured him had not softened, Marcus Whitman's winter trip across the mountains might never have been made, for it was Lovejoy who went with Whitman. For certain, Lovejoy would not have been a partner with William P. Overton in the founding of Portland, Oregon.

Dr. Elijah White, vain and officious, was coming west to be the first United States official in Oregon, a mere sub-agent of Indian affairs, so that the British would not be suspicious of Uncle Sam's intentions out this way.

Lovejoy, wishing to see the West, and then go to Honolulu, joined White's pioneers in Western Missouri. Lovejoy and Lansford W.

Hastings, another lawyer, who afterwards lived in California and Brazil, were alone on top of the rock. Their animals were tethered below.

Looking down, Lovejoy saw eight of ten Indians, the advance guard of a large force. The expedition had moved on and there was no help in sight. When Lovejoy and Hastings came down from Independence Rock, their rifles and animals were seized. Some of the Indians shook hands with them, while others made menacing gestures with their weapons. The first eight or ten were soon joined by forty or fifty more, who came throwing spears at the white men. More Indians came, until they numbered 500. Some struck Lovejoy and Hastings with the butts of their guns. One shot Lovejoy in the hand.

Then the Indians seated themselves in a wide circle. The white men were put in the center, kept apart, but permitted to talk. The pipe of peace was passed and smoked After that, the Indians amused themselves by tossing Lovejoy and Hastings and making them dance. This performance over, the white men started to leave to join their cow column, but the Indians had another plan. For a starter, they jumped about and let out war whoops.

With the precision of an army, the Indians formed a long column. Lovejoy and Hastings rode along with them, mounted and disarmed, but closely guarded. Toward sundown, they caught up with White's expedition. Their one fear, as they approached the group, was that their own fellows would fire on the Indians and start a battle which would have been fatal to the whole expedition as they had no idea the strength of the Indian's forces. Thankfully, the men and women only ran out to greet them.

That night, the Indians camped near White's party. The next morning, bought off with hot coffee and all the tobacco the white men could spare, the Indians returned the rifles, mounted their ponies and rode away.

The men and women of the covered wagons breathed easier, and Dr. White came on to Oregon to uphold the dignity of the United States Government and knock over a few whiskey stills--and so on.

HENRY E. REED, Portland, Oregon

"When Oregon Went Berserk"

EPISODE 2 of 6

An Account of Ten Spectacular Years (1855-1865) When the Northwest Was Host to War, Greed and Death

By JOHN W. KELLY, Staff Writer, *The Oregonian*, September 20, 1936

Introduction

Prosaic, peaceful Oregon had a phenomenal era so packed with thrills and melodrama that no similar period of the West surpassed or possibly equaled it.

In these modern days, it is difficult to imagine that there was a time when every white settler was in danger of murder at the hands of thousands of Indians. Every tribe from the Oregon Coast to the Rocky Mountains, armed with guns, bows and arrows, tomahawks, and scalping knifes took a terrible toll throughout the region.

It is also difficult to imagine thousands of miners and prospectors swarming over the creeks and rivers of Oregon, searching for, and finding, large quantities of gold and occasionally silver. The Klondike gold rush in Alaska didn't compare with the impatient stampede through Portland.

Crime, gone rampant, has never seen the equal of those ten sensational years between 1855–1865. Rampant until the law of the rope was achieved.

The first episode of "When Oregon Went Berserk" described the beginnings and extent of the Indian uprisings. At first the Indians had the best of the struggle, but they succeeded not with forthcoming battles.

EPISODE 2

White Man's Superior Equipment and Organization

Collapse of the great Indian uprising to exterminate the whites in the Pacific Northwest began only after the regular army changed its views respecting the treaties.

While war whoops resounded from the Shastas to British Columbia, and hundreds, probably thousands of white men, women and children were tortured and killed, even the highest military authority on the Pacific Coast said the people of Oregon and Washington were an organized army of mass murderers and government liars.

Joel Palmer, Superintendent of Indian Affairs, who made the treaties that led up to the outbreak, said that the whites forced the hands of the natives and asserted that "reckless land grants" had instigated the war.

With this attitude, expressed by the critics, it is not surprising that the Eastern press held the handful of white settlers as responsible for the ocean of blood being shed. Horace Greeley thundered about Oregon suggesting "a bill for scalping whites."

Kamiakin, "hias tyee" of the Yakimas, who plotted the war of extermination, must have smiled at the rancor and ill feeling between regular soldiers and the volunteers and the refusal of the regulars to recognize the citizen soldier as anything other than as a rabble.

Responsible for this attitude was General Wool, and not until he was relieved of command at Fort Vancouver was there amity between the military authorities and the Civil Government, represented by Governor George I. Curry of Oregon and Governor I. I. Stevens of Washington.

War parties besieging Gold Beach over a month after a massacre; Indians attacking a schooner in Puget Sound; killing of whites somewhere south of the Umpqua River in Oregon; business paralyzed throughout the region, and every white settler living in the fear of sudden death—none of these developments would swerve General Wool from his belief that the Indians were victims of the white man's greed.

One of the hostile chiefs to be killed was Peupeumoxmox. This chief of the Walla Walla tribe was killed while being held hostage by the Oregon Volunteers. In an engagement between the volunteers and the Indian tribe, Peupeumoxmox was shot by a hot-blooded citizen soldier who scalped him, cut off his ears and cut his skin into strips which were carried back to the Willamette Valley as souvenirs. The only excuse for the mutilation was that the engagement was near the old Whitman Mission at Waiilatpu where the Indians had massacred its inhabitants only a few years before. Sentiment still ran high.

In 1856, Kamiakin encountered the first real obstacle to his plans. This was the battle of Bonneville.

To be continued ...

~ 246 ~

Mexican Murderer Pays High Penalty

They are digging up the streets of old Jacksonville for gold. They are digging up the back yards in that little city of once-upon-a-time. They are telling tall tales of big strikes in pioneer days when nuggets as large as hen eggs were nothin'. If you didn't find one the size of an ostrich egg, there wasn't any use cackling about it.

But only a very few folk in Jackson County, Oregon today know the story of how Kaspar Kubli, father of K. K. Kubli of Portland, handled a Mexican murderer who killed a white man named Williamson. Kubli and Veit Schultz were noted Jacksonville pioneers. Among their early operations was a mule freight train between the busy gold mining town and Crescent City, California. They operated this line for several years, and were very lucky to quit with their scalps in their right places.

Just a short time before the end of these pack-train days, Kubli hired a white man who gave the name of Williamson to work with the caravan. The chap's right name may have been Williamson or Williams, or it may have been Miller or Hofflemeyer. In those days of the Wild West, no questions were asked about where a man came from, no one cared whether one's father was a judge or a horse thief.

A Mexican mule driver belonging to the crew took a great dislike to Williamson. This added to the mystery, for no one could see why this hatred sprang up so suddenly. No one will ever know, for all this happened back in the 1850's.

One day, the Mexican asked Kubli for powder and bullets. They were refused. The driver walked away muttering something no one near understood. A short time later, Williamson went out to round up the animals so the march could be resumed. It was not much of a chore to get the beasts together, so when the man didn't return after an hour's wait, Kubli began to worry.

After a while, he started out to look for the fellow. He soon saw a horrible sight down the trail. Williamson lay dead across the wilderness highway, the Mexican was standing over him repeatedly plunging a knife into his chest.

Kubli always carried his pistol with him. So he fired at the killer as quickly as possible. The shot missed. The Mexican high-tailed it for the timber, his employer right after him. The murderer reached the top of a steep hill, got behind a big tree and began throwing rocks at the boss. But the villain didn't have a good throwing arm, so he wasted a lot of time and effort.

Kubli just started a siege. The sun boiled down on the hill, and in time, the big, bad Mexican gave up. He wanted a drink. Out from behind the log he came with his hands as high up in the air as he could get them. His employer gave him a warning that if those dirty, bloody hands showed any signs of coming down, a shot would be in order.

The murderer was marched into camp. A company of soldiers was stationed for a short time on the Illinois River not far away and the killer was taken over to them. It didn't take Kubli long to tell the story. Then the Mexican was asked what he had to say about it. At first, he refused to speak. But when he saw one of the soldiers pick up a rope, the mule driver shouted: "If you do anything to me, you find out in Crescent City!" That was all he would say. He was given an opportunity to tell the world why he hated Williamson, why he killed him, and if he had any word to send to a relative. But he refused to speak further to the self-appointed judge and jury.

Soon the officer who was acting as judge at the hearing put the case up to the jury. It was an informal trial, no squabbling among attorneys, no calling of experts to testify—they kept it simple.

"All who are in favor of hangin' this damn fool, say 'aye,'" shouted the judge.

Everyone yelled "Aye." There was no dissenting opinion.

Williamson's pony was brought up. The Mexican looked at it a minute. A sneering look passed over his face. Perhaps he had expected to ride away to freedom on this very steed. He began muttering in a language no one present understood. His hands were tied behind his back and a rope looped around his neck. The murderer was then put astride the pony, and the other end of the hemp rope tied to the limb of a tree above him.

The pony was struck with a lash across his rump. He lurched, then trotted away. The calloused men shrugged their shoulders and slowly strolled away. The unmourned mule driver was left squirming, kicking, and swinging in the wind.

DAVID W. HAZEN, Portland, Oregon

~ 247 ~

Priest Takes Chiefs on Peace Mission

A lone man left Vancouver, Washington one fall day more than three-quarters on a century ago as a messenger of peace to the warring Indians of the upper reaches of the Columbia River. He was Rev. Pierre J. DeSmet, a Jesuit Priest, who had labored long and earnestly as a missionary to the natives of old Oregon.

The government had bought the rich Willamette Valley from its native owners for about 2½ cents per acre. Governor Stevens of Washington Territory had concluded a treaty at Walla Walla which had left the Indians sullen and resentful.

In 1855, the Indians of the Northwest went on the warpath. It was their last chance to strike before the white settlers outnumbered them. General Haller's soldiers were defeated. Seattle was attacked. Portland was in fear after the massacre near present Bonneville Dam, and made preparations to defend itself.

The blow came too late to do the Indians any good. Still their depredations formed the basis of over $6,000.000 claims for damages filed with the Federal Government. These were reduced nearly sixty percent in the national capital.

General William S. Harney took command at Vancouver in October, 1858, and ordered the Walla Walla country reopened at once. It had been closed to settlers and miners since the beginning of the war. Desiring that there be no more bloodshed, he rapidly approved Father DeSmet's suggestion for a trip of peace.

The mission was one of great danger. While the Indians were defeated, the embers of war still burned in the country through which the priest, unattended, must pass. Father DeSmet put his life in God's hands. General Harney wished him well in his "holy mission."

Father DeSmet passed the winter among the Indians of the upper Columbia River and convinced them that further opposition to the whites would be futile. He assured their chiefs that they would not be hanged if they would come to Vancouver and have a peace talk with General Harney.

Father DeSmet arrived in Vancouver in the spring of 1859 with seven chiefs of the inland nations.

Kamiahkin, the Yakima chief, who was one of the leaders in the war, came as far as Walla Walla. A government agent alarmed him and he left the party. General Harney sent word that he did not blame Kamiahkin and that he believed that the chief intended to be peaceful.

After the meeting with the military authorities, Father DeSmet and the seven chiefs were entertained in Portland in the home of G. Collier Robbins, which covered the block bounded by Southwest First and Second Avenues, and Southwest Couch and Davis Streets. General Ulysses S. Grant, General Winfield Scott, General Joseph Hooker and Lady Jane Franklin at one time or another enjoyed hospitality at the Robbin's home.

After the Portland visit, the chiefs were taken to Oregon City and Salem. Everywhere they were impressed with the numerical strength and vast resources of the whites. They were told that Oregon had just become a state and could wage a war of extermination against any who disturbed her citizens.

The visits over, the chiefs were sent home to tell their people of the power of the whites and that further resistance to the new civilization would be useless and devastating to them.

Father DeSmet was known to the Indians as "Black Gown." His historical mission bought even the fierce Blackfeet to their knees in prayer.

ALAN DONEY, Portland, Oregon

~ 248 ~

Secrecy Required in Boat Building

Utmost secrecy was observed in the building of the first schooner in the Oregon Country. The Hudson's Bay Fur Company, determined to dominate the country for some years to come, was opposed to any attempt at shipbuilding on the part of the American settlers.

Inasmuch as the materials needed were brought into the country only by the fur company's ships and handled by its company stores, it was quite a problem for the settlers to keep their enterprise a secret.

Nevertheless, in 1841, R. L. Kilborn, Charley Matts and P. Armstrong (who was afterward killed in the Indian War on the Rogue River in Southern Oregon), H. Woods, John Green and George Davis undertook the building of a schooner of forty tons burden on a little island some four miles above the present city of Portland. As head carpenter, they engaged Felix Hathaway, who had been saved from the wreck of the *William and Ann* and commenced their work.

Dr. McLoughlin informed them that he did not approve and would furnish no supplies, and so they were forced to resort to various subterfuges to get them. In order to obtain the necessary irons and spikes, they had it reported that they were building a ferryboat to cross the Willamette River.

To obtain rigging, they induced the French-Canadian farmers to go to Fort Vancouver and get ropes to use in the Old Dutch harness for plowing. They even produced a whipsaw from the mission.

When Captain Wilkes, commander of an exploring expedition, sent to the Columbia River to gather information, visited them and found that they had a substantial and seaworthy craft well under way, he furnished them such articles from his stores, as he could spare, and spoke favorably of their enterprise to Dr. McLoughlin.

Dr. McLoughlin became more liberal, and so with his and Captain Wilkes' assistance, the vessel, the *Star of Oregon* was launched. It made trips back and forth to California under the command of Captain Joseph Gale.

GEORGE COOK, Portland, Oregon

~ 249 ~

Happy Family Has Terrible Tragedy

It was a happy little family who lived in a cabin not far from Lower Burnt River in what is now southern Baker County, Oregon. Their name was Scott, and upon their marriage, some seventy five years ago, they had come over from Walla Walla into Burnt River country attracted there by the gold excitement.

Husband and wife together cleared the land and prepared it for vegetables, grain and fruit trees, for they knew that in the lively town of Rye Valley, eight miles distant, a good market awaited their produce.

Three years passed, during which two little ones came to brighten that rude pioneer home. Mr. and Mrs. Scott got up early one morning, loaded their wagon with vegetables and a basket of carefully gathered peaches, the first their trees had yielded, and started for Rye Valley.

The produce sold, they spent the night with friends and enjoyed a neighborhood dance. Next day, after making purchases, they started home, the two-year-old boy and baby girl safely in the bottom of the wagon bed.

They were about halfway home when a frightful Indian war whoop told them of imminent danger. Almost immediately Mr. Scott was hit and fell forward across the dashboard, dying. In falling, he dropped the reins between the horses and the frenzied animals started to run.

Mrs. Scott, with superhuman strength, dragged her husband's body back across the dashboard; then jumping out on the wagon tongue, she crawled along until she secured the trailing lines, then back over the dash.

Crouching low, bullets whizzing about her, she managed to guide the terrified, plunging horses down a different mountain road that was little better than a trail, but led away from her pursuers. Her troubles were not over however, for the Burnt River had to be forded, and fording that river with a spirited team was a man-sized job.

Before attempting it, she stopped and placed her husband's body in a better position, took up her children in her arms, trying vainly to still their crying; then headed her horses into the river, guiding them with firm hands, their heads upstream. She safely reached the other side and started up the hill towards home.

Several settlers had built their cabins near her home, and Mrs. Scott, thinking for the first time of herself, stopped at the first one. She climbed down from the wagon, tied the still frightened horses, lifted down her babies, and, pointing to her dead husband's body, said, "I reckon I'm hit too," falling to the ground as she spoke.

An examination revealed the fact that she had received two deadly wounds, her clothing being soaked with blood. She lay there, telling the family the particulars of the assault, made a will, giving instructions as to her children, saying they should be sent to her parents. She then asked that they might be brought for her to kiss good-bye, and saying. "I'm tired now," … and closed her eyes.

Next day, the neighbors dug a broad grave and stood about it with bared heads, rifles in their hands, while a simple service was held over the bodies of this pioneer man and his wife of dauntless courage.

DAISY C. GRISWOLD, Portland, Oregon

~ 250 ~

"Forty Thieves" Not Appreciated

"The Arabian Nights" have been a source of enjoyment to thousands of readers, and the enjoyment of the stories, which Shahrazad, the beautiful slave, related to her master, King Shahreyer, will forever remain. It will therefore surprise many to learn that in 1856, the convivial companions of the famous Ali Baba descended upon a small town in Oregon, where they made things miserable for the inhabitants.

Although the episode of the boiling oil was omitted, the thieves were pretty well roasted before their enforced departure, but it took years to erase the memory of the unbidden guests' depredations. In those days, towns were small and the inhabitants few, so that whenever extra men were needed, it became necessary to import them.

Needing some extra men at the Newport Mine, the owners wrote to General James M. Estill, who was in charge of the California State Prison at San Quentin, requesting him to send some laborers. The General loaded a lot of questionable characters aboard his steamer, the *Newport*, and started them on their way north.

As only a few were needed at Newport, the rest remained on the ship. On the return trip, the *Newport* cast anchor off Empire City. Rather than return to San Quentin, the men decided to honor the town with their presence.

History states, "They were a crowd of hard cases," and from all accounts they certainly lived up to their reputation. From the historical record, I quote the following quaint narrative:

"The unsuspecting and unsophisticated citizens scanned them curiously and returned with innocent confidence to their domiciles.

But consternation soon pervaded the community. Hen roosts suddenly became depopulated, freshly washed shirts that dangled from clotheslines abruptly disappeared. Anything and everything valuable took mysterious departure, until the confiding people were aroused to anger. They began to suspect, then 'go for,' these strangers, and emphatically advised their immediate immigration" The touching recollections connected with this interesting gang led the citizens to speak of them ever after as the "Forty Thieves."

A slight touch of romance was injected into this affair. One of Empire City's fair maidens fell in love with a member of the "Forty." She married, reformed him and they lived--"happily ever after."

GEORGE MARSH, Portland, Oregon

~ 251 ~

Lane and Nesmith Barely Save Necks

James W. Nesmith, who settled in the Willamette Valley over ninety years ago, was a noted citizen of old Oregon.

Nesmith had been in a campaign against the Cayuses following the murder of Dr. Marcus Whitman.

He was tilling the soil in Polk County when the Rogue River Indians took a notion to clean up all the whites in Southern Oregon in the summer of 1853.

The red warriors were ravaging and pillaging until their scouts told them that General Joseph Lane, the Territorial Governor, was among the white forces. Then they asked for a conference to arrange a peace. Nesmith, who was a United States Marshal, had come to the scene with more soldiers.

Lane, a fearless man, agreed to meet with the Indians, taking only ten unarmed men with him. The Indians, numbering seven hundred, in war dress and paint and fully armed, retired to a point on Table Rock where they could look down on the white soldiers.

Nesmith, who spoke Chinook perfectly, was selected as interpreter. He demurred, saying that the Indians could not be trusted. General Lane said if Nesmith be afraid, he could stay behind. A United States officer could not afford to admit fear, so Nesmith went along.

Into the hostile camp marched the eleven men, with no other arms than a hunting knife, which Nesmith carried. Nesmith felt that they were inviting a massacre.

The negotiations proceeded amicably until an Indian runner came into the camp and dropped to the ground exhausted. He brought word that one of his tribe was, that morning, tied to a tree and shot to death.

Seven hundred Indians instantly prepared for action. They made motions as if they would tie the white negotiators to trees and shoot them. With eyes flashing, General Lane arose. In a calm voice and without fear, he told the Indians that the murder had not been committed by any of his men. The offender, he said, was a bad man. He had broken the armistice and would be punished. Moreover, the relatives of the dead man would be compensated.

The Indians knew and respected General Lane. That was why they sued for peace when they learned that he was in the field against them. His words quieted them and the looks of anger passed from their faces. Negotiations were resumed, and a peace was made which lasted for two years.

That evening, as the sun was going down, the eleven descended the slope of Table Rock and rejoined the seventy soldiers and civilians who had watched the rock all day.

"General Lane," said Nesmith as they reached their horses, "we had a close call. The next time you go unarmed into a hostile Indian camp, you will have to get someone besides me for your interpreter."

"God bless you, Nesmith," said General Lane affectionately. "Luck is better than science."

Twenty years later, when the Modocs murdered General E. R. S. Canby and others at a peace conference in northern California, Nesmith knew that he was right about the Rogue River Indians.

HENRY E. REED, Portland, Oregon

~ 252 ~

Church Given $210 for Dorion Burial

When the Indians buried their dead, many of them were placed in canoes and secured to high places along the cliffs of the Columbia River Gorge. Others were wrapped in burial garments and put in trees or in the earth. When the white man came to the frontier, he too, held to his accustomed burial habits, but was restricted by the lack of accoutrements commonly in use. Adapting himself to conditions, he buried where necessary with exceedingly simple ceremonies.

Ewing Young, although a man of considerable means, was buried with little pretense upon his own farm, and his grave is marked with a solitary oak tree.

Jason Lee records his first funeral in the West. Of this occasion he comments: "July 28, 1854. Read the 90th Psalm, prayed, spoke at the graveside of the French-Canadian Catholic who was injured by a fall from a horse, read a part of the 15th chapter of Corinthians and read the burial service; nearly all the men from both camps attended the funeral service. Canadians put a cross on his breast; burial without coffin."

John McLoughlin Jr. was brought from Fort Stikine after his murder and his body interred at the Hudson's Bay Fur Company burial plot at the Columbia River fort. The funeral was a ceremonious affair with the mass being read by a priest in the presence of many friends and relatives.

Another pretentious burial was that of the wife of John Toupin, Marie Ayvoise (Madame Dorion), who was given an elaborate interment for those times. In an old account book, kept by the priests of St. Louis Parish, this hitherto unknown record is made--written in French:

"Revenue to the church for the Toupin interment, 100 p. (piasters), $210.00." This notation is made under the date of December, 1850, a few months after Marie Ayvoise's death, which occurred September 5, 1850.

In all probability, the old litter or bier was used for this inhumation that later carried so many of the settlers of this parish to their graves. The bier that had been so long a part of the funeral services in this part of French Prairie was still in existence up to a few years ago.

Still more pretentious was the last service for the "Father of Old Oregon."

There were no funeral cars in the country at that time, and a light spring wagon was pressed into service to carry the heavy oak coffin containing the body of Dr. John McLoughlin. On the way to the Catholic Church, in Oregon City, the wagon mired in the mud and the coffin was lifted to the shoulders of the pallbearers and carried to the place where masses were said. After these services were over, his coffin was placed in the churchyard beside the chapel, facing the Willamette River.

In later years, the church has been extended over the graves of both Dr. McLoughlin and his wife.

Pioneer and primitive people put away their dead in their own way, bestowing upon them the burial benedictions of their time.

M. LEONA NICHOLS, Portland, Oregon

~ 253 ~

Horse Trade Cause of Early Killing

In the early days of Oregon City, the first killing of white men was caused by a horse trade between a Negro and an Indian. In 1844, a Negro hired an Indian by the name of Cockstock to work for him for a given time, promising him a certain horse as pay. Before the time had expired, the Negro sold the horse to another Negro.

Cockstock, not knowing this, finished his time and demanded his horse. Learning to his chagrin that the horse had changed owners, and believing it a conspiracy against his rights, he resolved to take the horse by force, and he did.

Because of this, and because he was making threats against many different men, Dr. White, Sub-Indian Agent, posted a reward of $100 for his capture.

Cockstock, learning of the reward for his capture, rode into Oregon City with five companions, all horribly painted, and dared someone to capture him.

After defying the town, he recrossed the Willamette River to the Indian village and tried to get the Indians there to burn the town and kill as many white men as possible.

Failing to arouse the Indians, he obtained an interpreter and crossed the river again for the purpose of calling the whites to an explanation.

By this time, however, the whites were angry and armed and met the Indians at the landing.

The firing commenced simultaneously on both sides. George LeBreton was killed. Cockstock himself was killed. Mr. Wilson and Mr. Rogers were wounded by poisoned arrows and soon afterward died.

The main tribes of the Indians took no part in this. Cockstock's widow was appeased with a gift of two blankets, and peace was soon re-established.

TOM WINBOURNE, Scappoose, Oregon

~ 254 ~

Snakes Driven Out, Says Indian Legend

St. Patrick's Day being this month, the following tale of old Indian days may not be out of place, as it has to do with snakes.

Chehalem was a famous Indian Chief among the Wapatoo, and the Chehalem Valley out in Yamhill County in Oregon was his "il-la-hee," or land. He was a sort of St. Patrick.

At one time, so runs the legend, the Chehalem Valley was infested with rattlesnakes. They were everywhere and very poisonous. They would frequently bite the Indians, and thus many were killed by them. Chehalem told the snake king that he must stop this, but no attention being paid to these demands, Chehalem determined to stand it no longer. His people were dying too rapidly.

So he called together his medicine man and his warriors. The warriors drove the snakes into their den, a rocky point said to have been on Sam Kinney's Donation Land Claim. The old medicine man then made his medicine. He used magic to seal up the mouth of the den.

For a whole moon he watched that none might escape. He neither ate nor slept during the time. He was strong and vigorous when he began his vigil, but worn and wasted, yet triumphant, when he finished.

The rattlers were his prisoners forever--and the valley has never seen one of them since.

E. P. NORTHRUP, Portland, Oregon

~ 255 ~

Adventurous Trip Made by Youngster

When the scout, Tom McKay, was traveling from one Hudson's Bay Company post to another, in early times, he made many trips between Fort Vancouver on the Columbia River and York Factory on Hudson's Bay.

On one of these excursions, about 1837 or 1838, he brought his little niece as a surprise to her mother, who lived at Fort Vancouver. This little miss was also the niece of Sir Alexander McKenzie. She had been left at Red River with relatives so that she might go to school and enjoy the privileges of the settlement.

Little Mary was an attractive child and a general favorite in Red River, and when her Uncle Tom visited her, she begged him to take her to her mother in the Oregon Country. Moved by the pleas of the child, he agreed to take her on this long journey if she would promise to be obedient to him. She readily agreed. Her relatives prepared her for the event.

Sometime during this long trip, she became so weary that she wished that she had not begged Uncle Tom to take her to her mother. When she had almost despaired of ever reaching Dr. McLoughlin's fort, her uncle whispered to her that she must dress herself in her best ribbons and put on a smiling face, as Fort Vancouver was their next stop. And so she arrived, one of the very first children to make the long overland trip to the Oregon Country.

On arriving at this place, she was enrolled as a student in Covington's School, which was near the Hudson's Bay post in Vancouver. This little miss grew to be a most lovable and attractive young woman. In later years she was married to John Pambrun.

M. LEONA NICHOLS, Portland, Oregon

Prehistoric Indians of the West

Part 2 of 3

By JOHN W. KELLY, Staff Writer, *The Oregonian*

Improbable as the affiliation between the Oregon Indians and the Mayas appears, ethnologists show the connection through tracing the linguistic families. Government scientists make the assertion, and, link by link, have constructed their chain of circumstantial evidence through the languages, from the Columbia River southward to Mexico, to Central America. The linguistic hypothesis was set forth in Part 1 of this series as they traced the southward movement of the Shoshoneans or Snake group.

How long ago did the early Oregonians go south? Scientists are in disagreement on the age of man in North America. Dr. Ales Hrdlicka, foremost anthropologist, says not more than 10,000 years—probably 8,000--may be 5,000. Dr. Hrdlicka says geologic man was not present on this continent until the passing of the last Ice Age—approximately 10,000 years since.

Researchers say the Mayas flourished 4,000 years ago—the Maya calendar, a marvelous time machine, starts with the date October 14, 3373 B.C. Also should be considered the length of time—ages—required to develop agriculture.

Certainly centuries rolled by before crude savages developed a species of wild grass into maize and evolved into a highly intelligent race, possessed of scientific knowledge and proficiency in the arts. Perhaps the seeds of Maya culture began the southward migration from Celilo Falls 6,000 years ago. This guess is as good as another.

Ethnologists having established to their satisfaction that the Piutes and Bannacks of Oregon, as members of the Shoshonean linguistic family, are related to the Mayas. The archaeologists, with their spades, have dug up material evidence along the long, long trail from the Columbia to Maya land.

This evidence consists of artifacts and different cultures. In addition there are petroglyphs and pictographs. Finally, customs practiced by the Indians in the Columbia region and by the Maya people. The supplemental evidence will be presented.

Tribes of the Shoshonean family differed for "environmental factors that determine cultural development of various kinds and degrees are: 1.) Physical geography; 2.) Climate, to which primitive people are especially amenable; 3.) Predominant plants, animals and minerals that supply the materials of drink, food, medicine, clothing, ornaments, houses, fuel, furniture and utensils, and the objects of hunting and war, including arts, and items connected with travel, transportation and commerce."

What appears to have been the earliest wave of Shoshoneans drifting afoot to the south on the west side of the Cascades and along the Deschutes River were the people known to archaeologists as the Basket Makers.

The very existence of these people was not suspected until 1890, when two cattlemen, the Witheral brothers, found mummies of this race buried deep beneath graves of cliff dwellers. Basket Makers, this accidental discovery in Grand Gulch, Southeast Utah revealed, lived before the apartment house era of the pueblo's. Today they are known only as Basket Makers—nothing else.

Herbert W. Krieger, curator of ethnology, United States National Museum, discussing his exploration in the Big Bend country of the Columbia, says of Basket Maker influence:

"There is definite evidence that this culture extended far to the south and formed the nucleus of substratum of the Basket Maker culture of the Southwest." ("Prehistoric Pit House Village Site on the Columbia River at Wahluke, Grant County, Washington, and proceedings of the *U.S. National Museum*, volume 73, article II, pp. 1-29.)

Six miles from Bend, Oregon, in a lava cave locally known as Barlow Cave, Walter J. Perry, an officer of Deschutes National Forest, in 1930 found pieces of basket work, sandals, artifacts—the same evidences of Basket Maker habitation unearthed in the Southwest by J. S. Guernsey.

Additional artifacts were subsequently dug from the floor of the Barlow Cave by Judge Robert W. Sawyer and Phil Brogan of Bend. Mr. Perry's find is now displayed in the national museum. Basket Makers wore sandals—not moccasins, and used hair rope made from the locks of women.

Prehistoric pit houses on Miller's Island in the Columbia, at the mouth of the Deschutes, yielded indications of Basket Makers during a survey made by a University of California expedition.

Aside from indications found in the Columbia region of the presence of Basket Makers there are other reasons for the belief that these people were in the Oregon country long before they filtered south into Nevada, Utah and Arizona—where more abundant evidences of their existence have been unearthed.

There is no place in either North or South America where the art of making baskets attained such a degree of perfection as in the old Oregon Country. All the so-called Colombian tribes embraced in Bancroft's category from Alaska to the great river manufactured baskets and have continued this industry to the present day. Archaeologists give a specific name to the basketry of the Columbia—"klickitat."

Basket making is a more difficult operation then pottery. Basketry is the specialty of the Northwest aborigines and pottery the art of those in the Southwest. The Basket Makers did not learn how to weave twigs, roots, willows and bark in the Southwest, the land of pottery; they brought the art with them from the Northwest, where basketry was supreme.

Since the days of the Basket Makers and their crude but efficient sandals, matting and bags, basketry has attained its zenith in the klickitat production. Improvement was the fruit of years of endeavor and experimenting, just as the development of pottery from the rough, coiled type of the cliff dwellers to the exquisite specimens from Peru—specimens manufactured before the days of Julius Caesar.

When not resorting to caves, the Basket Maker build his shelter in the open, and there is a strong affinity between the sites of the Basket Maker almost to the Mexican line and the semi-subterranean pit houses of the ancient peoples of Oregon, both on the Columbia River and the still more ancient dwellers along the coast, the Kitchen Midden people.

Like the early Colombian residents, the Basket Makers dug a circular pit in the open and build an extension to the walls and roofed it. In the Oregon country and as far north as Kodiak Island the walls were normally made of hewn cedar planks. The same style of habitation was constructed by the Kitchen Midden people at the mouth of the Pistol, the Rogue and at the mouth of the Chetco Rivers, at Port Orford and on the Lincoln County coast. Ruins of similar dwellings are on Miller's Island in the Columbia. The pit house was ample and sufficient.

In the Basket Maker area of southeastern Arizona archaeologists have discovered that these people dug their pit, faced it with slabs and carried the walls above ground by using adobe. Essentially it is the pit house of the Oregon Country.

When the Cliff Dwellers succeeded the Basket Makers, the underground "kiva", which became the place of ceremonies, was a survival of the slab houses and these in turn were adaptations of the northern pit houses. Available material in the neighborhood caused the transition from the semi-subterranean, timber-walled houses of the north to the stone slabs.

Wood being scarce, the Basket Makers in the south substituted stone. In the half-underground pits the family huddled and propitiated the spirits as they squatted around the fire. From this the kiva was born and established as an institution. It, too, was carried south, becoming part of the Maya temples.

Before the day of the bow and arrow the primitive natives had a device known as a throwing-stick or "atlatl". The stick was used to hurl darts tipped with bone or flint, increasing the velocity and force of the flying dart.

Fragments of such a throwing stick were found by Keiger in his explorations in the Snake River Valley.

While traces of the atlatl are practically unknown in Oregon, caves in the south eastern part of the state may someday yield specimens. Only 60 miles south of the Oregon line, in Nevada, specimens have been unearthed. The atlatl eventually was supplanted by the more efficient weapon, the bow and arrow, the bow in the process taking the place of the throwing-stick.

Throwing-sticks were of several kinds, but the variety with the two-finger grip is associated chiefly with the Basket Makers. This particular spear-thrower was common in central Mexico, and from that point has been found northward to Coahuila; south to Panama.

There is a gap where no specimens have been recovered, then the two-finger grip type appears from the Pacific Coast, in the vicinity of Santa Barbara eastward across California, across Nevada, to northern Arizona and in western New Mexico. It is found in the southwest corner of Colorado, southern Utah, and has been discovered as far north as Churchill County, Nevada—in the vicinity of Lovelock--60 miles below the Oregon line. (*Bureau of American Ethnology*, Bulletin 65, page 203.)

Among the lava caves of southeastern Oregon, in Pueblo Mountains, Steens Mountains, and the rugged region immediately adjacent, spear-throwers may yet be sifted from the debris of caves by some expedition. A journey of two days would bring the atlatl users to a point due north of Denio, in Oregon, from the gypsum cave near Lovelock, Nevada.

The atlatl was used by the Nahua and the Maya. It can be assumed that the throwing-stick was carried south into Maya land by those first members of the Shoshonean family to penetrate that region.

The spear-thrower was certainly used by the aborigines who went south from the Oregon country, for the artifact has been found along the trail. It is significant, too, that the atlatl follows the main route of the pictographs and petroglyphs from lower Oregon across the state of Nevada into Arizona.

First attempts at irrigation in the Western Hemisphere were made in the region settled by the Basket Makers after their drift from Oregon. Scientists give these people credit for the irrigation idea, which must have started experimentally, but which later developed into extensive projects.

Many miles of canals have been traced to a project watering 100,000 acres. All this tedious, laborious struggle to create an agriculture was not long after Egypt was developing its wheat growing culture. One branch of the nomadic Shoshonean family was settling down, becoming farmers.

But Shoshonean tribes pushed ever farther to the south, carrying with them the knowledge of agriculture; retaining customs which were in a process of evolution; using there atlatl, their sandals, developing mentally, gradually emerging into a high state of civilization, and, in some respects, centuries ahead of India and Egypt—the rest of the world was trailing far behind.

As the hypothesis stands: The Shoshonean linguistic family extended from the Columbia River to Central America—from Celilo Falls to Chicken-Itza. The Basket Maker culture started on the Columbia and also went south, but existing ages before the Cliff Dwellers. Ethnologists and archaeologists of the American National Museum, the Smithsonian Institution and the Carnegie Institution agree on these points in numerous scientific reports and bulletins. Still another supporting prop to the theory is the evidence of picture writing.

Government scientists who have specialized in pictographs and petroglyphs traced these unintelligible and mysterious signs on the basaltic banks of the Columbia in the vicinity of Big Eddie and Roosevelt, Washington, straight southward. No system has been discovered of interpreting or translating these writings. They may mean nothing in particular!

But this is true--from the neighborhood of Celilo Falls, Indian writings or markings (some painted, some carved) follows the known trail of the Basket Makers, the area occupied by the Shoshonean linguistic family east of the Cascades and Sierra Nevada ranges.

These unique signs virtually blazed the trail from the northern boundary of present-day Oregon into Mexico and even deeper south, for signs identical with those carved on the rocks in Oregon are found in faraway Peru. They speckle the state of Nevada, of Utah and New Mexico--like footprints in the sand. These writings are signs of these prehistoric pioneers as they wandered south.

These markings are less authoritative than the testimony of the ethnologists and archaeologists, yet, is it mere coincidence that they cover the identical territory occupied by the migrating Shoshoneans and keep within the bounds of the linguistic group?

By JOHN W. KELLY, Staff Writer, *The Oregonian*

To be continued …

~ 256 ~

Making Dogs Smarter Simple Task

After the trouble with the Indians was pretty much over and they had become somewhat pacified and friendlier with the soldiers stationed around at various forts, one old brave became very much interested in a little, speckled, bob-tailed dog belonging to one of the soldiers. "Old Six," as he was called, spent hours watching the dog as he frisked around the camp, barking and snapping at everything he saw.

One day, Old Six said to the soldier, "Him heap smart dog, how make 'em dog so smart?" "Why," said the soldier, "Cut his tail off. That make him a smart dog." "H'mm," said Old Six, "We cutem my dog's tail off--make him heap smart."

Of course the soldier agreed with him, so the Indian hurried off to his wigwam, returning soon with an old, long-haired, mangy, flea-bitten cur, and said, "All right, now we fix 'em."

They took him out to a log beside the road. One soldier taking him by the tail, and one by the ears, they stretched his tail over the log. He told the Indian, "Take the ax and chop him, heap hard."

Old Six spit on his hands, swung the ax up, shut his eyes, and brought it down with all his strength. But the soldier holding the tail, being afraid of getting his hand chopped, jerked the tail back suddenly. The ax came down right behind the dogs shoulders.

Old Six looked at the two pieces of his dog a minute, and then said, "H'mm, cutem heap too short. Cookim!" His appetite overcoming his affection for his dog, he gathered up the remains and took them to his teepee. Soon the aroma of dog stew gave evidence that a feast was in preparation.

E. L. BARTON, Medford, Oregon

~ 257 ~

Scores Are Wiped Out by Massacre

In the late summer of 1864, a man near death from exhaustion and hunger staggered into the new gold camp at Ruby City, Idaho Territory. The story he related was one of the most tragic in the history of the Old Oregon Trail.

A wagon train of more than one hundred wagons and about four hundred people had been wiped out by Indians along the banks of the Snake River some thirty miles from Ruby City.

Some ten miles from where the skirmish occurred, at the mouth of Rabbit Creek, a low range of hills come down almost to the banks of the Snake River. Here was an ideal place for an ambush and here the wily Indians awaited the doomed travelers.

After a number of wagons had rounded the first hills and were out of sight of the rear of the train, the Indians charged, taking both sides of the trail so that each wagon was surrounded at once. So sudden and violent was the attack that but little defense was possible, and within an hour, the whites were dead and their wagons on fire.

The man who escaped, and who died a day or two after reaching the mining camp, had hidden in a clump of willows that grew along the river's edge. He had made his way across the thirty miles from the Owyhee Range of mountains to Ruby City.

A relief party went at once to the scene of the massacre. One woman was found alive, but was a raving maniac and also died within a few days.

These appalling details were made known to the writer of this article at the place where the massacre occurred by an old and grizzled mountain man who had been one of the rescue party.

Speaking the vernacular of the mountain trapper, he sketched a picture that still seemed fresh in his memory after twenty seven years:

"Here lay the lead wagon, overturned, its defenders scalped and stripped of their clothing. Farther up the trail, twenty or more women and children horribly mutilated lay in one heap."

As we came to the place where the last of the wagons had been destroyed, my companion turned and looked back down the ghostly old road, still visible here and there. Into his faded blue eyes came a somber shadow, and it seemed as if he visioned again that ghastly sight, long buried in his mind. His hand fell to the butt of a .45 Colt pistol he wore on his hip, and he said, "Them damn varmints!"

This was the last wagon train to cross the Indian country without an armed military escort. The American Civil War ended the next spring, releasing many adventurous men who preferred fighting the western Indians to the humdrum existence of workaday life.

JAMES R. KEITH, Grants Pass, Oregon

~ 258 ~

Wool Fragments Are Made Into Socks

Matilda Zumwalt Howard tells many stories of her early life in Oregon. None of them gives a clearer insight into the frugality of those pioneer women's lives than does the tale of her children's first wool stockings.

This pioneer daughter lived with her husband and family at Wilsonville, on the Willamette River, in the 1860s. She and her husband operated a ferry at that point, and one day, during her husband's absence, a stockman came along with a large band of sheep.

When the sheep owner observed the frail little woman, he asked if she could operate the ferry without her husband. She assured him that she could, so the work of ferrying the sheep across the river began. When the last wooly was across, this thrifty mother noticed that considerable wool clung to the bushes and thorny berry vines where the animals had milled about waiting for the transport across the river.

Gathering her apron into her hands, she began picking the bits of wool from the bushes, kind of like picking cotton, I imagine. Soon she had filled, not only her apron, but several bags as well. This wool was washed and spun into yarn by this patient little woman and then knitted into warm woolen stockings for her children.

M. LEONA NICOLS, Portland, Oregon

~ 259 ~

Girls Get Fright from Indian Fracas

In the Oakville community in Linn County, a few miles east of Corvallis, Oregon, is the Donation Land Claim of the Honorable Joseph Hamilton, who settled there in the fall of 1847.

The winter of 1846-47 was spent in preparation for the trip across the plains. Among the many things that were prepared for the journey was a barrel of handmade lye soap, which proved to be instrumental in saving the train from destruction. The next spring saw the assembling of wagons and oxen and soon the long procession was on its way.

Things went smoothly for a while, but before reaching Fort Hall, the train was attacked by Indians. It seemed for a time that the whole train was doomed. The Indians ran from wagon to wagon to pilfer, when one Indian spied the barrel of soap. He, of course, supposed it to be molasses.

He gave a yell of glee as he ran his entire arm into the barrel of soap and then proceeded to lick off his arm. In no time the lye took effect and the performance the Indian went through began. The other Indians stopped and watched with surprise, and finally, thinking evil spirits had overtaken him, they hurriedly rode away. The train was saved. Most all of the food supplies were taken by the Indians, so by the time Fort Hall was reached, there was much sickness and little food.

After a rest of a few days, the immigrants proceeded on their way. The train then divided, the Hamiltons and others choosing the Applegate Route. On reaching the Rogue River, they found the Indians were even more treacherous, and orders were given for everyone to stay by their wagons.

It was in the fall of the year, when the Evergreen blackberries were ripe, and in spite of the warning, young Mrs. Hamilton and another young woman went for a short distance to pick some of the delicious berries. They wandered farther than they intended, when they heard a disturbance in the direction of the wagons. In a few minutes, they realized the train was being attacked by Indians.

They were very frightened and dared not return to the wagons, so proceeded to find a hiding place. They crawled behind a large log which was densly covered with thorny berry vines. There they waited. The noise and fighting seemed to come closer, and within a few minutes they realized that their hiding place was the center of the battle.

Many times the Indians and whites went back and forth over the log where the girls were hiding. Even after the fighting had stopped, the girls were afraid to leave, and remained there until nightfall. They were also worried that the wagon train would move on while they were away and leave them to the mercy of the Indians.

In the meantime, the camp was all astir when it was discovered the girls were missing. It was finally decided that the girls had been either killed or taken captive. Imagine their surprise when the girls came slipping into camp. From that time on, it was not necessary to warn them about leaving the wagons.

The Hamilton family finally arrived in the Willamette Valley, settling near Oakville, where they raised a family of six children.

MISS MERLIE GILLIAM, Corvallis, Oregon

~ 260 ~

Battle of Table Rock Declared to Be Myth

Stay in Medford or Jacksonville, Oregon for any length of time and you are sure to hear of the battle that raged between settlers and the Rogue River Indians on the summit of the lower Table Rock, a natural citadel whose only approaches are a narrow trail on the east side and from the rear. You will hear how the tide of battle ebbed and flowed when the settlers stormed and gained the upper hand, through sheer audacity, the summit of this huge rock formation. You'll hear that the despairing warriors leaped from the towering cliffs into the river below, some meeting death, but many escaping to fight another day.

Well, it's a good yarn, but as I stood on the brink of the cliff and gazed at the Rogue River some fifteen hundred feet below and about a quarter of a mile away from the base, I had my doubts. For a long time it seemed as if that was the story of the local historians who were stuck with it and would always stick to it.

Finally, my good friend, Edward E. Gore, son of R. E. Gore, pioneer of 1852, told me the story of the affair as his father, who participated, told it to him. Mr. Gore's integrity and veracity are above question.

In August, 1853, there was a band of Indians camped on Bear Creek, east of the elder Mr. Gore's cabin, which stands today on the west side of the Pacific Hwy. north of its junction with the Phoenix-Jacksonville Road.

These Indians seemed peaceable, and were not molested until a man named Edwards, who had a cabin further up the creek, was found very dead, his own ax having been the lethal weapon.

The settlers thereabout became uneasy, lest such procedure, if let to pass, became a native mode of operation. They gathered at Gore's house, armed for the purpose of rounding up the Indians camped on the creek in an effort to apprehend the guilty party or parties.

The reason for Mr. Edwards' sudden demise is now known, but as it has nothing to do with the subsequent "battle", suffice to say, it was one of the very first actions to be taken in that part of the state for alienation of affections.

The Indians saw the posse coming and decided not to be home. Upon finding the village deserted, the punitive expedition set out in pursuit, and soon overtook the fugitives. The Indian braves whirled around to face their pursuers and assumed a bellicose attitude. The posse leveled their rifles, but refrained from tickling the triggers. That being the days of muzzle-loading weapons, they had no desire to unload their guns upon slight provocation and thereby give their noble adversaries such an advantage.

The native sons also were loath to begin hostilities, so as soon as the women and papooses had made yardage, they turned and went trotting after, while the posse trotted along behind.

From there on, it was a pantomime battle, the afore-described procedure being re-enacted whenever the posse pressed too close. When they reached the Rogue River, the braves made another stand while the women and papooses forded the stream, which, prior to the construction of the Gold-Ray Dam, was fordable above the mouth of Bear Creek.

At the foot of the trail leading to the summit of Table Rock, this "you don't" and "I won't" act again was staged until the noncombatants gained the summit. Whereupon their rear guard nimbly hot-footed it up the trail. The settlers, in pursuit under forced draft, were determined to engage at close quarters. Consequently, they gained the summit before the Indians could select defensive positions.

Ever enthusiastic adherents to the adage, "discretion is the better part of valor", and with a somewhat winded but thoroughly irate posse in their front, and a long, long drop through space in their rear, the red brothers threw down their arms in unconditional surrender.

As the settlers were herding their prisoners back down the narrow trail, one of the older women, who had not read any of James Fenimore Cooper's books, and as a result had not cultivated the stealthy tread and sure-footed grace of his fictional Indians, turned her ankle on a rock and tumbled over the edge of the cliff. This incident must have given rise to the legend of the soaring leaps.

Thus was the "battle" on Table Rock--fought and won.

LYNN M. BRAGG, Silverton, Oregon

~ 261 ~

Broken Friendship Patched by Romance

Francis Payette, a Frenchman, brought with him from the Far East in the early 1860s a wife and two children, son and daughter, to live at Fort Boise where he was employed by the Hudson's Bay Fur Company as a trader.

Here his children grew to adult life and here they married; the girl to a Frenchman by the name of Pattee, and the boy, Pierre, a Bannock Indian maid. In turn, each bride bore a daughter and both girls when thirteen were sent east for three years to schooling.

Julia Payette was as striking a beauty as her full-blooded French cousin, Elizabeth Pattee. Upon their return to Fort Boise, comely maids of sixteen, they were viewed with favor by all the young men at the fort; among them George Goodhart, a lad only a little older than the girls, but steadily employed as a trapper and as a guide.

George had met a man named Osburne, sometime before, at Fort Hall on the Snake River. To Osburne he had pledged everlasting friendship because of an earlier favor granted to him. The two were for months inseparable companions; then nature took a hand and their ways parted. Osburne fell in love.

Drifting into an Indian camp at Salmon Falls, he found several Indian women drying fish. Among them was the comely daughter of the chief. Osburne was immediately infatuated, and, having no ponies to trade for a bride, he sought other ways of winning her.

Several ponies had been stolen by the Blackfeet from Chief Mox Yahwatin, a Shoshone and father of the girl he loved. Yahwatin, known to the whites as Two Belly, was furious because his braves had failed to find the missing stock, and when the daring Osburne offered to find and bring them back, his services were immediately accepted.

Several days later, the ponies again within bounds, Osburne was given his reward, the lovely Bright Face. After a customary Indian ceremony they left for his cabin. They lived happily for two years.

Then, on a visit to Fort Boise, Osburne encountered Payette's granddaughters and fell in love with Miss Pattee, to the consternation of his young friend, George Goodhart, who had preceded him to Fort Boise. Goodhart also loved the beautiful girl, and, knowing of Osburne's Indian wife, and in friendship for her, remonstrated with his rival. Fighting mad,

Osburne threatened his friend with death if he told of the Indian bride. Loyal to his love, the youth went to Elizabeth's father and told the story. Osburne, vowing vengeance, took Bright Face and left for his trap lines.

The time came for the annual arrival of the company's pack train. Osburne, in the company's employ, failed to appear with his catch from his camp on the north fork of the Boise River, and young Goodhart was sent to search for him.

Not finding him at his permanent camp, the youth pushed over his trail into the wilderness, knowing that he might meet death at the end of the trail. He found Osburne, alone and injured, in a meager shelter of willows, with one foot frozen. Immediately upon sighting Goodhart, Osburne, half crazed, reached for his gun, but was overpowered by the younger man.

In all haste, Goodhart built a trivoy upon which he loaded his irrational patient for the long trek back to help, where Osburne recovered. Nothing was known of Bright Face, and upon recovery, Osburne again disappeared.

Soon after this happening, a priest doing missionary work among the Indians arrived at the fort and plans were made for an immediate wedding for George and Elizabeth. Before the day came, three Indian tepees were put up one night, just outside the adobe wall around the house in which Grandfather Payette lived.

Next morning, when the guests had assembled for the wedding, a loud rapping startled them. The door opened to reveal Osburne and the smiling Bright Face. Osburne clasped the hand of young Goodhart and explained that he and Bright Face had come to be married the white man's way.

Both couples took their marriage vows and all four sat together at the wedding feast. Mr. and Mrs. Goodhart were the first white couple to be married at Fort Boise.

MRS. A. J. KING, Merrill, Oregon

~ 262 ~

Mother Watches Daughters Perish

To residents of the Willamette Valley, the year 1861 meant not only the American Civil War, but "the great flood." The Willamette River grew until it was claimed that steamboats could have run from Corvallis to "Hamilton's Timber," several miles to the east and normally too shallow for large boats.

To the family living on an island, about three miles above Corvallis, the flood brought tragedy. There were five of the Georges; Father, mother, two little girls and a boy, living in their two story farmhouse.

One winter afternoon, people on the Linn County side of the river, to the east, heard the marooned family calling desperately for help. The farm of Captain John Smith, afterward Indian Agent of the Warm Springs Reservation, was near the river. His son John and some other boys heard the cries for help and started a rescue of the Georges.

In the meantime, water was pouring into the second story of the island home and its owners abandoned it for fear it would soon be swept away and destroyed. They loaded into the small boat they used to go back and forth across the river and tried to reach the west bank of the Willamette.

Logs and wreckage threatened the small craft, the swollen river boiled around it, and then, a whirlpool engulfed the boat, spinning it around and around and finally turning it upon end so that the passengers were thrown into the cold and muddy water.

Mr. George swam to the west bank and grabbed a fallen tree. He had just climbed upon the tree when he saw his wife in the river below him.

He reached down and caught hold of her, took off his belt and fastened her wrists to the tree so that the current could not carry her away. The children had already been swept downstream beyond his reach.

Mrs. George, hysterical and nearly out of her mind, was taken to a nearby farmhouse.

"When I saw my little girls, they were clinging to bushes and praying," were the words in which she described the last sight of her daughters, and the boy was never seen again.

The pitiful part of the story was the fact that the drownings were unnecessary. The two boys from Linn County reached the empty farmhouse but finding it too dark to return home that night, stayed safely until morning in the attic.

At any rate, if the young rescuer named John had been drowned, Vancouver and Clark County, Washington would have never had their tireless and beloved pioneer doctor, Dr. John Randolph Smith.

ELIZABETH C. YATES, Vancouver, Washington

~ 263 ~

Lone White Man Puts Indian Band to Rout

John Wesley Howell crossed the plains to Oregon by ox team in 1843, arriving at Howell Prairie in October. Howell Prairie is about nine miles northeast of Salem, in Marion County and was so named in his honor.

In the early summer of 1845, Mr. and Mrs. Howell were at their cabin. Mrs. Howell was preparing the noon meal and their baby boy was sitting on the floor near the center of the small room.

Mr. Howell saw two Indians coming across the prairie on cayuses from the northwest. He took his muzzle-loading rifle, which he called "Old Snyder," down from the wall and closed the door. He stepped to one side so he would be behind the door when it was opened and told his wife to only partly open the door if they knocked.

They pounded heavily on the door. Mrs. Howell opened the door a few inches and asked what they wanted. By this time they saw the baby on the floor. They said they wanted white papoose and shoved the door half open.

Mr. Howell stepped out, shoved Old Snyder's muzzle against the lead Indian's chest and told them to "clatawa."

He followed them out. They walked backward out to where they had tied their cayuses to a bush. Then they mounted and rode back in the direction they had come. Within just a few minutes, hundreds of Indians were riding out of a belt of timber headed for his cabin.

It was several miles to the nearest neighbor or settlement, and Old Snyder their only weapon of defense. Mr. Howell said he felt that if they barricaded themselves in the cabin, the Indians would likely set it on fire. So he resolved to step out and meet them face to face with Old Snyder at his shoulder, which he did.

The Indians were armed with bows and arrows. Those in the lead rode up within about a hundred yards and stopped. Suddenly they wheeled their cayuses to the northeast and rode away.

Mr. Howell decided that each Indian thought he himself would be the one killed, and would not run the risk. John Wesley Howell was a kind-hearted, good-natured, honest man and very courageous. This writer was well acquainted with him.

J. T. HUNTLEY, Dallas, Oregon

~ 264 ~

Rawhide Ropes Stop Harassment

Blackfeet Indians constantly harassed early trappers in the Rocky Mountains. Joe Meek and two of his companions, Jim Flett and George

Igo, were camped along the Green River when a band of fast riding warriors from this tribe attacked the trio and chased them into the tall timber. None of the men were harmed, but they decided that they needed a plan to, hopefully, stop future attacks.

The men made rawhide ropes, sixty feet long and stretched three of them twenty feet apart across a timbered trail that the Indians often used.

The next time the Indians made an appearance, the trappers jumped on their horses and rode off in the direction of the awaiting ropes. The wild chase continued until the trappers reached the ropes. The Indians didn't notice that the trio maneuvered quickly around the ropes, then darted back on the trail.

The fast running Indian ponies ran their riders into the ropes with such force that a number of the Indians were either killed or injured. A dozen ponies were left for the trappers, who wisely decided to get out of the area.

ROBERT MOULTON GATKE, Salem, Oregon

~ 265 ~

Funeral Trek Made Across Plains

Robert J. Hendricks in his book, "*Bethel and Aurora*", tells about a hearse (not a horse) that led a wagon train in 1855 from Bethel, Missouri to the Washington Territory.

Dr. William Keil, the founder and leader of the settlement of Aurora, Oregon was busy with other members making preparations for the long and tedious journey to the Oregon Country to found a Utopian settlement like the one in Bethel.

Day by day, Dr. Keil's nineteen year old son, William, watched and took part in the preparations. Imagine Willie's consternation when he became ill with malaria. He pleaded until his father promised not to leave him behind.

Dr. Keil had the carpenters build a comfortable bed to fit in a light wagon. Willie was to ride in this "plains ambulance" and lead the procession westward.

Four days before the caravan was to leave, Willie died. The members feared they would be delayed by the funeral, but Dr. Keil had the carpenters change the ambulance into a hearse. A wooden coffin lined with lead and filled with alcohol, one of the products produced by the colony in Bethel. The body was placed in the coffin and sealed.

Dr. Keil carried out his promise to his son as the hearse was the first wagon in the column across the plains. The hearse seemed to be a protection to the caravan as it slowly traveled westward. They had very little trouble with the Indians. It is known that the Indians are superstitious of the dead.

About six months later the wagon train arrived at Willapa Bay, Washington, on November 1, 1855. William Keil was buried on December 26, 1855, on the Giesy farm near Crockett's Landing. This little cemetery, the resting place, over the years, of other members of the commune, is about halfway between Raymond and Menlo, Washington.

This was the closing scene of the longest and evidently the only funeral march in American history conducted by a covered wagon traveling two thousand miles.

HARVEY C. ABELING, Portland, Oregon

"Northwest Empire Builders"

SIMEON G. REED

A Versatile Empire Builder and College Founder

By ANNE MELLETT KEEZER, Wife of Reed College

President Dexter M. Keezer. April 7, 1935

Eighty odd years ago, a young pioneer arrived in Portland from East Abington, Massachusetts, via Panama, to make his fortune. He came equipped with a small working capital, a young wife who had been the belle of Quincy, and more ideas rolling around in his head than most of us have in a lifetime.

He was not an "adventurer" nor a scapegoat, but a shrewd, solid Yankee who saw in the far west the opportunity to build a new New England and to grow up with the country. If the notion that gold could be had for the picking up crossed his mind, he evidently dismissed it in favor of the old Yankee principle that hard work is the key to fortune, and that real fortunes come out of the soil via the plow and not the gold pan.

So he hired himself out as a clerk in Mr. W. S. Ladd's general store and set about the business of building the West and himself along with it. Thus quietly Simeon G. Reed established himself as a citizen of Portland.

Within four years, Simeon Reed was a partner in the store, the firm name becoming Ladd, Reed & Company. The city was growing at a terrific rate, and business opportunities were opening up rapidly for those who had the courage and enough capital to seize them.

Reed had both, and the journals of his dealings in those years show how he was buying real estate at strategic points in the little city very quietly and persistently. Also he was buying fine livestock. Probably no man ever loved horse flesh with more passion than did Simeon Reed. He eventually had the means to gratify that passion that made possible the great legacy he left to the Northwest in the fine strains he incorporated into the local stock. But in these early days, his dealings were on a small scale.

The great potentialities of the territory east of the Cascade Mountains were obvious to a man of Reed's farsightedness, and the immediate answer that occurred to him was the part that the Columbia River must play in developing the vast interior.

Reed was one of the small groups of men who organized the old Oregon Central Railroad Company and a prime mover in the formation of the Oregon Steam Navigation Company, which practically monopolized the traffic on the Columbia and poured a steady stream of gold into the pockets of its founders for years on end.

Inasmuch as the Oregon Steam Navigation Company played such a vital part in the development of Portland as a great city, it seems appropriate here to mention it in some detail.

The men who went into the venture with Simeon Reed were John C. Ainsworth, R. R. Thompson, W. S. Ladd, Jacob Kamm and a few others. They were all a courageous and hard-headed lot, financially speaking, and, having created a "good thing," hung onto it until the development of the railroads practically doomed the enterprise.

At that time, while others still did not see the "writing on the wall," the incorporators of the Oregon Steam Navigation Company sold out to the Northern Pacific Railroad Company for a good price and went on to other things. But while the Oregon Steam Navigation Company was in its heyday, these men controlled the traffic on the Columbia River and dictated freight rates without fear of competition.

The steamship company built many of its own boats and ran them on the lower Columbia below the Cascade Mountains, on the middle river between the Cascades and Celilo Falls, and on the upper river above Celilo, including the lakes of Pend Orielle and Cour d'Alene and the Snake River. It owned and operated portage railroads at the Cascades and Celilo and also operated boats on the Willamette River.

Whenever the Oregon Steam Navigation Company had a vessel to sell it stipulated in the contract that it "should" never be run on the Columbia or any of its tributaries. Many of Mr. Reed's letters indicate, with forceful clarity, the firmness with which the steamship company maintained this stipulation. There are evidences left that "alien" ships which put their noses into the Columbia were dealt with, with dispatch, either by being bought out of hand by the company or made so uncomfortable that they sought other waters.

Another industrial enterprise, in which Mr. Reed was a moving spirit, was the Oregon Iron & Steel Company, which operated a plant at Oswego and successfully produced iron products from local ore for a number of years.

After some time, however, reduction of freight rates on iron and steel from the East made the operation uneconomical and the furnaces were shut down. Oswego Lake probably is the most lasting benefit to Portland remaining from this enterprise.

In the early days of the Northwest, mining was, of course, a consuming interest and an extremely profitable one. Simeon Reed knew mining and a good mine when he saw one, and even when he hadn't seen it. Reed sent a friend with $15,000 to Baker to buy the Connor Creek mine. Reed had never seen it, but it produced more than a million dollars and repaid the original cost in a few months. He was the owner of the immensely wealthy Bunker Hill-Sullivan Mine for several years and also owned a large number of shares in the Crown Point Mine in California. About the only activity of the community in which he was definitely not interested was banking. Apparently he left that to his two close associates, W. S. Ladd and John C. Ainsworth.

As a result of these activities, the young man who had come west to make his fortune had made it, as fortunes went in those days, but the investments he had made kept adding automatically to its size, enabling him to branch out into fields where the return was a matter of longer waiting and was much less sure-fire.

In going over the many journals that were left in the possession of Reed's relatives and in the archives of Reed College, one salient fact stands out very clearly. And that fact is that, however expansive his operations became (and they came to include practically every phase of business and industrial activity of the Northwest), Mr. Reed never took his hand off the throttle.

He knew where his money was, what it was bringing in, the technical details of operating steamboats, railroads, coal mines, iron and gold mines, how to drill for water, how to build a box stall and a hay shed and ... how to cure the common cold.

As the common cold has been the subject of much research of late years, it seems only fair to the scientists laboring in their laboratories to reveal the secret buried so many years in a pioneer notebook between entries of the latest dividend payment of the Oregon Steam Navigation Co., and a notice that the pedigreed cow, "Clematis," had dropped a white bull calf named "Mount Hood." Here is the recipe for any brave soul who would like to try it the next time he starts sniveling and sneezing:

2 oz. Peruvian bark
1oz. Wild Cherry bark
1 dram Cloves
1 dram Cinnamon
1 dram Nutmeg
1 oz. Sulphur

1 teaspoon Cayenne Pepper
2 quarts of Port Wine
Dosage: Drink ½ wine glass every ½ hour till cured.

Can anyone deny that our forebears were made of stern stuff?

The wide range of Mr. Reed's interests can best be indicated by a few sample excerpts from his notebooks. In 1865, he writes: "Mr. Angus McDonald, trader of Hudson's Bay Fur Company at Fort Coleville, says that in the year 1846, an old Indian Chief, then seventy years of age, informed him that when he was about twelve years old, (which would make it the year 1788) there was an eruption of Mount Hood which covered the whole earth, as far as the Snake River, with ashes to a depth of from two to eight inches and destroyed all grasses and verdure."

In 1866: "Good water at any point on the sound four miles below Olympia, Washington. Wharf or dock could be built so a ship of any draft could lie alongside the warehouse. Good coal beds at Seattle in inexhaustible quantities."

In 1867: March 21: "Paid William Kohl for six hundred cigars, $85.00." May 5: "Sally Come Up' trotted the mile in 2:51." December 15: "Water came onto wharf. Removed goods from cellars."

In 1868: "Estimate cost of running steamship from San Francisco to China, via Sandwich Islands and Japan—ninety days' round trip--$130,000, of which $15,000 is interest, $22,500 is wear and tear—estimate revenue, not including meals, $103,000."

In 1870: May 1: "Telegraph line completed to Walla Walla." July 30: "Sold out interest in 'Evening Commercial' this day to C. Dolson."

In 1871: October 30, he paid $11.50 for a pair of English pheasants and $15.00 for a handkerchief holder.

All during the year and following years, his interest in plans for a new house, which actually was built in 1875 on the corner of First and

Montgomery Streets, occupied him. At this time, he has been figuring out how many gallons of water it will take to keep an outside fountain, and one in the conservatory, going seven hours a day. At Mr. Reed's death, this property was left as an Old People's Home.

That Portland was still frontier in these days, is indicated by a memorandum for "killing coyotes and wolves" in an 1871 notebook.

In 1871: On July 17th, Mr. Reed seems to have fallen victim to the book salesman, for he notes: "Agreed to take 26 volumes of New American 'Cyclopedia for $120, bound in sheepskin."

March 22, 1872: "Prices furnished Rev. C. W. Shaw of Albany for excursion: Astoria and back, $3.00; Cascades and back, $2.00, The Dalles and back, $4.00; meals 50 cents extra."

April 18, 1872: "Sold phaeton and harness to E. Corbett for $800. Telegraphed New York for landau and harness last Saturday."

April 25, 1872: "Gave dinner party to Norris, Holladay, Ladd, Montgomery, H. Green, General E. R. S. Canby, Halsey, Judge Upton, Judge Deady, Green, Lewis, Mitchell, Failing and Judge Strong. Had cucumbers--our own raising."

October 7, 1872: "Started up Columbia River to Wallula with Northern Pacific Railroad party."

November 28, 1872: "Experiments on new grasses at Five Oaks. As none of them seeded this year, I think they should have been sown in the fall—say early in September."

December 22, 1872: "Fire in Portland. Memo: To find the net weight of an animal, multiply the square of the girth in inches by the length from top of shoulder to tail in inches and divide the product by 7,344, and the quotient will be in stones of 14ths." (Or put it on a scales).

January 22, 1873: "San Francisco. Dined with Holladay, Ainsworth, Gov. Goodwin, and Rumford. Queen pigged--l boar, 1 sow, two died."

February 24, 1873: "Ballad, 'The Bell Ringer,' words Jno. Oxenford, music W. V. Wallace—four sharps."

August 5, 1873: "Martin Holbrook, Yakima City—wants a purebred shorthorn bull."

August 24, 1873: A sketch of an original bookcase.

August 27, 1873: "To kill fern: Cut it from this day till fourth of September and it will bleed to death." (Sounds rather cruel)

July 30, 1876: "William Currier bets me $20 that *Ophir* will sell in San Francisco for $100 a share before the first of February, next. Also bets me $20 that *California* will sell at the same price in the same length of time."

In 1877, his notebook has pages of trotting times for some of his horses and intricate figures on costs of fencing and area of pasture with different types of fences.

Mr. Reed also notes instruction for planting corn: "Plant King Philip's corn with some red grains in it. Plant three kernels in hill four feet apart when the white oak leaves are as big as squirrel's ears."

After thumbing through these notebooks in which Reed jotted down the things that he thought about, one has a feeling that he had an almost childlike curiosity and diversity of interest, until cold figures jump out of the page and impressively show how well he turned these interests into paying propositions.

No detail was too small, and no proposal was too staggeringly large for him to pass it by. In a letter written during the 1870s, he remarks to a friend that he has fourteen farms in the Willamette Valley. There are those who would say that managing one farm is a full-time job, but he carried all fourteen as a sort of side issue to his activities as an industrialist and business executive.

On these farms, he experimented with new types of agricultural implements, orchard grasses, well borers, stock breeding, drainage systems, tree grafting and knew exactly, to the last detail, the progress of these experiments. Long before the invention of the internal combustion engine, Mr. Reed wrote to a British manufacturer to inquire about the "steam plow" for large-scale farming. His experiments with alfalfa have borne fruit (or rather more alfalfa) in our day.

Purebred stock was his greatest passion. He spent fortunes on importing fine bulls and stallions and putting them at the service of the community at a very low fee in order to improve the livestock of the Pacific Northwest. W. S. Ladd, his first business partner in Portland, also was associated with Mr. Reed in this activity. The last years of his life, especially after his health forced his retirement from business, was devoted to stock breeding.

A letter written about 1890 stated that the Oneonta Stud Farm alone cost $90,000. In 1892, Mr. and Mrs. Reed went to Europe for the "grand tour—old style," but the time was unhappily spent for Mrs. Reed as the trip was mostly made up of months spent in London attending stock fairs and sales. Over a dozen mares and stallions were shipped to Oregon from Liverpool as a result of this "pleasure" trip.

The Reed farms specialized in Short Horn and Ayreshire cattle, Cotswold sheep, Clydesdale and trotting horses, Hampshire hogs and exotic poultry.

But the running horse was his greatest delight. A note in one of his dairies says: "In racing colors, black shirt with gold stripes," and scattered throughout his notes are tables of running times of his trotters and race horses, prize moneys at various tracks, weights and racing forms, and notes, such as, "Wm. Black of Peoria, Illinois, has best pacing stallion." "Get boot for Boston's hind leg," and "sent six horses to pasture today."

For years, he was Secretary of the Oregon State Agricultural Fair and never missed a fair day even if he had to rush across the country from lobbying for the Central Railroad in Washington D.C., to do so.

The Reeds evidently planned, for some years, before moving to Pasadena, California, to build there the house of their dreams, mansard roof and all.

During their European trip, Mrs. Reed must have spent days on end choosing her carpet patterns, damasks for curtains, tapestries and ormolu clocks. All were the most splendid accouterments for the Victorian mansion. This was a shopping tour for any woman to turn green with envy over.

Mr. Reed was as interested as she in the plans for the house, and, although he had a battery of architects working on them, he collected in his notebooks, sketches of facades that pleased him—as the front of the hotel in Brighton where they stayed.

Evidently this edifice was mostly of glass and Mr. Reed meticulously sets down dimensions and elevations, with the notations, "suggestions for conservatory." This house still stands in Pasadena and is now a small museum set in seven acres of lovely park, originally laid out by Mr. Reed and planted with shrubs, many of which he introduced himself.

When Simeon Reed died in 1895, he left practically all of his estate to his wife, with this suggestion:

"Feeling as I do, a deep interest in the future welfare and prosperity of the city of Portland, Oregon, where I have spent my business life and accumulated the property I possess, I would suggest to my wife that she devote some portion of my estate to benevolent objects, or to the cultivation, illustration or development of the fine arts of said city of Portland, or to some other suitable purpose which shall be of permanent value and contribute to the beauty of the city and to the intelligence, prosperity and happiness of its inhabitants."

In response to this suggestion, Mrs. Reed, who died in 1904, provided in her will that the bulk of the estate should go to the founding of "an institution of learning having for its object the increase and diffusion of practical knowledge among the citizens of said city of Portland and for the promotion of literature, science and art."

Hence comes Reed College, whose beautiful Gothic buildings now stand on the original Ladd farm in Eastmoreland, a large part of which was presented to the college by the Ladd estate, and where future citizens of Portland now enjoy benefits they might have missed had it not been for the devotion of a real pioneer and empire builder to the home of his choosing.

ANNE MELLETT KEEZER, Wife of the President of Reed College, Dexter M. Keezer, April 7, 1935

~ 266 ~

Lost Steer Saves Train From Grief

In 1853, a little band of wagons and ox teams left St. Louis, Missouri, traveling westward. Heading the party was one William K. Smith, who later was to establish a sawmill business in Portland and to build the city's first large, brick home, on Ash Street, between Front and First Avenues.

As the caravan proceeded westward, the danger of an Indian attack grew constantly greater. The aborigines at that time were still semi-hostile throughout the greater part of the West. Sullenly they watched the advancing wagons with the plows tied to tail-boards, and it was but slowly that they learned to accept those wagons as destiny.

On the Humboldt River, the party ventured off on a new mountain trail. One night, as they camped, one of their steers strayed away. As they broke camp in the morning and discovered the loss, Smith dispatched one of the men on horseback to scour the country for the missing animal. In the meantime, the caravan moved on.

Smith had been apprehensive that a band of Humboldt Indians was planning an attack. That morning his fears proved well grounded. As the wagons were filing through a narrow pass, the way suddenly was blocked by painted, well-armed Indians who commenced whooping and firing.

The outcome of the battle remained uncertain. Suddenly the white man who had been looking for the lost steer came riding over the brow of the hill. When he spotted the activity below, he stopped and frantically started waving his arms.

The Indians hastily concluded that he was the advance guard of reinforcements and they fled in confusion.

ALBERT HALL, Portland, Oregon

~ 267 ~

Wits Rescue Young Pony Express Rider

When the late Judge Thomas Hurley Brents of Walla Walla, Washington was twenty-two-years old, he invested his small capital in provisions and supplies, and accompanied by several friends, set out for the Powder River Mines near Baker, Oregon.

Their equipment was meager, consisting of a pack horse each, loaded with bacon, beans, dried apples and mining tools.

The heavy snows of the previous hard winter still covered the Blue Mountains and the old trail up Birch Creek was almost impassable. But, undaunted, they dug a trail through drifts three feet deep for a distance of twenty five miles and reached Auburn after two months of hardship.

In June of 1862, they trekked across the mountains again to a tributary of John Day River, which they named Canyon Creek. There they located mining claims and built the first cabin in Canyon City.

Shortly after their arrival, young Brents and a friend established a pony express business from the new settlement to The Dalles, Oregon. The trip was made weekly and was 225 miles from Canyon City, by the old road.

Even though fifty cents was charged for delivery of letters and newspapers and 3 percent for gold and silver treasure, the project was much more hazardous than profitable.

Hostile Indians in the mountains and highwaymen nearer civilization provided enough thrills in one trip to last the rider a lifetime. Few stations for change to fresh horses along the route had been established at that time.

One evening, fearing to swim his tired horse across a swollen stream, the young rider, in making a wide detour, came upon a bright campfire at nightfall and decided to seek the companionship of the travelers. He was fairly upon them before realizing that one of the campers was Berry Way, a notorious outlaw, who had recently escaped from the California Penitentiary, his wife, and another desperado.

It was too late for retreat, so he boldly unsaddled his horse, carelessly threw his gold-dust filled canteen on the ground, and made preparations for the night. Chatting with his curious hosts, he was asked if he carried much treasure, which he denied, saying usually he did, but this time was to meet the incoming express train and had with him only small irons for repairs.

Needless to say, he did not sleep, and lay all night with his cocked revolver in his hand. His careless manner apparently deceived the outlaws, for in the morning, he was allowed to depart without hindrance.

Later he met a sheriff's posse searching for his companions of the night before. They had found the body of a man named Gallagher concealed in the brush up the trail and laid the blame for the robbery and murder on Berry Way.

Brents directed them to the camp, where the desperadoes were captured. Later, Way was taken from the jail by vigilantes who hanged him without trial or ceremony.

On another occasion, when changing horses at a station, the keeper told him that Jim Romaine and three other desperadoes had inquired, not long before, when they might expect the pony express to ride in. Though the moon was high, Mr. Brents continued on his way. He was thinking of what would be his fate if he fell into their hands. Behind him he could clearly hear hoof beats and plainly see the four horsemen approaching him.

Whipping up his horse, he hastened on, and after crossing a creek heavily fringed with brush, he suddenly turned off the trail and watched them dash by. Until the moon set, he rode cautiously and made a detour upon spotting their campfire ahead. Pressing on, he reached The Dalles, over one hundred miles, ten hours later, with only three horse changes.

Sometime later, the bandits, after committing a series of diabolical murders, were caught and hanged by the Vigilantes.

ADELE GOFF McEWEN, Walla Walla, Washington

~ 268 ~

Little Becky's "Big Fish" Story

During the later years of the great Western emigration the government provided small detachments of armed soldiers to escort the wagon trains to their destination in the Oregon Territory. This protection kept most of the life threatening elements away from the weary pioneers and allowed for a more relaxed attitude about allowing children to be children. The following story was not a typical series of events for the children of Thomas "Too Tall" Jensen and his wife Sarah.

My great-grandmother Rebecca and her older brother Ebner had finished their daily chores early so they decided to go fishing in the Willamette River south of Oregon City near the wagon train's evening camping spot.

Ebner had a nicely carved fishing pole with stout line and a hand-bent hook made from a sharpened piece of wire—and a collection of fat, juicy earth worms to tempt the fish. Rebecca had just celebrated her tenth birthday the day before so Ebner, fourteen, decided to let her to go along. She sat quietly on the river bank playing with a stick in the water.

Ebner crawled out on a large snag that had fallen into the river and created a nice spot for the fish to hide. After just a few minutes, he had his first fish jerking on his stout line. He held a firm grip on the little trout as he ran a short cord through the fish's mouth and gills. He called to Rebecca to climb out on the tree a short way so she could hold the cord and let the little fish swim around. Ebner then went back to fishing until he heard Rebecca made a strange squeal and then the words, "Eb, there's a big fish trying to catch your little fish. What should I do?"

Before he could answer, he saw her give a mighty pull on the cord as she yelled, "No, you can't have Eb's fish". Out of the water popped the big fish still clutching the little fish in its mouth. They landed in the crotch of a limb and tightly wedged there. Rebecca quickly pounced on her surprised catch and held the squirming fish against the tree until her brother could help her. He quickly secured the other end of the cord around the bigger fish's tail. Eb congratulated her for her nice catch, a beautiful 21½ inch wild "cut-throat" salmon trout.

"Okay Becky, let's get back to the wagon. You gotta carry the fish back 'cause you caught the biggest one. Mom and Dad will really be surprised."

Rebecca could hardly wait to tell her parents the fish story. She ran all the way back to the camp with their breakfast tightly wrapped in her arms.

Oregon's largest "cut-throat" trout on record is 20 inches in length. Becky's fish, later found hand outlined on a wrinkled scrap of paper will sadly never be recorded correctly as the state's largest "cut throat".

Alex Rogers, Silverton, Oregon

~ 269 ~

Surrender Not Understood by Raiding Party

As the first wagon trains attempted to trudge across 2,000 miles of plains, deserts, rivers, mountains, and valleys--they knew not what to expect over the next hill or around the next corner. Certain death might be lurking just ahead. But these determined pioneers dreamt of getting to Oregon--or bust. And to Oregon they would go—thousands of them.

The Indians watched as these white men, many with their families, moved onto hunting grounds occupied for centuries by various tribes, and then watched them build homes that were never intended to be moved. The Indians regularly moved from the valleys to the foothills and back again as their food supply changed with the seasons. They just didn't understand the ways of their new neighbors, the white man. Such a misunderstanding is told here:

One small party of 22 wagons and less than 100 souls held frequent meetings around the campfires at night to discuss plans for the next day. Early on in their journey they had decided that if attacked by Indians they would risk surrendering to them rather than be killed. No one knew exactly what would happen to them as prisoners, but it surely couldn't be as bad as dying. Besides, they might get rescued. But, by whom they had no idea.

Early in the month of July, the party crossed the hunting grounds of one of the most dangerous tribes they would encounter. Seven mounted Indians appeared on a gently sloping hillside about 200 yards away from the wagons. Behind them were estimated to be a band of fifty or more warriors armed with bows, arrows and spears. As soon as the mounted band was spotted, the whites sprang into action. Everyone grabbed white flour sacks, white shirts or white underskirts, tied them to poles and gun barrels and began vigorously waving them. The waving of a white flag meant surrender to the pioneers, but had no meaning to the Indians.

The chief held up his right hand to stop the approaching warriors. The seven riders out in front circled around the chief to discuss the situation.

They repeatedly shrugged their shoulders not knowing what the travelers wanted. Were they just excited to see them with their painted faces and bodies? Were they trying to scare the warriors away? Were they just hungry or thirsty? Or were they extremely anxious to do trading with them?

The chief, seeing no apparent hostility in the small group and no guns being fired at them, decided that trading must be the purpose of their strange behavior. He immediately ordered the braves back to their camp to gather up dried fish, roots and berries and many beautifully tanned animal skins. Trading was brisk and many good deals were made on both sides. The satisfied Indians mounted their horses and headed back to their camp.

Many of the white settlers fell to their knees with tears streaming down their faces. They thanked God for saving them from certain death that day. He visibly acknowledged their thankful prayers that night with a "sign"--a beautiful two inch ground cover of clean, pure white snow—in July.

James T. Blount, The Dalles, Oregon

~ 270 ~

Brandy Protected by Unique Cache

Westbound travelers on the Overland Trail in the old days became accustomed to scenes of tragedy along the way. Newly dug graves were commonplace sights, and this fact was put to good use by a shrewd trader who was overtaken by ill fortune on this westward trip.

It was in 1848 that this fellow started on the long journey with his prairie schooner piled high with casks of brandy for which he hoped to find a ready market in the West.

Near Fort Laramie, Wyoming, two of his oxen died of exhaustion. Without them, the other two were unable to pull the heavy load by themselves. He was stranded with a load of liquor. He realized that to cache it along the trail would be to invite disaster the minute some thirsty emigrant or Indian happened along.

But he had a bright thought. He dug a hole for each barrel and covered them over with earth to look like freshly filled graves. He then took boards from his wagon, printed fictitious names on them, added the words "died of cholera" and hand drew a skull and crossbones symbol on each marker.

The naming of that dreaded disease and the symbol of death did the trick, and although the "graveyard" was passed by scores of travelers, they all gave the site plenty of space.

The trader continued on until he was able to buy fresh oxen. When he returned to the grave site, he found it undisturbed.

He dug up the valuable barrels of brandy, reloaded them on his wagon, burned the markers for his evening campfire, and the next morning continued on his journey to Oregon.

H. WOODWARD, Portland, Oregon

~ 271 ~

Farmer Kills Own Pig in Cornfield

When my mother was a very little girl, she lived with her parents, two sisters, and two brothers on a large farm on the Columbia River

Slough. There were not many families along the slough then, and all were great friends and neighbors except for one man, who seemed unable to get along with anyone.

My grandfather's farm adjoined that of the unneighborly one. The latter was continually complaining that Grandfather's pigs rooted under the fence and got into his corn field. Grandfather was sure his fences were "hog-tight" and told him so.

One day, the surly neighbor declared he would shoot the next one of Grandfather's pigs he saw on the wrong side of the fence. Feeling pretty sure his pigs couldn't stray through the enclosure; Grandfather just shrugged his shoulders and said, "You have my permission."

A few days later, the neighbor came running over to Grandfather and yelled, "I just shot one of your pigs. It was in my corn field again!" Grandfather went to look at the remains.

When he saw it, he laughed and pointed out to his neighbor that the dead pig was one of his own. He never again threatened to kill Grandfather's pigs.

The motto here should be: "Check your own pig-pen before you go shooting off your mouth".

MARY L. STEIN, Portland, Oregon

~ 272 ~

Swimmer Loses Pants in Water

In the early 1850's, one of my ancestors, Joseph Randles, had this strange experience on his way to Oregon:

The covered wagon train had reached the Humboldt River, and after a conference of the leaders, part of the train went into California, lured by gold, but the larger part, bent on agriculture, headed for Oregon.

On the banks of the Humboldt, the train camped for several days. Soon the grass on that side of the river was exhausted, but there was an abundance of it on the other side. Grandfather was a strong swimmer, so he was assigned the job of swimming across the river with the cattle each morning and bringing them back again in the evening.

One morning, dressed in an old pair of pants, he was swimming through the stream, swollen by recent rains, when suddenly he felt himself seized and pulled as if by some unseen monster. Such was the force of the suction that his body was held, as if in a vise, while a downward pressure was exerted all over him.

He was trapped in the whirling vortex of one of the numerous sink holes of the swiftly moving Humboldt River. Suddenly, his pants, not too well fastened on him, disappeared. On the home side of the river stood a crowd of sympathetic women, who sensed trouble, but were ignorant of the fate of his pants.

No men were present to come to the rescue, for all were at some distance, either hunting or engaged in other work. Finally able to extricate himself from the sink hole, Grandfather stood on a flat rock in a depth of about five feet of water. The ladies were vociferously offering suggestions.

My ancestor finally recalled having seen some old clothes in an abandoned camp site near the river on the other side. So he plowed through the water to that side, and then, amidst the hilarious cheers of his fair audience, he leaped up the opposite bank and raced behind whatever offered concealment and protection.

NEIL SUTTON, Oak Grove, Oregon

~ 273 ~

Woman Recounts Early Happenings

In 1852, my parents crossed the plains by ox team and covered wagon to Oregon. I was the youngest of seven children making the trip. We had two yoke of oxen and two milk cows for our slow, but sure, means of transportation.

I recalled that Father said we made only nine or ten miles per day. One of the oxen got such sore feet that Father took him from the team, put some kind of shoes on him and turned him loose. He could not keep up with the wagon train, but would catch up with us when we stopped at night.

In the early spring, we left Farmington, Illinois, where I was born. I will be eighty five on April 6, 1935. We made our first real stop a few miles south of Corvallis, Oregon, where we remained for three years, then moved to Monroe, Oregon.

Later, Father decided to move to Eastern Oregon in search of a homestead. We stopped about three miles from the Oregon/Idaho line. One day, everyone had gone to town except two of us girls, and my sister was sick in bed with smallpox. We had a bedroom window open and I heard a noise about the window. Turning around, I saw an Indian with a hunting knife in one hand and a whisky bottle in the other, trying to crawl through the open window. He was evidently drunk.

A thought struck me. I went to my sister's sickbed, turned the covers down and showed him where her face was broken out, and he left at once.

One morning, a few months later, one of our neighbors drove to our place, his team and wagon on the run. He told us to get in quickly, as the Indians were on the warpath and burning everything as they came.

We went several miles to a sort of fort being built in a barnyard. The men hurriedly worked to build the log fort while the women rushed to make lead bullets over camp fires and prepare meals for the hungry. We were there several weeks, but finally, when the excitement had quieted a little, we packed up, and wisely moved back to the Willamette Valley.

MRS. ADELIA BAIRD, Newberg, Oregon

~ 274 ~

Grave of Indian Hidden by Sheep

In the early days of Oregon's settlement, many peculiar and tragic events took place. Foremost in my memory is the following story, which might prove that truth is truly stranger than fiction.

It was on a spring day in Eastern Oregon that a sheepherder drove his flocks to pasture. He was riding the usual type of pony and was armed with a Winchester rifle. Wearying of riding, he dismounted, hobbled the pony, and, leaning his rifle against a pine tree, seated himself in the cool shade.

As the day wore on, he moved away from his gun. He fell asleep, only to be awakened by a shout. He beheld an Indian, dressed in a chief's regalia and riding a pure white pony. The Indians of that day were not friendly, and the herder was looking into the business end of a rifle.

Although the Indian spoke a jargon, it was clear that the herder was expected to dance to the tune of bullets fired perilously near his feet. The herder danced in circles, ever nearing his rifle by the tree. The Indian was so intent on his fun that he didn't notice what the herder had in mind.

At last, the herder made a dash, and, using the tree for a shield, swung his gun into play. The Indian sensed his danger and started to ride away as the herder shot. The Indian rolled to the ground, dead, and his pony galloped away.

Knowing that the chief's tribe would soon be hunting him, the herder dug a grave, buried the Indian, and knowing the grave would likely be found, he decided to bed his sheep at this location. So, for several days, he allowed his flocks to trample the grave site. Soon, no trace was left of his deed.

G. A. ROCK, Svensen, Oregon

~ 275 ~

Tragedy Averted by Indian Wife

Chief Gobaway, a powerful Indian leader of Western Oregon, lived at The Dalles. One of his daughters was married to Dr. Solomon Smith, a prominent pioneer of Clatsop County. They had five children.

Mrs. Smith adapted herself readily to the ways of the white people, and was well liked by her neighbors of both races. One day, a local Indian was killed by a white man. Of course, this called for revenge. The Indians decided to surprise and massacre a large crowd of men who were gathered to raise a barn for a new settler.

Mrs. Smith heard of the plan and went out in a pouring rain storm to stand in the trail the Indians must use on their way to their rendezvous. She intercepted them, one by one, and threatened them with the punishment of the powerful Chief Gobaway. One by one, they turned back on the trail they had come.

In this way was averted what would have been a great tragedy.

ELNA ANDERSON, Portland, Oregon

"When Oregon Went Berserk"

EPISODE 3 of 6

An Account of Ten Spectacular Years (1855-1865) When the Northwest was Host to War, Greed and Death

By JOHN W. KELLY, Staff Writer,
The Oregonian, September 27, 1936

Introduction

With suppression of the Indian uprising planned to exterminate all whites from the Pacific Ocean to the Rocky Mountains, and from Mount Shasta to British Columbia, the country east of the Cascades was thrown open to settlement. This marked the second phase of Oregon's most sensational decade. It was the gold rush. The word "rush" can be defined as "an eager movement of many people to get to a place." This second phase was followed by an orgy of crime, reaching a climax and closes with the "disciples of direct action"—the Vigilantes.

EPISODE 3

The Great "Reckless" Gold Rush

Gold had been found in Southern Oregon. Miners were murdered in that region during the Indian uprising, but the great gold rush was to come later, starting in 1858 and continuing for eight riotous, rip-roaring years in the area east of the Cascade Mountains.

After the regular army officers officially stated that peace was declared and that east of the Cascades was open for settlement, there were reports of gold discoveries north and south of the Columbia River. Gold was found on the Malheur, John Day and other Eastern Oregon streams, on the Wenatchee River and in the vicinity of Colville, Washington. The Dalles, recovering from the Indian scare, was the jumping-off place for the Frazier River mines.

Joel Palmer, who made the treaties with the Indians and established the reservations at Grand Ronde, Siletz and elsewhere, blossomed out as a trader. R. R. Thompson, who had been an Indian agent at The Dalles, and Laurence W. Coe built a steamer at the mouth of the Deschutes River and christened it *Colonel Wright,* after that hard-boiled soldier who punished the hostile Indians with an iron hand. In April, 1859, the little steamer made its first trip to Fort Walla Walla (Wallula) with a cargo of supplies which Palmer was taking to Priest Rapids for the miners there.

Walla Walla, which had been named Steptoe City, now became a rival of The Dalles as a point of departure to the mines. Miners prospected the Columbia as far as the Bitter Root Mountains making $5 to $6 a day. Captain Weller's expedition in the Malheur country found gold and his troopers successfully panned the streams. These were preliminaries to the grand stampede and all discoveries to come.

Word came to Portland in October, 1859, of the Pend Oreille (pon-de-ray) strike, and merchants began organizing companies to grub-stake prospectors. Quickly the news was carried to Jacksonville, still jittery from the recent Indian outbreak, and miners from the diggings in that vicinity hurried to Portland en route to the discovery. Joel Palmer opened a road from Priest Rapids to Similkameen. The *Colonel Wright* carried supplies to the rapids, the freight moving from there over Palmer's road in wagons.

It was five hundred miles from Portland to the mines, but impatient, gold-crazed men started from the settlements on the Willamette River in canoes. Next were the rich Caribou placers in British Columbia, and then a discovery by E. D. Pierce, trader, one hundred fifty miles east of present Milton-Freewater, Oregon—vastly increasing the excitement.

In March, 1861, more than 1,000 miners from Portland and California were on Oro Fino Creek. To accommodate the gold hunters, additional steamers were placed on the run between San Francisco and Portland. The route was: From Portland by steamer to Fort Walla Walla, by stage to the city of Walla Walla, then pack horses to the mines. These mines were four hundred miles from the little village of Portland. It took 2 – 3 months travel from California.

The *Colonel Wright,* in May, pioneered to the mouth of the Clearwater River and twelve miles up that stream from the forks-- forty miles from Pierce City. Lewiston was founded at the joining of the Snake and Clearwater rivers in June, 1861, and Mr. Ankeny of Oregon City built a wagon road to Pierce City. A man named Mulkey of Washington County drove the first team of freight into Oro Fino City.

A perfect frenzy seized the male population. By August, 2,500 miners were on the creeks. 4,000 other workers were at the mines, receiving $8.50 a day for common labor and $9.50 for carpenters. Lumber was 20 cents a board foot and nails, 40 cents a pound. Saloons saved on building material by using blankets for roofing.

The Willamette Valley was drained of settlers by the craze. Portland began supplying miners by steamer to Lewiston and The Dalles lost most of this trade. Portland was hectic. The Oregon Steam Navigation Company laid the foundation for several family fortunes including John C. Ainsworth of Oregon City. Drays stood in line day and night to load freight on the up-river boats. Drivers dozed in their seats. The few hotels and boarding houses were crowded. Prospectors slept on the docks waiting to take passage.

More discoveries were made. There appeared to be no limit to the gold fields. Scouting prospectors looking for the mother lode found the Salmon River mines and Millersburg sprang into existence. Two weeks after this discovery, 1,000 men were on the creeks. Men panned from $75 to $100 a day. [There are twelve "troy" ounces of gold per pound, thus making one pound of gold, at that time, worth $240. The price was approximately $20 an ounce. Compare with today's prices]. All the newspapers of Oregon carried accounts of the vast treasure chest. Every news item stirred more prospectors to search.

The Oregonian of November 14, 1861, reports: "John Munroe of Yamhill took out $180 in an afternoon." "Others, unnamed, reported panning $600 and $1,200 in a day." [2¼ - 5 pounds]. *Portland Times* told of $1,800 [7½ lbs.] taken in three hours by two men working a rocker; and of $150 in one pan. The *Times* said a man named Weiser of Yamhill owned the claim where $1,800 was found. Weiser took 45 pounds of gold dust in pickle jars to Portland [worth over $10,000]. Estimates said that $3,000,000 [12,500 pounds] came to Portland from Oregon creeks and the Clearwater River in Idaho in 1861.

During the winter of 1861-62, the Florence, Idaho mines were found, and the route of the stampede was the Old Oregon Trail to the Grand Ronde Valley, then an Indian trail to the Snake River and beyond. Terrible conditions prevailed this winter in the overflowing mining camps. There were heavy snows and floods. Lewiston, six months old, was in tents. Miners were starving at Florence. Between October, 1861, and March, 1862, seventy inches of rain fell. Roads were impassable, landslides frequent and misery constant.

And still the fortune hunters sped to Portland from the Oregon valleys and from California. The town of Portland boomed with business, furnishing accommodations for the Argonauts and equipping the prospectors. On February 13, 1862, the steamer *Cortez* steamed into Portland harbor with seven hundred miners from California.

Regular steamers were almost swamped with passengers seeking the new fields.

The great Klondike rush in Alaska of 1898 was small in comparison to the migration to Portland and then on to the mines in Idaho, just across the Oregon border. Three steamers raced up the coast with anxious miners; they raced up the Columbia River and then up the Willamette to Portland. These vessels, the *Sierra Nevada, Panama* and the *Oregon* disgorged 2,400 gold hunters. Next day, May 6, the steamer *Brother Jonathan* hove to on the Portland waterfront with 600 more heading for the mines. Three days saw 3,000 California miners arrive.

Everyone was delirious with the gold fever and anxious to get up the Columbia River. The severe weather which was causing suffering in the mines did not spare The Dalles. In March, snow was from two to four feet deep from The Dalles to Lewiston, Idaho. The Oregonian and other newspapers published warnings that there were neither food, fuel, nor other supplies; that no pack animals were available and hikers would freeze. Food ran short at The Dalles, prices soared; hungry men, desperate, organized into mobs and looted stores. At Walla Walla, flour was $24 a pound. [That's $1,200 for a fifty pound sack--if you could find one].

Tinkling bells were heard at The Dalles, March 17th. Breaking through the deep snows came a saddle train from Walla Walla, the first to arrive since January. In the saddlebags were four hundred pounds of gold [valued at $100,000]. Snowbound miners at The Dalles wildly organized caravans to hit the trail opened by the saddle train and were on the road before nightfall.

Five days later came a dreaded "Chinook" [heavy rains and warmer weather with rapid snow melt] bringing floods and making bad roads even worse. The *Colonel Wright* poked her nose into the mighty Columbia and chugged with passengers up-stream to Wallula [old Fort Walla Walla], where the Hudson's Bay Fur Company had dumped its store of gun powder into the river in the uprising of the confederated

Indian tribes. Pack trains moved to Powder River in April; famished miners on the Salmon River met the pack train to obtain food. Came May with more floods, swamping Lewiston, The Dalles and Portland.

Somehow news from the mines trickled through to Portland. Excitement increased, if possible. Weiser of Yamhill took out $6,000 one day at Baboon Gulch and $3,000 the next. Despite floods, 25,000 prospectors and miners were on the John Day, Salmon and Clearwater rivers in June. In its issue of June 2, 1862, the *Oregon Statesman* said half a million dollars in gold passed through The Dalles weekly. The steamer *Julia* brought 1,000 pounds of gold from The Dalles to Portland on its trip July 30th. One creek worked by 500 men for eight months yielded $2,785,000 [about 12,000 pounds of gold]. The miners averaged $4,000 per season.

H. M. Comstock of the famed Comstock Lode came into Oregon from Nevada. He located and built a road on Powder River and petitioned the Oregon Legislature for a charter. Failing in this, Comstock opened a quartz vein on Powder, according to the *Oregon Statesman* of June 16, 1862, and discovered a lode from which he took $450 the first day. Comstock was not alone prospecting the John Day. These John Day River mines were being worked in August, and in September a thousand men were on the middle fork and five hundred on the north branch.

Apparently every river and creek east of the Cascade Mountains was a source of gold. New strikes were being made monthly, and miners hurried from one discovery to the next, packing pan, pick, shovel, blankets and grub on the backs of horses or mules. It was a transient population. One day a thousand miners would be working a creek and the next day news of another rich strike would see half of the miners decamp for the latest find.

Prospectors spread out over Oregon, Washington, Idaho and the western part of Montana—the Old Oregon Country. Camps and mining towns sprang up overnight. Traders followed the discoveries. From distant Portland came an uninterrupted stream of supplies and additional recruits to the army of miners. The supply train was uninterrupted, except for six months, when pack trains could not negotiate the crude roads and trails or flood swollen streams.

Sailor Diggings and other camps in Southwestern Oregon—the Jacksonville country—were largely neglected for the more alluring discoveries. Seasoned miners deserted Galice and Applegate Creeks, and the Illinois River to join the myriad of gold hunters who were panning all the streams in Eastern and Central Oregon and across the Snake River in adjacent Idaho. There was agitation to have Oregon's boundary extended eastward to include the fabulous diggings in Idaho, but changes were never made.

Such quantities of gold, which were flowing into The Dalles with the ultimate destination the mint at San Francisco, started a campaign to have the government build a mint at The Dalles. Dust could be coined into "fives," "tens" and "twenties" as well at The Dalles as at San Francisco. The government thought so well of the proposal that an appropriation was made, and part of the mint building was constructed, but the government decided to abandon the plan. [Perhaps the potential loss of the lucrative river and ocean shipping business had, in some way, influenced the government's decision. Ships bringing men and supplies from San Francisco would lose the highly profitable income from gold shipments on return trips].

The Oregon Steam Navigation Company was waxing fat. It had almost a monopoly on the Columbia River below The Dalles. Between handling passengers and freight, [and gold shipments to San Francisco] the O. S. N. Company was a goldmine in itself. California steamers arrived with overflowing passenger lists, stages rolled north through the valleys from Sacramento, jolting and shaking their occupants. Over new-made roads moved saddle trains and wagon trains. Miners on foot were everywhere on the march.

There was competition in building and operating ferries on such streams and rivers as the Snake, Owyhee and Deschutes. Portland was expanding as a village; it boasted a few street lamps, the illumination coming from oil. Its streets were ankle deep with dust in summer, knee deep with mud in winter and a mixed consistency in spring and fall. People discussed new gold discoveries rather than the Civil War. The allure of raising livestock, growing potatoes, or harvesting wheat would never surmount over gold. Gold was king.

Never before had Portland experienced such thrilling days—and nights. Its two parallel streets, Front and First, were thronged with roughly clad strangers; its stores were busy and quantities of supplies were piled up on the rickety wooden sidewalks awaiting a drayman to load them and cart them to the wharf, where the O. S. N. Company boats were preparing for the up-river trip. Other steamers were coming down from The Dalles carrying orders for more supplies, carrying pounds of gold nuggets and dust in the purser's iron safe. Upon the counter of every store was a pair of gold scales; behind the counter a strongbox—and usually a pistol. Upon the streets of Portland, passed the hopeful prospector, headed for the gold fields, and the miner returning from those fields with a stake or at least with highly colored stories of strikes, phenomenal discoveries and fortunes in every gold pan.

The "Frisco" steamers were a sight to behold. Their decks were lined with men, each anxious to step down the gangplank and outfit himself at a Front Street store. Four-horse stages, swaying and jolting, lumbered through the valleys, pausing at Wolf Creek, Canyonville, painfully toiling through Stagecoach Pass, rumbling into Roseburg, Eugene City and finally arriving, with everyone aching and tired, in Portland; a bone jarring trip of well over two hundred miles.

And all these thousands of miners and laborers negotiated the portage up-river and poured into The Dalles, which in turn had to obtain its supplies from Portland merchants. This stream of gold-hungry men flowed through Portland and The Dalles for several years, each prospector seeking an El Dorado.

The greatest discoveries of all were still to come, and with these richest finds came sudden death to many, for the Indians were again becoming restless. The red men had forgotten the loss of life among their tribesmen in the uprising to exterminate the whites in the years before 1858, and how Colonel George Wright had shot and hanged leaders without mercy. Murderous as the Indians were, they were no worse than the bad men, the influx of killers, highwaymen and horse thieves who participated in the madness, spreading terror on the land.

And still, in the immediate future, were the men to wipe the slate clean by free use of the lynch law—the Vigilantes.

To be continued ...

~ 276 ~

Melon-Stealing Indians Fooled

My grandfather and grandmother, Caleb and Elizabeth Chapman, crossed the plains to Oregon in 1848, and settled on Howell's Prairie, between Salem and Silverton, Oregon. Grandfather was a Christian minister and helped build his own church, which is still standing near Silverton; the Bethany Christian Church.

Grandmother planted watermelons in her garden, but the Indians raided her patch as fast as the melons ripened. Those mince pies and fruit cakes that were made in those "good old days," had to have candied citron in them, which had to be grown at home and candied there. So, Grandmother raised some citron in her garden. A citron is somewhat like a melon in appearance--but not in taste. They are quite acidic tasting.

One day, along came some young Indians on their ponies and stopped to pick up a few delicious melons. Grandmother went out and told them the citrons were not melons and were not good to eat. She tried to make them understand, what they were and that they were hard and bitter. But they couldn't be stopped. She watched them break them open, scrape out a handful and eat the bitter fruit.

Their faces pictured mingled surprise and chagrin, but most of them saw the joke and seemed to understand what she had tried to tell them. There was much laughter as they mounted their ponies and rode away.

She raised her melons, without further raiding, after that incident.

MRS. J. L. PARRETT, Dundee, Oregon

~ 277 ~

Bully's Daughter Saved by Indian

Hank Walters (a fictitious name, since this is a true incident that took place over 70 years ago in Southern Oregon), was the owner of the largest retail trading store in a village of 500 inhabitants.

He was also the town bully.

One day an Indian came to the store to trade a blanket for a set of animal traps. Hank Walters could easily have realized more profit from the blankets than from the traps, but he offered the Indian only a scant trade-in value.

One thing led to another and Hank, in a fit of temper, beat the Indian with a pick handle and drove him out of the store.

Six months later, Hank Walters' only child, a four-year-old girl, wandered away from home and climbed into a flat-bottomed boat, tied none too securely, to a branch on the shore. Moving about in the boat, the child was set adrift. Upon realizing her peril, she began screaming for help.

The river was wide and her cry would have gone unheard but for an Indian who was dragging his canoe up the opposite shore.

A half hour later, Hank had the embarrassment of having his daughter carried into the store, in the arms of the same Indian he had beaten with a pick handle.

KEITH SOESBE, Portland, Oregon

~ 278 ~

Cougars No Joke in Pioneer Days

One afternoon, 70 years ago, my grandmother saw from the window of her cabin, near Bellingham, Washington, where she lived with an old aunt, two huge cougars stalking a young pig, one of her prized possessions.

Grandmother dashed from the cabin with all the rashness of youth and rushed across the clearing toward the beasts, armed only with a dishpan, which she banged and waved frantically.

The two cats watched her with malignant eyes and twitching tails, but held their ground. She was halfway across the clearing when her danger dawned upon her, and she stood paralyzed with fear while the cougars growled menacingly.

To retreat might have been fatal, and anyway Grandmother felt unable to run. Suddenly one of the big cats started toward her.

Just at that instant, there was a sharp report from the cabin. The doorway framed her aunt with a smoking rifle in her hands. The shot went wild, but it scared the cougars away, and no doubt saved Grandmother's life.

LEONORA STAMPS, Bellingham, Washington

~ 279 ~

Initials in Rock Seventy Three Years Found

My great-grandfather, Robert C. Tunison, was born in Michigan in 1825. When thirty-years-old, he left for Oregon by the Oregon Trail. One of the many adventures related to the family, after his return home, took place at Massacre Rock, near what is now known as American Falls, Idaho.

One day, he dismounted from his horse to carve his name upon Massacre Rock where hundreds of other pioneers had written. He had just carved "R. C," and the first two letters of his last name when a party of renegade Indians came into view. Fearing trouble, he mounted up and rode away--never to return to finish carving his name.

In 1928, his son, John G. Tunison of Portland, now eighty two, took a trip to Michigan by automobile. On reaching Massacre Rock, he stopped and located the initials carved by his father seventy three years before.

WARREN TUNISON, Portland, Oregon

~ 280 ~

Settlers Escape by Clever Ruse

Lon Chadwick and Ames Williams were captured and disarmed by three marauding Bannock Indians on the Snake River, near what was later the Eagle Rock crossing, in 1857. The Indians were candid if not friendly.

By means of the sign language, they gave Chadwick and Williams to understand that a dugout canoe was needed and that the white men were to be the builders. Afterward, two scalps would be set to dry on Bannock ridgepoles.

The Indians were armed with trade muskets and knives, while the white men had only an ax and a wedge, with which they were to fell and split a cottonwood tree.

They were certain to die if they made the canoe, but they were equally certain of a probably less pleasant death if they did not. So, they worked.

By a good deal of sign talking and by accomplishing little in shaping the log, they, at least persuaded the Indians to lay aside their guns and help with the work. But the Indians were watchful, and the white men knew that knives could be far more dangerous than smooth-bore muskets.

Williams opened a crack in the log with the ax and wedge, while Chadwick slipped his fingers into the crack and pulled to spread it wider. The log did not split.

Williams told the Indians that two men could not split a log of that size, that they must help Chadwick. At last, the Bannocks agreed to help spread the log while Williams drove the wedge deeper. One Indian stood near Chadwick, his hands almost touching those of the white man as they tugged at the log. The other two stood opposite, watching Williams closely as their fingers clutched in the open seam.

Williams nodded to Chadwick as he swung the ax, striking the wedge on the side rather than the end and knocking it from the log. The cottonwood came together on three pairs of hands. Williams and Chadwick escaped into the brush before the Indians could pull loose.

This story is contained in a diary kept by my great-uncle during the period mentioned.

DICK ROBSON, Thornton, Idaho

~ 281 ~

Greenbacks Not Money to Indian

While teaching school in the Klamath River country of Southern Oregon, in 1908 and 1909, I became acquainted with an old Indian woman who was fond of relating tales of the early days. Old Dolly lived in an old log cabin with a great mud fireplace, just across Little North Fork from my school. After school, I often loitered there to admire her baskets and weaving, or just listen to her stories.

The Indians along the Klamath and Salmon Rivers near Somes Bar did not meet up with the white man until sometime after the first gold was discovered on the American River, farther south in California.

Dolly said the white men came looking for gold and it did not take the Indians long to learn that gold would buy even the most valued trinket. The white man's guns were the chief ambition of each Indian, and his watch or personal trinkets were the envy of the Indian maids.

The Indians did not try to mine themselves. They would watch, and steal from the white miners whenever possible.

One day, a young white man came to the Klamath country. Dolly watched him from the bushes as he worked, and at dusk saw him dig a hole and bury a baking powder can beneath a large rock.

Eager for the things that the gold would buy, Dolly watched her chance and stealthily dug up the treasure. To her disgust the can contained nothing but worthless green paper. It meant nothing to her so she threw it, can and all, into the river.

Should that white man still live, and read this account of Dolly's theft, it might, perhaps, clear up the mystery of his missing greenbacks.

RUBIE PHELPS MATTESON, Gaston, Oregon

~ 282 ~

Liquored Captain Has Good Alibi

The Peoples' Transportation Company, with headquarters at Salem, Oregon, years ago, hunted down their missing boats with a team and buggy. There were no telephones, telegraphs, radio, trains, or other rapid means of communication, so when a boat did not appear within a day or two after schedule, a man with a team was sent from Salem to look for it.

This company had one captain who imbibed freely, sometimes. He was a splendid captain when sober, and the company endured much from him before finally letting him go. However, when he was drunk, he knew enough to tie up the boat somewhere until he was sober again. So when he didn't show up on time, the company always knew what was the matter and a man was sent out to find him and get him sobered up and going again.

One time, he went south from Salem with a boat, and nothing further was heard from him. He failed to come steaming into port on schedule, so the office sent a man up the Willamette River after him. He was found, boat and all, tied up between towns, where he had evidently stayed several days. The rescue party hailed him and wanted to know why he didn't steam up and move on. "Indians!" was the reply. "There are a million of them up at the bend, and they are all on the warpath."

"Never mind the Indians," shouted the rescuer, who knew that this was just an alibi. "Two million couldn't hurt you in that boat. Just get inside the cabin and let them shoot their arrows or muskets at you. Not a shot will go through the heavy boards of the cabin."

"I know that, old man," replied the captain, "but they'd stick in it. I've got a big load now. I ain't goin' to have the old tub sunk by an extra load of bullets and arrows."

GUY HUGHES, Harrisburg, Oregon

~ 283 ~

Pioneer Lives to Tell of Scalping

In February, 1936, in McMinnville, Oregon, there died a man well versed in the lore of the Oregon Country, and his stories of the pioneer days were all from personal experience.

One was a painful experience, an experience that nearly cost him his life. W. A. Van Gothem was partly scalped by Indians when a young man--yet he lived to be eighty. The scalping occurred one day when the young man and a friend were riding range, on the banks of the Snake River.

Suddenly, a band of Indians came upon them, and although they tried to escape, the attempt was useless. A shot from a gun in the hands of one of their pursuers killed the friend instantly and stunned young Van Gothem so that he fell to the ground, unconscious.

The Indians triumphantly scalped his partner, and duplicated the operation upon Van Gothem enough to encircle his head with a knife gash. Before they could tear the bleeding trophy from his head, however, a wandering priest appeared, and the Indians, fearing retribution, fled.

The priest picked up the unconscious youth and administered such aid as he could. The young man's strong constitution turned the tide toward recovery.

He lived through many other dangerous days with his fellow pioneers, and lived to die calmly in bed--in a land where Indians were friendly.

VENUS L. BUNNELL, Hillsboro, Oregon

~ 284 ~

Empty Guns Bluff Indians

In the spring of 1845, my great-grandfather, Rev. Leander Belien, and his wife and six children, left Missouri with a covered wagon train for Oregon on the Oregon Trail.

A man named Meek attempted to guide them through a shorter route than the wagon trains before them had taken. They somehow became lost and wandered around for several weeks. In the meantime, they ran out of ammunition. One evening while making camp and placing their wagons in a circle as they always did, they looked up to see at a distance a large band of Indians coming, yelling their war cry.

They quickly placed the women and children inside the wagon circle. My great-grandfather told the men that if they had ever prayed in their lives to pray then.

They placed their unloaded guns on their shoulders and marched boldly out to meet the Indians.

As the Indians were afraid of guns in those early days, and believed they were always loaded, the chief rode out in front of his band and threw up his hand in a gesture of peace.

They all stood and talked for a while. Some of the Indians came back to camp with the whites and sat around the fire, smoking the "pipe of peace."

The members of the train gave the Indians some of their small supply of food and they left peaceably. They never knew the rifles were not loaded

STANLEY STOCKTON JOHNSON, Portland, Oregon

~ 285 ~

Indians Ransack House for Sugar

In 1870, my great-aunt, Martha Dougherty, was living with her husband and children near the Wallowa River in the lower valley of Wallowa County, Oregon. The Nes Perce Indians often came up the river to this site for summer fishing.

One day, my uncle, Winn Dougherty, went to Elgin to get provisions--a sixty mile trip. Shortly after he had gone, Aunt Martha was terrified to see a band of Indians enter the yard. Several Indian women entered the house, leaving the men reclining on the cellar door in the sun, and rummaged through everything, turning things upside down and muttering "shugh."

They paid no attention to Martha or the children and after the women had satisfied their curiosity, they departed.

Several days later, Aunt Martha learned that the Indians had been hunting and calling for sugar--which they loved.

RACHEL JOHNSON, Wallowa, Oregon

Prehistoric Indians of the West

By JOHN W. KELLY, Staff Writer,
The Oregonian January 20, 1935

Introduction

This is the last of three articles describing the evidence pointing to a probable connection between pre-historic northwest Indians and the Mayas of Central America. Previous articles discussed the linguistic and physical evidence that such a connection existed.

John W Kelly gathered much of the material for these articles while residing in the Northwest and later checked his findings with ethnological authorities at Washington, D.C.

Part 3 (Conclusion)

Circumstantial evidence linking Oregon Indians with the Maya Indians is summarized thus:

1. Ethnologists connect the Snake Indians with the Mayas through the Shoshonean linguistic family. This stock extended from the Columbia River Valley, east of the Cascades, to Mexico and beyond.
2. Anthropologists trace the little-known vanished race, "Basket Makers," over the area occupied by the Shoshonean groups.
3. Petroglyphs (Indian signs) form a blazed trail from Celilo Falls to Yucatán.
4. Pit houses of prehistoric people in the valley of the Columbia were used by the Basket Makers in the Southwest before the days of the

Cliff Dwellers. These semi--subterranean houses evolved into the kiva of the Pueblo culture and the temples of the Mayas.

5. Certain customs and culture are found at each end of the Shoshonean

When one realizes the high state of civilization attained by the Mayas at a time when Europe was in slavery; when it is known that the Maya scientists used the concept of Zero 500 years before it was invented by the Hindus of the old world, it sounds improbable that such intelligent people were of the same stock as the ancestors of the Piutes in Harney County, Oregon.

Improbable as this affiliation may appear, ethnologists show the connection through the tracing of the linguistic families, Government scientists make the assertion, and, link by link, have constructed the chain of circumstantial evidence from the Columbia to Central America.

It is not unthinkable that the advanced arts of the Mayas had a common starting point in an archaic, or intermediate people, which had the germs of agriculture, sculpture, weaving; that these germs later developed into the greater skills of the Mayas.

The germs of sculpture (the monkey heads of Celilo Falls and the petroglyphs); weaving (sandals, baskets and blankets); agriculture (undertaken by the Basket Makers); architecture (pit houses and cliff dwellings), were all possessed by the Shoshonean family in Oregon and gradually blossomed as they worked their way further south—coming to full ripeness in Honduras and Yucatán.

For a modern parallel, consider the hill people of the southern states: old American stock, illiterate, unambitious, living in hovels, having few wants. Compare these backward people with other early Americans who have advanced, built cities, developed sciences and arts.

The spread between Piutes and Mayas is no different and the span of time permitting the development is greater. The Maya of today is no more intelligent than the Piute.

Scientists agree that the valley of the Columbia is one of the oldest homes of man on this continent; it is asserted that the Columbia was the starting point for the peoples who populated the east and south.

In corroboration, they trace the Shoshonean linguistic family from the Columbia to Central America; trace the Athapascan linguistic family from the Pacific Coast to Hudson's Bay, and from the Arctic to the mouth of the Rio Grande—extending more than 40° latitude and 75° longitude. The Athapascans also were in Oregon.

Mayas had their origin somewhere. Dr. Ales Hrdlicka says North America was peopled by way of Alaska from Asia. This imminent authority says he has unearthed the same cultural seeds on Kodiak Island as were common with the Mayas.

As for the sculpture of the Mayas, it does not surpass some carvings of the Haida, Tlinget and Kwakiutl Indians of the north west coast, excavated by scientists from the village sites of the north coast.

Assuming the first adventures from the Columbia began their nomadic wandering along the Deschutes and south of the Snake River Valley 6,000 years ago, there were two or three thousand years for them to loiter as Basket Makers and eventually trickle into Central America.

The Christian era is but 2,000 years old and note to progress and declines of many races in that brief period—brief, compared with the age of the Maya people.

There is no chronological record of the migration from the Columbia, nor of the waves of Basket Makers, nor the more modern Cliff Dwellers—but scientists have thus far identified eight different cultures between the Basket Makers and the later Cliff Dwellers.

Not until the 1890s were the Basket Makers discovered and they caused a new chapter of early settlement of the West to be written; they were an ancient and forgotten people who were developed into or vanquished by the Cliff Dwellers. The Basket Maker's influence is a matter of scientific record in the old Oregon country.

If the trained minds of government men are not in error and the Shoshonean-Maya reports are correct, it should give a sense of pride to know that a great scientific genius—one of the greatest the world has known—was a Native American of the Shoshonean linguistic family; that unnamed individual who invented the Mayan calendar of 13 months of 28 days each. Not even the name of this mastermind, and intellectual giant, has survived.

"In Central America during the pure stone age, the Mayas developed arithmetic astronomy and city planning and swept in advance of anything the Egyptians could do in the sculptural treatment of the human body.

"They had no beasts of burden and no use of the wheel in mechanics and their economy was based on domesticated plants not known to the old world before Columbus.--" *Reduction of Maya Dates*," papers of Peabody Museum, Harvard University.

Scientists hesitate about fixing definite time and dates unless they have an indisputable record. They deal with the progress of the Maya people from nomads to civilization in some such fashion as the following from bulletin 57, Bureau of American Ethnology:

"How long a time had been required for the development of their complex calendar and the hieroglyphic system to the point of graphic record it is impossible to say, and any estimate can only be conjectured.

"It is certain, however, that a long interval must have elapsed from the first crude and unrelated scratches of savagery to the elaborate and involved hieroglyphs found on the earliest monuments, which represent not only the work of highly skilled sculptors but also the thought of intensively developed minds. That this period was measured by centuries rather than by decades seems probable."

That there was a kinship between the Maya in costume, customs and habits and the ancient dwellers of the valley of the Columbia is apparent to anyone delving into the subject. Perhaps these were a mere coincidence, yet they existed.

Outstanding authority on Mayan mode of dress and customs is Diego de Landra, who is a fountain of knowledge, for this clergyman collected and described all that is positively known of the Mayan calendar, its science and habits of the people. It can be found in "Relacion de las Cosas de Yucatán."

Until the manuscript by Landra was found in Spain, there was not enough known of the Mayas to fill a small notebook. By means of this manuscript latter-day scientists have been able to identify and interpret a number of Mayan dates, but the scientists themselves are not in accord on the method of fitting in the Maya dates with comparative dates in the old world.

One calendar date of the Mayas is 850 B. C. To gain an idea of how far advanced the Maya people were on that date, Biblical students will note that while there are Mayans that were building and planning cities, it was the period of the prophet Elijah; famed Jezebel was painting her face (Mayans painted the entire body red); it was the age of Homer in Greece.

Rome was not founded for a century after the Maya date was carved and it was three centuries after the Mayan date was placed on the stone that the Chaldeans, under Nebuchadnezzar, made Babylon the home of the highest civilization developed in the old world. That date was 200 years before Cyrus, the Persian, defeated the Medes and 500 years before the Great Wall of China was built.

And be it remembered, the Maya calendar starts with the identified date of October 14, 3373 B. C. Expeditions are digging up ancient and forgotten cities in the old world which had not been started when the Mayas were already abandoning some of their older cities and establishing newer ones.

And how the ethnologists, the world detectives, had managed to convince themselves that the Maya and the Shoshonean are distinctly related is not for the layman to question. It should not be more surprising than the established fact that a high state of civilization developed in Central

America in remote Biblical times, that there were magnificent cities an exact science in the new world when Babylon and it's hanging gardens and tower had not even been thought of.

King Solomon had been dead only 85 years when the Maya date of 850 was chiseled, and the Phoenician alphabet devised in 1000 B. C. probably came into use about the time the Maya scientists were developing their hieroglyphic system.

All Biblical dates are approximate before the middle of the seventh century, B. C., 100 years after the known Maya date. The Basket Makers had, apparently, moved south from the valley of the Columbia before the children of Israel entered the wilderness; before Moses gave the Ten Commandments.

Aside from the Maya people having Oregon ancestry, the Aztecs, who conquered the Mayas, may have lived for a time in that region. The annual report of the Smithsonian Institution, 1927, declares that the Indian tribes of the northwest coast appear to have been related, at one time, to Mexican tribes, "with whom they show startling physical and cultural resemblances," and notice is taken of the San Blas Indians of the Pacific Coast of Panama, who form a cultural link between the Mayans and Peruvians— the San Blas Indians erected small totem poles.

From descriptions by Landra, the Maya costume was not dissimilar from the inhabitants of the Columbia Valley; the wrap around the waist, which hung in front and back like an apron; woven sandals; encircling bands on legs and arms; lambrets in the lips, plugs in the ears; elaborate headdress (a weakness of the Maya); coats of armor—the Maya using quilted cotton soaked in a salt solution—the Colombians elk hide or sticks woven together.

On the Columbia and in Honduras, spears were used before the bow and arrow were introduced, the spear being thrown by using a throwing-stick called an "atlatl." The natives played with gaming bones. Maya and Colombian had similar customs as slavery, head flattening of babies, prisoners used for human sacrifice; cremation was practiced and with the late departed were placed small figurines carved from stone.

Tattooing, less common on the Columbia, was a favorite decoration with men and women, and north and south these members of the Shoshonean linguistic family daubed themselves with paint as Diego de Landra tells and as the paint pots dug from cremation pits of the ancient Americas of the Columbia Valley confirm.

Evidence of the various scientists when woven together, appear to make a strong case to support the theory that the highly civilized Maya people had their original homeland in the Columbia River Valley.

By JOHN W. KELLY, Staff Writer, *The Oregonian* January 20, 1935

~ 286 ~

False Molars Scare Indian

My grandfather, with my grandmother and three children, settled in Tillamook County, Oregon, in the early 1880s.

One day, late in the fall, Grandfather, who was in a hurry to get the buildings finished and a well dug before the winter rains began, asked some Indians if they would do some work for him. One big buck had his eyes on a large mirror which Grandmother had brought with her from Illinois--a trip that had not been easy on it, as it was now chipped in several places.

It had taken the Indian's fancy, however, and at last, although obviously reluctant to do so, he agreed to help Grandfather for two days in exchange for the mirror. Grandfather started him to work, helping him dig the well, which was already started.

They worked steadily all day. It was very hot, and during the afternoon, Grandmother appeared with some cool blackberry juice to quench their thirst. When she arrived, Grandfather was working at the bottom of the well and the Indian, who was at the top, had just hauled up a bucket of dirt and was emptying it. The air was thick with dust and Grandmother inhaled it and sneezed. As she did so, her false teeth clattered to the ground.

Grandfather climbed out of the well just in time to see the Indian drop the bucket and light out.

But his desire for the mirror was stronger than his fear, an after Grandfather promised him that he would keep his wife in the house, and not let her come out to the well again, he returned, carried out his part of the bargain and disappeared, proudly bearing the chipped mirror.

K.D. EVANS, Portland, Oregon

~ 287 ~

Rash Horseman Taught Caution

Upon one of my father's trips across the plains, during the 1840s, there was an elderly man in the party named Koontz. Although repeatedly warned of the danger of an Indian ambush, he took upon himself the task of scouting in search of wood, water, and good grazing.

After crossing the Platte River, the company found itself in the land of the Pawnees, at that time, a hostile tribe. One afternoon, the drivers of the lead wagons saw Mr. Koontz coming down a slight rise, with his horse on the run, waving his hat and shouting, "Corral, boys, corral!"

A band of Indians, shaved and painted, apparently were attempting to cut off his retreat. The warriors then divided into two groups, one on either side of the wagon train, racing their horses and giving war whoops.

There was no time to corral the wagons, but the oxen were unhitched to prevent a stampede. After circling the train again, the Indians withdrew to a nearby knoll. Then a lone Indian rode out and made it known that his chief wished to talk with the captain of the train.

The captain went forward to meet the "Indian chief," who proved to be "Peg Leg" Smith, a white man, and a character familiar to all students of western history. Smith explained he had been on the lookout for Koontz and certain other members of the expedition whom he had known before going to live with the Indians. He had heard of Koontz' indifference to danger, and planned to scare him, as a lesson.

Smith was warmly welcomed by his old friends in the party. He told them of a place he knew, a short distance from the trail, where there was plenty of grass and water--and assured them that their stock would be safe there also.

JOHN M. UMPHLETTE, Amity, Oregon

~ 288 ~

Indian Raid Only Horses

A few years after the last of the Indian uprisings in the Northwest, my great-grandparents, Mr. and Mrs. Oscar Libbetts, and their four children, lived near Lexington, Oregon. Although Grandma had lived all her life in Indian country without being harmed, she was always afraid of them and made elaborate precautions in case of attack.

Grandfather was a Justice of the Peace and occasionally had to be away all night. Early in the evening, one night when he was away, the family heard loud hoof beats. Frightened and silent, the family waited. It wasn't long until they saw galloping horses coming over the hills. True, they were still a long way off, but they were too close for Grandma. She gathered the children together, and, taking a few blankets, ran out into a field of tall wheat to spend the night.

After they were well hidden, she remembered the dog was tied up close to the house. She knew that when the Indians came, they would turn the dog loose, and of course, he would run right out to the children.

It must have been a long night. But when daylight came, and nothing more had happened, they went home. Nothing was disturbed--there were also no signs of Indians.

When Grandfather returned, he said there were no Indians in the neighborhood. Later he learned that dynamite blasting, back in the hills, had frightened a large band of wild horses--and it was these Grandma had mistaken for hard-riding Indians.

AURELIA ALLEN, Portland, Oregon

~ 289 ~

Boy Didn't Like Indian Girl

This story, my grandfather, James Langlois, tells as happening in 1853, when he was about five years old. They were living at Oregon City when his father decided to move to California to search for gold. They took a river boat from there to Astoria, and from there, took an ocean schooner.

The schooner stopped at Port Orford, Oregon, for supplies. There had just been a gold strike near there and everyone was excited about it. So his father decided to stay there instead of going on to California.

One sunny day, the family decided to join a group of Indians fishing in the ocean nearby. When they got to the beach, there was a fire already built of drift wood with logs on both sides to sit on. There were friendly

Indians all around. In the middle of a log, young Jimmy sat down. An Indian chief put his young daughter beside him.

Grandfather did not like her, as "she smells like fish and smoke," he grumbled. He edged down the log a little way, and with her father's encouragement, she moved down the log, beside Grandfather.

They kept this up until they got to the end of the log. Jimmy thought he had stood enough, so he turned and slapped her on the face. His father was going to spank him, but the Indian chief said, "No, make heap brave warrior."

HAZEL BUCKINGHAM, Monroe, Oregon

~ 290 ~

Indian Woman's Recipe Wasn't Pleasing

One day, and old Indian woman called at my grandmother's house and asked to borrow an iron pan that was setting on a bench outside the cabin. She said she wished to use it to boil a mixture to grow hair on her papoose's head. Grandmother's thoughts flashed to her husband's increasing baldness.

She invited the woman inside and gave her permission to use the kitchen stove. Soon the kitchen was filled with an aroma, described by Grandmother as not unlike the odor of boiling pumpkin.

In a short while, the brew was finished, and the Indian woman generously left a quantity for Grandma. That night, when Grandfather returned home, he was forced to sit, while his wife smeared his head with the sticky concoction.

The directions given by the woman were, that the medicine should remain overnight on the head and not be washed off the following morning. At the end of a three night treatment, Grandfather's head was thoroughly saturated with the brew.

Several days later, the Indian woman returned to the cabin. Grandfather happened to be in the back yard and came in to find out what was in the recipe for the hair tonic. She gave him this recipe: Place the bodies of three frogs in Ollalie (berry) juice and allow to stand until the frogs have jelled into the liquid. Then bottle in a tight container and heat before applying. The words were hardly out of the old woman's mouth before Grandfather had his head submerged in the wash basin, vigorously scrubbing his bald spot. It was a full week before he and Grandmother were on speaking terms.

HERBERT KEITH, Portland, Oregon

~ 291 ~

Indian Racketeer Gets Sandwiches

My grandmother, who with my grandfather, settled near Roseburg, Oregon, in the early 1880s. She loved to tell of one of the early cases of racketeering in this country.

It started one day, when a scrawny, hungry-looking Indian appeared at my grandfather's place at breakfast time. Grandmother could never see anyone go hungry, so she offered him some sausage between a couple slices of bread. He accepted it and ate it greedily. It was evidently his first experience with a sandwich.

A few days later, Grandmother became alarmed when my father, then a small child, wandered away into the woods. She was about to set out to look for him when this same Indian appeared again. Learning of the child's disappearance, he offered to look for him, and in a short time, reappeared with the boy perched in front of him on his cayuse. Grandmother, greatly relieved, again gave him a sandwich.

A short time later, this episode recurred--but this time under rather suspicious circumstances. The Indian appeared again and asked where the boy was. She realized that she had not seen the child in some time, and a hasty search failed to disclose him. The Indian then suggested that if his strength were fortified with a "sam'ich," he could probably locate the lad. Grandmother again complied. He left, to reappear soon with the child.

Several times thereafter, the child disappeared--and each absence was followed by the immediate and suspicious appearance of the Indian, who, for a "price", offered to look for him. Grandmother knew he engineered the affair every time, but she was never greatly alarmed, and the Indian seemed quite fond of the child—and her "sam'iches".

BLANCHE THIELE, Portland, Oregon

~ 292 ~

Little Girl Foils Indians' Attack

My great-grandmother came across the plains in 1852, in a covered wagon. Like other children her age, she wished that Indians would attack the wagon train so she could use the rifle her father had given her.

One day, as the train stopped for a rest, she left the group and went "hunting for Indians," never dreaming she would find them. After she wandered just out of sight of the wagon, she saw a band of Indians holding council.

Without thinking, she fired in the general direction of the Indians, hitting no one, but surprising everyone, including herself. The people of the wagon train, hearing the shot, prepared for battle, while my great-grandmother ran back to the train, accompanied by a shower of arrows.

Fortunately, she received no serious wounds, and, she had saved the wagon train--for when the Indians attacked, the pioneers were ready and drove them off.

HOMER C. BAER, Portland, Oregon

~ 293 ~

Feather Bed Rescued From Bay

When the little schooner *Honolulu* sailed into Portland, Oregon, in 1848, it brought the news that gold had been discovered at Sutter's Mill in California, five months before. Uncle Tom and Aunt Martha Shadden, Oregon pioneers of 1848, chucked a stock of provisions and a feather bed into a large wagon and rolled off for California, where, in time, Lady Luck dealt the two a joint hand of $50,000 in gold dust.

$49,000 was from a trading post business that Uncle Tom established on Feather River. The remaining $1,000 Aunt Martha made by raising and selling watermelons to the miners for $1.00 apiece. A trading post was, by no means, a safe repository for $50,000, so in 1852, Uncle Tom sold his store, stuffed the 120 pounds of gold dust in their feather bed, and took it to San Francisco, where he and his wife embarked for home on the old side-wheeler *Ajax*.

Here, misfortune all but overtook the priceless feather bed. While being trundled aboard the steamship, it fell overboard. But for Uncle Tom's offering a boatman $20 in dust for its return, it would have beaten its owners through the Golden Gate.

"It's like this," said Uncle Tom persuasively to the boatman, "I just got to have that bed. I killed half the wild geese in the Oregon Country to make it, and to go back home empty-handed means a straw tick for my wife and me, on a rawhide bed, until I kill the other half."

It takes a mighty "skookum" man to grabhook a water-soaked bed with a deadweight of gold and pull it into a skiff on a fast running tide.

Twenty minutes later, however, the almost exhausted boatman staggered up the gangplank with the roll of bedding on his shoulder and cast it on the deck. "That's the heaviest bed I ever toted!"

[$49,000 of gold dust would have weighed 205 pounds at the value of $20 per oz. Perhaps the boatman had help lifting and carrying that much weight in a feather bed. Feathers are light—and not that heavy when wet!].

TOM H. ROGERS, McMinnville, Oregon

~ 294 ~

Night Visitor Not Indian

The gray gloom of a rainy night had settled over the circle of wagons camped on the banks of a beautiful lake. One lone sentinel, Joseph Randles, paced to and fro, guarding the horses and oxen. Indians had been seen in the vicinity the day before, so he was especially alert.

A sudden restlessness among the bedded animals caused him to turn. Through the thin underbrush, on the edge of the lake, he saw a hazy figure approach the water's edge. Through the gloom, he could discern what were apparently the dark trousers and light shirt of a man creeping on his hands and knees.

"Halt!" he shouted.

No answer. The figure stopped, and then moved slowly forward again.

"Halt or I shoot!" again called the sentinel, fearing an attempt was being made to stampede the cattle and leave the camp helpless. The same order was repeated, even louder a third time, but still there was no answer from the shadowy figure.

The guard raised his gun and fired at the approaching figure. It rose slowly, nearly upright, and then pitched forward into the waters of the lake. The gunshot brought other armed settlers to the scene, but no further movement in the bushes was observed.

Early next morning, the men found in the lake, the body of a huge timber wolf--with a dark coat and white underbody. A large bullet hole in his chest definitely established him as the previous evening's visitor.

JANE WARD, Oak Grove, Oregon

~ 295 ~

Teamster Hides Gold in Salt

Years ago, my father, Eli E. Keith, drove a freight wagon from Wallula, Washington to old Fort Colville. It was a long, hard trip and often took him more than a month.

One time, when he was preparing to leave Colville on the return trip, a very rough-appearing man approached him and wanted to make the trip with him. The stranger said he didn't have much money, but was willing to help with the cooking and camp chores to help pay his way.

Dad did not like the looks of this fellow, especially as Dad had several hundred dollars in gold coins in his money belt. But the trip was long and lonesome, so Dad said he could come.

The first night out, after the team was taken care of, Dad sent the man to gather firewood. As soon as he was out of sight, Dad emptied the salt out of a large salt can, put the gold in the bottom and then filled it up with the salt. When his companion returned with the wood, Dad was very busy mixing flapjacks.

So it went, on all the long journey, with the stranger doing most of the cooking and camp work.

Dad was careful with his money belt, so the stranger never once suspected the value of the can of salt, into which he dipped several times a day.

Dad admitted that he was rather worried at times that the stranger might find the gold, but he knew his life was safer that way.

No doubt Dad's nonchalance saved his life, for it was only a short time after the trip that Dad heard of a man being killed attempting to holdup a miners camp, presumably from the description, by this same man.

HATTIE KEITH MORGAN, Kelso, Washington

"Northwest Empire Builders"

PETER FRENCH

PART 1 of 2

The Northwest's Greatest Cattle King

By ANNE SHANNON MONROE, Author of "*Singing in the Rain*" and other fine Oregon books. April 14, 1935

David Crow, a gasping, half-frozen rider from the P Ranch, having been in the saddle 48 hours with never a pause but to change horses—which he had done nine times—galloped into Winnemucca with barely breathe enough left to gasp out, "Pete French is murdered!"

He had ridden 225 miles in late December, 1897, through bitter cold, to get word off to the world by way of a telegram to *The Oregonian*—which reached its destination five days after the event. Wonderful time in that period of our history.

Pete French, multi-millionaire, was owner of more land than any other man in the Northwest. The "Cattle King of Central Oregon" had been murdered in cold blood, shot through the back of the head, in broad daylight, as he was riding into his own ranch. He had stopped to open the gate for his vaqueros (Mexican cowboys), never seeing the deadly danger.

His murderer, Ed L. Oliver, was said to be a good man, married, with several little children. His ranch sat in the midst of one of Pete French's holdings and French wanted it--but Oliver wouldn't sell.

Oliver, a quiet, mild mannered man, was never in any "trouble" before the killing. He considered it a "good day's work done" as he rode calmly back to his ranch home, and went to bed for a sound night's sleep.

Never afterward was he really molested no punishment meted out, nothing at all done about it. Possibly the only case of its kind on record where a multi-millionaire has been shot to death while men (his vaqueros) looked on--with no punishment for the killer. When men are killed, especially multi-millionaires, someone usually makes a row about it. All the world wondered.

Pete French's brother, Bert French, took the body back to his father's home, near Red Bluff, California for burial. "Little Doc Marsden," a highly developed physician of the ranges of that day, had his brain removed and weighed to see if he could find the secret of the man's peculiar power. But though it weighed more than usual brains, the "secret" was not there.

"He always expected to be murdered," said Rye Smith of Happy Valley to me. Rye, the oldest man now living who knew Pete French, was with him during the Indian fighting when the Bannocks and Piutes were on the warpath. "A great feller," he went on. "Not afraid of nobuddy, or nothin'! Never saw such eyes—brilliant—wrap right around your head and tie knots behind! But they got him. Guess somebuddy had to--I dunno. A pity! Smart—smartest man ever in the country in them days. Some said he always wore a metal vest under his shirt--I dunno. Anyway, a killer'd have to shoot him through the back of the head. Couldn't nobuddy look in Pete's eyes and shoot him. He generally went armed—quickest man on the draw ever in the country, but wasn't armed that day. Leastways, they said he wasn't.

"But when they brought his body in, his coat was buttoned up crooked. Now, Pete French never in his life buttoned his own coat crooked. Smart dresser, always. Looked like a prince. My theory? Well, it looked to me like his vaqueros—they all loved him—kneeled beside him and pulled out his gun, on the idea it would go harder with his murderer to have shot an unarmed man. Then they buttoned his coat back crooked ... I dunno. They'd do anything for Pete—worshiped him."

The old man sighed deeply—after all the years the deed was still a sadness with him. "But he had to be killed, I guess. Only a question of who's have the honor. 'Bout everybody in them days wanted it. Nothin' else to do."

A strangely complex character. Everybody admiring him, but he had to be killed. The curious fact is that his partner, Dr. Hugh Glenn, had been murdered in much the same manner a few years earlier, but his murderer was tried, convicted of manslaughter and sent to the penitentiary. What made the difference? It's an interesting story.

Peter French was born on his father's ranch near Red Bluff, California in 1849, coming in with the gold rush. His father was a successful, practical farmer, who expected his boy to grow up to the same business, but young Peter was of a different make-up. Early, he ran away from home, seeking a livelier life, and was afterward employed by Dr. Hugh Glenn of Chico, California.

Here he learned all about land holdings on a larger scale, and the art of wrestling them away from the government. Imaginative Californians who hadn't caught the gold fever, caught the land fever. The old Spanish and Mexican governments had made great grants freely to private individuals. As much as 30,000 or 40,000 acres, with no survey other than a measuring off by two men on horseback, using a seventy foot riata and piling up a heap of stones at the corners. Usually the ocean, mountains, hills and rivers constituted the boundaries.

When California was admitted to the Union in 1850, the swamp land act gave the state title to all the overflow land, more than two million acres. Vast areas were allotted for school purposes. The state began at once to dispose of these lands commercially for a very small sum. The gold rush broke up the old hacienda life, brought confusion and resales.

The earlier Mexican and Spanish governments had taken over the mission holdings, breaking up the missions, scattering the "fathers,"

Indians and such settlers as were there, so that altogether, such an opportunity for empire grabbing was open to the people as never had been in the history of the world before.

Henri Miller, of the afterward famous firm of Miller & Lux, came in from Germany about this time via steerage, with five dollars in his pocket, little English on his tongue, but a huge ambition, and a real value in him, for he was a wonderful butcher and knew land.

He'd grown up with a soil-working mother, a grandmother who gathered fagots (bundles of firewood kindling sticks) from the hills, and was accustomed to tilling small strips of land for all that was in them. Often in those first California days, when getting his start, he took his pay from his butcher employers in stock—intestines, which he prepared and sold to sausage makers.

He began acquiring holdings at once, which, at the time of his death a few years ago, amounted to several million acres, and an estate valued at fifty million dollars.

Other "master minds" were busy at the same game. The gobbling-up went merrily on. No one was to blame, there was plenty of land and anybody could sit in the game who had the will to do so and the initiative of young Miller—and later of Pete French, who was a new-born baby when Henry Miller began his operations.

Then, fence laws were enacted in California, and this created range problems for the big cattlemen. They began to look to Central Oregon with yearning eyes. It was easy to drive up into the northern country, for there were many passes, and no fence laws. The invasion began. It was only natural for it to come this direction as the great Cascade Mountains lifted north and south through Oregon, making access from the west difficult, and the Blue Mountains lifted to the north and east.

Anyway, western Oregonians were not then range-conscious. They didn't realize the wealth in grass, water and climate "east of the mountains." They were busy getting homes in the Willamette Valley, building schools, colleges and starting churches. To clear the mighty timber was an absorbing task. And they were a home-loving people.

It had been said that California chose her state emblem wisely—a bear, that forever wanderer in high places. While Oregon chose hers with equal fitness—the beaver, that forever builder of a home and raiser of a family.

Dr. Hugh Glenn was among the Californians who had an appetite for large land holdings. Along with others, he drove his stock north and purchased an extensive stock ranch, in what was then Grant, but later became Harney County. In 1873, he made young Peter French, then but twenty four, his manager, and sent him north to look after his interests.

French was fired with all he found in the raw new country—the high plateau, the quantities of native hay, the streams, lakes and springs, the sunny, winey air—such as he was used to in California, only so much cooler and crisper by reason of altitude, perfect location for the best cattle, disease-free, and the largest calf drops.

It is said that Henri Miller was first attracted to Oregon by seeing in the Sacramento Stock Market one day, some cattle, of which he said excitedly: "Those are the finest steers I ever saw! Where they come from?" On being told, "From Central Oregon," he straightway headed north and became so interested that he purchased, immediately, holding after holding.

Oregon now had swamp lands for sale at a very small down payment. These were being peddled all over Northern California by one "Hen" Owen, known as the "Oregon swamp rat."

There was plenty of this so-called swamp land in Central Oregon, and it sold at $1.25 an acre. He had also been the means of getting John Devine interested. John Devine was a famous horse racer, of those days, whose specialty was raising fast race horses. He moved up, and with the financial backing of Tom Todhunter, a capitalist of Sacramento, California, became a large Oregon land owner and an outstanding leader of the country—a cattleman with immense herds on the open range.

Rapidly they all came in. There was Colonel Hardin, an imposing figure, weighing between 350 and 400 pounds, sitting up on his high buckboard, called "Colonel" by right of his power to command. They formed a sort of cattle-land aristocracy among themselves, dividing up the range, establishing their ranch homes, bringing in their vaqueros, their Spanish names for everything—the mecarte, the riata, the single-cinch saddle, the silver-mounted trappings, their bright colors, gay shirts and kerchiefs and the carefree southern spirit. None of this ever reached north of the Columbia River or the Blue Mountains.

William Hanley, the last of the younger of these cattle kings, who drove his struggling herds across the mountains as a boy from his father's ranch near Jacksonville, Oregon and found all this splendor of the ranges, tells of his first impression of the California cattlemen. He says, having driven into camp during a round-up:

"Pete French was there, and John Devine and Maurice Fitzgerald, Ike Foster, Tom Allen, Mart Baker, John Smith and many others, including their vaqueros. The vaqueros were well-dressed, showy men, wearing bright colors—the best equipped for vaquero life of any that ever rode the plains—all had fine, well-trained saddle horses, with silver-mounted bridles, hackamores, mecartes and riatas. Mostly the vaqueros wore rosideros, a buckskin apron that fits like a tailored pair of pants, tied around the legs with buckskin thongs.

"These were all the stockmen there were in the country at that time—that's what a round-up meant—all the stockmen coming together out on the range. With their wide sombreros and bright colors and good form and the sun shining on them, they made quite a picture.

"I was a tramp boy, ragged and dusty with weeks of driving, and pretty well worn out. The old camp cook, among his steaming pots, began to beller, 'Come and get it!' and they all started for the mess wagon.

Pete French turned to me and said: 'Turn your horse loose, boy, get a plate and get you something to eat.' It was here I got my first impression of a powerful cattleman."

Dr. Glenn soon made young Peter French his partner, and French began his famous acquisition of land. Before anyone had legal title, he bought out a man named Ruby, whose brand was a diamond, and later what was known as the Diamond Ranch became a part of the great P Ranch property. He gave Ruby a large sum, for those days, between $20,000 and $30,000, besides his price on cattle and horses, and not a titled acre was in the deal. It was Ruby's only by right of occupation.

Ruby had come into the country earlier and had built the officers' and soldiers' quarters at Camp Harney and operated a store there. Their buildings, painted white, set on the side of a hill on Rattlesnake Creek, shining in the sun. They were the only imposing buildings in the whole country. Here a few white settlers took refuge during the Indian wars.

Pete French was now intensely interested in building up the French-Glenn holdings. Also a center for everything on the P Ranch. He built a great house, painted white like the camp buildings, known as the "White House." Huge for those days, when you consider that every stick of lumber had to be hauled by mule train, over soft dirt roads from the Blue Mountains, averaging 150 miles away.

He had ten to twelve-mule teams hauling three or four wagons each consistently on the road. He also had supplies being hauled in from the south. It is said that the jingling of their chain harnesses could be heard as far as their dust could be seen.

He established a store, all sorts of ranch buildings, cookhouses, bunkhouses, barns, breaking corrals and common cattle corrals. There was a fireplace—not a large one, but still a fireplace. A few years ago, I sat before it, with other ranch guests, and deciphered the hieroglyphics burned in a frieze all around it—the brands of every big operator ever in the country.

I understand that the wonderful old "White House," truly the "White House" of the plains, has been torn down by more recent outsiders who are in control, and the lumber used for other smaller buildings.

What, I wonder, became of the old frieze around the fireplace? It's a museum piece, and as such should be found by George Himes for the Oregon Historical Society, unless, of course, it is being kept intact in the original location.

Around this fireplace, gathered, not only the great cattlemen of the country, but all visitors of note, or with "influence" in the outside world. The aristocracy of cattle land met here more as fellow club members than as guests. But Pete French's hospitality was boundless—no traveler was ever refused a meal at the cookhouse.

It wasn't long until two men were nosing out ahead in the race for empire leadership—Peter French and John Devine. Always a friendly race.

John Devine had built a similar large white house at the old Alvord Ranch on the west side of Steen's Mountain, while the P Ranch lay on the east side. But you couldn't go over the mountain—nature had seen to that. Steen's Mountain not only afforded protection so that everything grows there in prolific abundance—there was never a finer garden spot—but it's a geologic wonder, one of the few spots of up-turned original earth-surface, so that while the eastern side ascends steely, like a wall, the western side presents a lovely gradual ascent.

Thus it is that one is compelled to go around the mountain—you can't go over. Also the Blitzen River bursts in a great gush of water right out of the side of Steen's Mountain—a wonderful site—and this river is the source of most of the P Ranch water. One could write a volume on this mountain alone.

But we must get back to these two outstanding men—Pete French, with all his fine hospitality, was never, in the usual sense, a "mixer." He was friendly, pleasant and courteous, but still he was always a bit aloof, choosing his associates carefully and having quiet visits with them when he went into the little cattle towns, such as The Dalles, and later on, Burns, Oregon. Devine was a big, jolly, good-natured fellow. He was always "one of the boys" in the saloons, in card games and racing groups.

Pete French rather awed the usual man whereas John Devine, with his hearty laugh, brought a smile to every face. He was always busy with horse races, running his own horses on the dried-up levels of old lake beds that abound in this region.

Pete French was forever busy among his tule-and-willow-lined springs and rivers, his thousands of water birds, his greyhounds—he bred high-class ones—and with his ranch planning and fencing. He loved to work with his own hands, and did so until he died. He never asked a man to do a thing he wouldn't do himself. He drove men hard, but no harder that he drove himself, and men liked to work for him.

It was organized man's work, everything done well and in a big way. His fences were solidly constructed, many standing unimpaired to this day. He hauled juniper posts from the hills. Juniper has never yet lived long enough to show decay. He bored holes, through which he strung barbed wire. He built rock walls, filling gaps in the natural boundaries of rim rock.

He built stockade corrals, the strongest made, by setting juniper posts close together in a trench, and then lashing willows on top with rawhide, building them round like a basket.

But as time went on, Devine overreached himself in his land acquiring. Also, he lost heavily on races. A famous horse of his, "Compromise," "flew the track" and this let him down.

Devine became Henri Miller's great Oregon opportunity. Miller took over all his Oregon holdings, handing him back, as a gift, I am told, the old Alvord Ranch. Here Devine remained until he died at a very ripe old age, but a few years ago.

He made the wonderful ranch into a sportsmen's paradise, as game birds were there in huge quantities and the fishing not excelled anywhere.

Here, every autumn, friends came for the shooting. Many, in recent years, came by plane. He never regained his leadership, but he undoubtedly had the better of it.

Pete French now became the acknowledged leader, with the largest holdings of any man in the country, with the P Ranch, and with the greatest herds. There were always large calf drops, few, if any serious cattle diseases, fine range grass, and an abundance of clear, cold, pure water. He controlled three-fifths of French-Glenn Company's holdings, and a bank in California.

He married the daughter of his partner, Dr. Glenn, and a fine little son was born to them. Peter French was handsome, genial, and young—only a trifle past thirty, in perfect health, looked up to everywhere he went and possessed a native pride in his achievement, being strong even among those he had outdistanced. He really seemed to be a man at the top of his world.

By ANNE SHANNON MONROE, Author of "*Singing in the Rain*" and other fine Oregon books.

To be continued ...

~ 296 ~

Soft Words Didn't Work

In the early days, there was a camp meeting grounds near Glencoe, Oregon, and one day the minister who was holding the meetings there, decided to drive his horse and buggy to the town of Glencoe for supplies.

A little Indian boy saw him coming and poked his head through the railing of the bridge that the minister must cross, to watch the vehicle pass. When the minister's horse saw the head poking through the banister, it reared up and refused to cross the bridge.

"Go away, little boy, my horse is afraid of you," suggested the minister, kindly. The child, not understanding English, just grinned and stared.

"Please, little boy, go away," urged the minister, and repeated his request unavailingly, several times.

Just then, Joe Meek, a pioneer trapper, came along on his horse, just in time to hear the parson's most recent appeal to the Indian child, and to assess the situation.

"Klaut-a-wa, you little devil, and make it quick," Meek yelled at the lad, in a fierce tone. Almost before he stopped speaking, the child was gone.

MRS. GERTIE MEEK, Cornelius, Oregon

~ 297 ~

Indian's Horse Follows Hearse

My grandfather ran an undertaking parlor in a small western town. One day, an Indian appeared and asked permission to leave a cayuse in the stables where Grandfather quartered the horses that he used for pulling the funeral coach.

Grandfather consented. Several weeks passed and the Indian finally sent word to keep the cayuse in payment for feed. In a short time, the cayuse had taken a liking to Grandfather. It would follow him wherever he went. The animal was exceptionally intelligent, and Grandfather was glad to be able to keep it. They were fond of each other.

One afternoon, a funeral procession left the parlor. The body of the deceased was carried in state, within the coach, and Grandfather sat upon the driver's seat, leading the procession.

As he rode along, Grandfather became aware that those he passed seemed to be amused and exhibited a lot of giggling and pointing. His curiosity got the better of him so he stopped the procession and looked behind to see what everyone was pointing and laughing at.

What Grandfather saw made him laugh as well. Following in the wake of the coach was the cayuse, with its head bent low, in an unmistakable gesture of mourning.

HERBERT KEITH, Portland, Oregon

~ 298 ~

This Indian Was Prankster

"It always appears to me," said Wilson H. Todd, an old-timer who lives a couple of miles southwest of Clackamas, Oregon, "that when folks hear a story about Indians, they don't think it's much good unless there is some scalp lifting in it or the Indian is pictured wrapped in a blanket in glum silence, figuring up some kind of deviltry.

"I had that same idea one time," he continued, "and it made quite a runner out of me. On our way west, my folks went into camp on the Missouri River, where Father had found a job railroad building between Council Bluffs and Omaha, Nebraska. We were much alone, except for a number of Indians, camped for the winter, among the willows along the river bottoms. Our water had to be carried about half-a-mile to our camp. I was a husky lad of nine and had to carry most of our water supply myself.

"Late one afternoon, I was returning with my buckets of water. The grass was almost shoulder high on both sides of me. Suddenly there rose from it an old Indian with the ugliest face I ever saw. He drew a bow from under his buffalo blanket and, setting an arrow, pulled back the thong, aiming right at me.

"He didn't let it go, but had he done so, I don't believe it would have touched me. I never thought I could run so fast. There wasn't much water left in my pails, when I got home, but it had to do until morning.

"Later on, I got to playing with the Indian boys. We ran foot races and hunted cotton-tail rabbits. Some of 'em could talk 'Boston.' (English) Imagine my surprise when one of them told how his grandfather laughed until he nearly fell over when describing how I looked and ran--the time he was just foolin' and pointed his bow and arrow at me."

F. J. CLIFFORD, Portland, Oregon

~ 299 ~

Penalty Paid For Murder

In the 1870s, I was acquainted with a minister named Rev. Samuel Snider, near Iowa City, Iowa. One evening, as we were visiting together, he told a true story about seeing a young man skinned alive.

He started to cross the plains with a wagon train bound for Oregon from Omaha, Nebraska, when he was nineteen-years-old. Another young man and he walked and talked together. The train had been only a few days out when they were passing an Indian village. There were only the women, children and old men in the village, as the younger men were out hunting.

Among them, there was an Indian woman and her sixteen-year-old daughter, sitting side by side near the trail. As they were going by, the boy with Snider exclaimed, "Well, I haven't killed an 'Injun' yet. Here's my chance."

They were walking behind a wagon, in the back of which was a loaded rifle lying on a bedtick. The boy drew the gun out of the wagon, stepped out and shot the girl dead.

This made a great commotion in the village and also among the immigrants. They went on a few miles and made camp and waited for results. Soon, they saw a cavalcade of Indians coming. Several of the men went out to meet them. One of the Indians said, "We want man who shot girl." There was no alternative, so they delivered the young man to them. They removed his clothes and proceeded to skin him while still alive.

Rev. Snider said that he decided then and there to make arrangements to return to Omaha with the first freighter they met. He said the incident was more than enough of the Wild West for him.

I have often wondered if there might be some descendants of someone in that train, living in Oregon, who could tell more about this occurrence.

A.W. HINDMAN, Woodburn, Oregon

~ 300 ~

Drunken Indians Get Orders Mixed

Paul Fleker and his wife were part of a band of pioneers who came from Oklahoma to Oregon in the fall of 1869. They settled along the banks of the Columbia River, close to the present site of Rainier, Washington.

The following spring, Fleker built a comfortable log house, barn, and chicken house. Before long, his place looked quite homelike.

Soon after, another caravan of pioneers came from Oklahoma. Among them were Jim Lawler and his family. The Flekers and Lawlers had been neighbors in Oklahoma, and for a number of years, hatred had been brewing between the two men. Fleker claimed that Lawler had once cheated him in a land deal.

One evening, Fleker treated three Indians to whisky until they had lost all sense of responsibility. When the Indians were well under the influence of the "firewater," he told them to sneak up to Lawler's house and set it afire, promising them more "firewater" for doing so. Willingly they complied with Fleker's orders. Fleker rode through the woods on a pretended hunting trip to allay suspicion.

The following morning as Fleker was riding homeward, he was shocked to see the Lawler home intact, and cursed the Indians for having failed him.

But, coming in sight of his own place, he was horrified to see that every one of his buildings had been burned to the ground.

MRS. W. L. FOUMAL, Oregon City, Oregon

~ 301 ~

Prospective Romance Goes on the Rocks

In 1858, which was a year or two after the death of his good wife, a prominent pioneer of Oregon began paying marked attention to a widow who was in no way admired by his two young sons and thirteen-year-old daughter.

Desiring to show his esteem for the widow in some material way, he picked a number of his choicest Bartlett pears from a thrifty young tree that had just come into bearing. He carefully packed the ripe fruit in a basket between layers of soft, freshly carded wool to prevent bruising.

Slyly the children later decided to remove the choice Bartletts, putting in their place several Pound pears, which were as hard as rocks. They, too, were careful to cover them well with the soft wool.

Their father, with his best compliments, sent the basket of fruit to the widow. He never did learn why from that day hence she would not so much as speak to him or answer the door when he came calling.

Later on, he found a more suitable companion--one that the children loved--and married her. All those concerned lived happily ever after. Many years later, one of the children, then an elderly woman, told me the story of the "woolly pears" and how an unacceptable union was spurned.

MRS. H. A. LEWIS, Portland, Oregon

~ 302 ~

Concomly's Grandson Has Great Travels

Few of the boys who run away to sea ever attain such distinction as did Ranald MacDonald, grandson of the old Indian Chief, Concomly. This lad's father was a Scotchman in the service of the Hudson's Bay Fur Company at Fort Vancouver, Washington. His mother was the Princess Sunday, daughter of the Chinook chieftain.

The boy was sent to St. Thomas, Ontario, Canada to learn banking in the business house of his father's friend. During his stay, he discovered that he was of mixed blood, and he felt so chagrined that he stole away, under the darkness of night, and made his way to a seaport. There he secured a berth on a sailing vessel. After some time and many experiences, he finally reached the vicinity of the, then closed, empire of Japan.

Persuading the captain of a whaling vessel to sell him a small boat, he entered the forbidden territory after a rather well-staged boating accident.

He was fortunate to be taken in by the islanders and although they restricted his liberties and held him prisoner, he was the first man to teach the English language to the Japanese. To him also belongs the honor of making a simple lexicon of Japanese and English words.

Ranald MacDonald recorded in his own dairy that his first desire to see Japan was born when three shipwrecked Japanese were brought to Fort Vancouver and placed in the school established by Dr. John McLoughlin.

[Eva Emery Dye, an Oregon City author, wrote the book *McDonald of Oregon, A Tale of Two Shores,* Published in 1906]

M. LEONA NICHOLS, Portland, Oregon

~ 303 ~

Stampede Upsets Mormon Caravan

A German lad and an English boy were the cause of a stampede which all but disbanded a company of Mormon immigrants consisting of over fifty wagons. In a diary dated 1857, Jim Robson, then sixteen years old, tells how he and a companion, Fred, stampeded first the cattle herd of the pioneers and then the driving oxen.

Jim and Fred, who had been assigned to watch the cattle herd, found that one of the fifty cows under their care was sufficiently gentle to be approached and milked. They knew that every possible source of food was to be reported to the captain, but they knew, also, that the cow would be taken from the herd and assigned to a family, if they obeyed orders. Rations had become short among the immigrants. They considered their own immediate need of food above that of the group, so they kept the cow and said nothing to the captain.

In his diary, Jim wrote: "We had difficulty in telling the milking cow from several others in the herd, so we caught her and slipped a woolen jacket, belonging to Fred, over her horns. She was quite docile and paid very little attention to the object on her head."

"However, a long-horned steer pulling the wagon of the Elder Patterson saw the cow with the jacket flapping on her head, like the wings of a giant bird. The steer gave one terrified bellow and charged across the prairie, spilling the elder, his wife, and their various possessions from the wagon."

"The herd cattle became frightened and began to nervously mill about, frightening the oxen and cows pulling the wagons. Soon all of the cattle stampeded. Fifty wagons jolted across the prairie in every direction, tossing household goods, woman and provisions from over the end boards at every bump." No one was seriously injured, but the wagon train was halted for three days, gathering up supplies and pieces of the wreckage. Neither Captain Ballantyne, nor the Elder Patterson, ever learned what had frightened the long-horned steer.

Dick Robson, Thornton, Idaho

"When Oregon Went Berserk"

EPISODE 4 of 6

An Account of Ten Spectacular Years (1855-1865) When the Northwest was Host to War, Greed and Death

By JOHN W. KELLY, Staff Writer,

The Oregonian, October 4, 1936

EPISODE 4

Hostile Indians Became Increasingly Aggressive

Bonanza discoveries came in July, 1862, and simultaneously the Indians became hostile, resenting the invasion of their lands by the palefaces. Forgotten by the redskins was the suitable punishment meted them by Colonel Wright when he suppressed the great uprising four years earlier.

Most important of the developments was the discovery of the Boise Basin mines. In July, George Grimes of Oregon City, headed a party from Auburn, Baker County. Others were John Phillips and David Rogers from Linn County, a Mr. Wilson of Portland and four Portuguese.

Moving east to the Snake River, they ascended Sinker Creek above the mouth of the Owyhee River. They penetrated Boise Basin, twelve miles from the present Idaho City. Attacked by Shoshones there, Grimes and a Portuguese chased the warriors. As Grimes killed an Indian, a redskin, who had been a guide for the party, shot and killed the prospector from Oregon City and the Portuguese man.

Terrified by the Indians, the survivors retreated to Walla Walla with $4,000 in gold dust panned before the Indian attack disturbed them. At once, upon hearing their story, fifty four men, all well-armed, started for Boise Basin. They buried Grimes between Grimes Creek and Elk Creek and staked a claim for Grimes' widow. Subsequently, the caretaker sold the claim for $8,000 and disappeared. At a gathering of miners in Boise City, the widow was given $3,000, subscribed by miners who had profited by her husband's contribution to the wealth of the world.

Bannock Indians became troublesome on the Old Oregon Trail. They attacked the stations of the Overland Stage, stealing and killing horses. Forty miles west of Fort Hall, an emigrant train was cut off and attacked. There were no regular soldiers available in the area as the Civil War had attracted the troops of the Federal Government and only home guard companies were in the Pacific Northwest.

Miners continued to arrive in Portland from California by stage and steamer. Merchants shipped supplies up the Columbia River to Walla Walla and packers took them through the Grande Ronde Valley and over the emigrant trail across the Blue Mountains to cross the Snake River by ferry. Lewiston merchants fought for this trade. Four-horse stages operated between Wallula, Walla Walla and Lewiston. A. S. Gould, who had worked on the Portland Times newspaper, started the Golden Age newspaper at Lewiston.

Transportation of miners and supplies was a problem. Two companies organized to build a portage railroad at the Cascades—the Middle Cascade Portage Company and the Washington Railroad Company. Neither did anything. In Boise Basin, supplies from the Willamette Valley, plus steamboat rates, plus pack-train, cost more than Salt Lake City prices.

Henry W. Corbett of Portland, A. P. Ankeny, a former Portlander, but who had become a leading citizen of Lewiston, and D. S. Baker, built the small steamer *Spray* to run opposition to the O. S. N. C. (Oregon Steam Navigation Company). The *Spray* managed to ascent the Snake River fifteen miles above Lewiston. Umatilla Landing came into existence and took the Boise Basin trade away from Walla Walla. The route was three hundred miles by pack-train or wagon and opened a new road across the Grande Ronde Valley.

Miners were still afflicted by the gold fever. Newspapers printed items saying there was $80 to the pan on Grimes Creek, and that three men cleaned up $1,500 a day for a year. The basin was thirty miles square, and every foot of it, apparently, was pay dirt.

Malheur River Indians began raiding. They killed miners near Olds Ferry, on the Oregon-Idaho line. Miners in self-defense, two hundred strong, left the creeks and searched for the raiders on the Malheur, Payette and Snake rivers. On the Malheur, they located the refuge of the hostiles. Camouflaging themselves with shields of grass and reeds, the whites crawled toward the Indian fortifications, took it by storm and massacred every living soul, except three small boys. This punishment disciplined the Indians for but a short period. The red men sniped lonely prospectors at every opportunity afforded them.

From Umatilla Landing to Boise, Idaho, was a thirteen day trip. Some idea of the traffic can be had by the statement that there were ten pack-trains and five wagon trains daily on the road. A pack-train consisted of fifty horses. The Wells, Fargo & Company, eventually suspended operations because of numerous holdups along the route. Tracy & Company of Portland sent the first express to Boise.

George F. Thomas, resident of Portland, and Vice-President of the California Stage Company, established a line from Sacramento to Portland. Later he went to Walla Walla, Washington and operated stages, and also built a stage line over the Blue Mountains in Oregon with J. S. Ruckle. The Oregon and Idaho stages began operating from Umatilla Landing to Boise.

Miners came by coach from Sacramento to Portland, by steamer to The Dalles, then took the road to Umatilla Landing to the mines—a two months trip. A new road up the John Day River to Canyon City and thence to Boise was opened in June, 1863.

Meanwhile, just across the Oregon line, gold quartz mines were found, some running $20,000 to the ton. H. M. Comstock, who had found rich quartz on the John Day River, like all other followers of the gold rush, sought ever-new discoveries. He was early on the scene. Michael Jordan (whose name still lives in Jordan Valley), discovered the silver mines on Jordan Creek, Owyhee County, about the time the *Boise News* made it's bow—printed on the first *Oregonian* press.

Despite the richness of the gold fields, the miners, lucky and unlucky, and the traders complained that the freight rates were exorbitant. There was resentment in Boise Basin, and a plan was evolved to boycott Portland merchants and the Oregon Steam Navigation Company. Caravans of freight wagons moved north from Red Bluff, California via Pit River, Goose Lake, and the Malheur River. One outfit was lost in the Warner Lake region east of present-day Lakeview.

Hill Beachy, who operated stages out of Walla Walla, and a councilman when Lewiston was incorporated, established a stage line to California. This venture was abandoned when Indians along the eastern edge of Oregon, where the stage line was located, stole the horses at the stage stations. Unafraid of Indians or highwaymen, Ben Holladay took a mail contract from the U.S. Government for the route from Walla Walla, Grande Ronde, Burnt River, and Payette to Salt Lake City. Years later, Holladay sold out to the Wells, Fargo & Company and moved to Portland, where he began promoting railroads and steamer lines out of the, then, overgrown village.

Increasingly aggressive and threatening were the Indians. They engaged miners in Central Oregon and killed prospectors between Harney and Warner Lakes, west of the Steens Mountains, and in the Hart

Mountain region. Mike Jordan's ranch was attacked, and that hardy miner perished in an attempt to save others. The Militia finally came to the aid of the freighters and miners. The 1st Oregon Cavalry operated between Alford and Mud Lake. Washington infantry were moved to Catherine Creek in the quartz mine district.

Captain Charles McDermitt, with the 2nd California Volunteer Cavalry, established Fort Bidwell near Goose Lake. McDermitt was with Colonel Ben Wright in the slaughter of Modocs in 1852. Wright was decoyed, tripped and killed by Enos at the mouth of the Rogue River in the wholesale uprising plot of Kamiakin, the Yakima chief. Captain McDermitt patrolled the road guarding the caravan of supplies until killed in a skirmish with Indians in August, 1865, on the road between the Owyhee River and California. His name is perpetuated in the town which sprawls across the Oregon-Nevada state line. Meanwhile, near Farewell Bend, on the Snake River, hostiles attacked wagon trains on a continuing basis.

Murderous Indians frustrated efforts to make the eastern mining region independent of Portland merchants and the O. S. N. Company. Hostiles destroyed the stage coach stations, stole the horses, murdered the station agents, killed the drivers of freight caravans, slew the men with the horseback trains, butchered stray prospectors, and the 1st Oregon Cavalry. The Washington Militia and the 2nd California Volunteer Cavalry could not make the roads safe.

With the bloodthirsty Indians in control of the Oregon border, from the Nevada and California line to the Owyhee River, the only safe route for freight and passengers was from Portland, up the Columbia to Wallula, Walla Walla or Umatilla Landing, then across the Blue Mountains to the Snake River. But for the obstacle of the Indians, the proposed new trade route might have held back the continued growth of Portland and hastened the development of Boise. California merchants and steamboats on the Sacramento River reduced rates and made concessions in the hope of establishing the road from Red Bluff through South Central Oregon into the Boise Basin.

Gradually the first prospectors skimmed the cream of the gold laden creeks and rivers and moved on. Unless there was rich pay dirt, the impetuous and restless gold diggers looked elsewhere. They came, created camps and left ghost towns. Their methods were crude, but sufficiently efficient for their immediate needs. They didn't work the creeks closely, the patient Chinese who followed the whites were much more thorough, and prospered. Like the whites, the Chinese also fell victim to the gun and tomahawk of the hostiles, and, like the whites, they were robbed by the bands of organized criminals who, by this time, had become a menace to every honest, hard-working, and law-abiding citizen in the region.

Toward the end of the American Civil War, the mining excitement had materially subsided, and miners, as is their habit, wandered away or settled, as many did, in Eastern Oregon.

There have never been compiled reliable statistics showing how much gold was taken from the ground of Oregon and its neighboring states in the six or seven years which definitely mark the gold rush period. It is known that many of the diggings were more valuable than the mines of 1849 in California. Some of the finds were fabulous, yet none are set down in cold print in the newspapers of that period. It is interesting to note that most of the discoveries, which caused stampede after stampede, were made by residents of Oregon, whether the mines were in Eastern Washington or Idaho.

The unfortunate George Grimes, who left Oregon City and led a party from the forgotten town of Auburn, Baker County, to the treasure house of Boise Basin, made a discovery comparable with that of Marshall's at Sutter's Creek in California. For nearly a score of years, emigrant trains had passed through the gold fields without suspecting that the wealth of the Indes was all around them. The only train that we know of, who found gold was the lost caravan, who wandered in Central

Oregon, and the gold found consisted of a few large nuggets which were tossed into a wagon box. Later, this find became fabled as the lost "Blue Bucket Mine" that is probably in Harney County.

Except for the quartz properties near Jordan Valley, practically all of the fields were "poor men's mines"—diggings where no capital was required other than a strong back, health, perseverance and hope and a few simple implements to enable the gold to be panned or rocked from the streams. With no more equipment than that, hundreds made their fortunes. Handling the quartz required machinery to remove the gold or silver.

Authorities appear to agree that the rush swept up all of the good gold fields before the restless Indians resumed their warfare against the palefaces. The Indians were again subdued, and soon the period of hit-or-miss mining was over. The industry settled down to a business rather than an adventure. The mining craze drew so many people into Idaho that Congress raised it to a territory, with Oregon residents attracted to the mines taking a prominent part in its official life.

Who now knows the location of Malheur City, built by miners high in the mountains, with a water system, wooden sidewalks and buildings housing a population of six thousand? Who knows of the ditch one hundred miles in length, costing a million dollars to construct, funded by John C. Ainsworth and friends to bring water to dry mining discoveries and all done by pick and shovel, located somewhere in Eastern Oregon? Some few camps survive, such as Canyon City with its Whisky Gulch, but mining towns with Wells, Fargo & Company offices built of brick and with telegraph lines (fastened to trees) connecting with The Dalles, are all gone. The stage coach and pack-train trails have become arterial highways today, smooth autobons of oiled macadam or "hot top," in no manner suggesting the tortuous roads of the gold rush era.

Nothing remains of Auburn from whence George Grimes had departed, seeking gold and discovering the Boise Basin. The dozen men who first reached Auburn diggings recovered several million dollars each.

The by-product of the gold excitement in Oregon was the epidemic of crime. Intermingled with the rough-handed miners, the hopeful prospectors and the daring traders were killers, fugitives from justice and crooked, smooth-handed, smooth talking gamblers. As the mining fever subsided in California and new fields were found in the Pacific Northwest, the rough and rowdies who infested the California camps crowded into Portland among the honest men. Their activities became such a stench that drastic measures were taken against them by a long-suffering citizenry.

The outlaw's operations during Oregon's gold craze and their nemesis, the Vigilantes, close a time unmatched for the theatrical tragedy and downright melodrama of the most sanguinary description.

To be continued ...

~ 304 ~

Patriot Spoils July Fourth Meal

In 1849, my father, with a group of young men, left Washington D.C., and came across the continent to seek their fortunes in the gold fields of California. Before reaching California, they came upon a woman and a small child, almost starved and wandering alone in that wild country. The woman told of an Indian raid and said that she and the child were the only ones that escaped.

The men took these two unfortunates into their wagon train and took them to California. Near the end of the journey, the woman, to show her appreciation for their kindness, said she would help them celebrate the Fourth of July by cooking a big dinner. She spent much time and ingenuity making a holiday dinner out of their limited variety of food. My father said that it looked and smelled so tempting, they could hardly wait for the dinner horn. But finally it was spread out and ready to eat.

Just then there was a loud explosion. Earth and rocks shot up in the air. The men were covered with dirt and pelted with flying rocks. But, worst of all, that much-anticipated dinner was completely ruined.

One of the group, overly patriotic and not thinking of the consequences, had set some black powder off in a hole nearby. He was discovered and life was made miserable for him during the remainder of the trip.

MRS. W. E. HANSON, Salem, Oregon

~ 305 ~

Enraged Woman Beats Indian

My grandparents crossed the plains from Ohio, arriving in 1849, to settle on a donation land claim along the Columbia River. They named their place, Martin's Bluff. At first, they lived in a houseboat because of the danger from Indians that roamed the shore. My grandmother once told me of an Indian who came paddling his canoe out to the houseboat while Grandfather was away. He demanded bread and "firewater." Flour was scarce in those days, and, as my Grandmother could speak a little Chinook, she argued with the Indian, refusing to give him bread and tried to explain to him that she had no whisky.

On the table was a jug of vinegar which she had made from wild crabapples. The Indian spied the jug and grabbed it, thinking it was whisky. He took a long drink, realized his mistake, and in a rage, spit a mouthful into a big kettle of crabapple butter boiling on the stove. Grandmother had scoured the nearby hills for the "makings" of that apple butter, which was to have been a treat for the family during the winter.

The Indian's wanton pollution of it made her so angry she lost all fear of him, and, grabbing up a broom, beat him over the head with it until he ran for the safety of his canoe.

Grandmother said that he never returned.

CLARA MARTIN MADDEN, Centralia, Washington

~ 306 ~

Indian Woman Drinks Washing Fluid

An Indian woman was employed as a laundress by the owner of Clarke's Hotel, back in the days when Corvallis, Oregon was a mere village beside Mary's River.

One day, Mrs. Clarke prepared some washing fluid, and, a whisky bottle being handy, used it to store the liquid. She noticed the Indian eye the bottle several times, but thought nothing of it at the time.

She had occasion to leave the room, however, but was no more than outside until she heard a hair-raising scream from within. She was almost knocked down by the wild-eyed, howling Indian woman, who headed for the river, shedding her clothes on the way.

She reached the river bank and dived right in--hoping to wash the horrid-tasting "whisky" out of her system.

MRS. CHARLES M. SHIPLEY, Monmouth, Oregon

~ 307 ~

Pioneers Escape Indian Attack

In 1851, a party of men looking for a passage from the Oregon Coast to the Rogue River Valley, became lost and finally found themselves a few miles from the mouth of the Coquille River, in a state of near-starvation after having nothing to eat but roots and berries for several days.

They induced an old Indian in a large canoe to convey them down the river. When near the mouth, one of the party, Mr. Tevalt, wanted to land and procure some food from the Indians, even if they had to fight for it.

Others in the party strongly protested, fearful of an encounter with the Indians on shore.

While they were disputing, the canoe drifted into shoal water, and the feared Indians rushed into the water, grasping the canoe.

Some of the men left the canoe and rushed for the shore, while others were killed at once. A young Texan, by the name of Brush was struck down by a blow of one of the canoe paddles, the sharp edge striking him in the head, glancing down the side, carrying a large piece of his scalp with it. He fell back into the canoe. Tevalt managed to escape, reaching Port Orford the second day after the disaster.

Williams and Hedden ran from the canoe and reached the shore, fighting there was as best they could. Williams was shot by an arrow. Hedden grabbed it, broke it and pulled out the shaft, leaving a three-inch piece, the shaft, to which the arrowhead was attached.

Hedden had escaped without a wound, but was bruised by the blows of clubs. They escaped to the brush, holding the Indians at bay with their rifles.

On the ninth day after the massacre, they reached the mouth of the Umpqua River, then on up to where Scottsburg is now located. In the spring of 1856, five years later, at Roseburg, Oregon, the shaft and arrowhead were extracted from Williams' body.

Williams was County Clerk of Douglas County for many years. The man who had saved his life, Cyrus Hedden, made his home at Scottsburg until his death.

FRANK B. TICHENOR, Port Orford, Oregon

~ 308 ~

Marauders Leave Trail of Feathers

In 1854, my great-great-grandfather, led a covered wagon train into the Oregon Country. My grandfather, son-in-law of the captain, a young married man of twenty one, with a wife and child, accompanied this train of sixty wagons. After an eventful journey, in which hostile Indians had been encountered several times, the train finally arrived in the Northwest.

On a sultry afternoon, the train pulled into what was evidently a recent settlement of whites. The topsy-turvy condition of the buildings pointed plainly to a successful onslaught by the Indians. Careful inspection of the country revealed the presence of no Indians, nor could definite tracks be located.

Just when the pioneers were getting ready to give up the search for the marauding Indians, my ancestor spied some feathers. He peered among the sagebrush for more. A definite line of feathers was established. A leaky feather mattress was among the things pillaged and carried off. Soon they were hot on the trail of white feathers.

Reaching an elevation, they saw a small camp of tepees nestling at the base of a hill some two miles away. Carefully planning a surprise attack, they encircled the encampment and found the white members of the pillaged settlement had not been slain, as assumed. Rescued to a man, they naturally thought their salvation a work of Providence.

At the base of Grandfather's thumb he carried a large scar. In that battle, an Indian arrow had passed through his hand, tearing through bone and sinew. To his death, and unchanged by time, he told this story to his grandchildren.

RUTH E. KING, Merrill, Oregon

~ 309 ~

McLoughlin Murder Early-Day Mystery

One of the unsolved murders of the Northwest was that of John McLoughlin, Jr., son of Dr. John McLoughlin, the "white-headed eagle." Young McLoughlin was in charge of Fort Wrangle, located, at that time, at the mouth of Sticken River on Dundas Island, a Hudson's Bay Fur Company post.

His subordinates were some of the worst desperadoes of the Northwest, Indians, white men and blue men (Kanakas painted themselves blue), whom he had kept under control only by frequent use of the blacksnake. They hated and feared him, and they all plotted for his death.

A short time before his murder, Pierre Kanaquassee, one of the men employed at the fort, attempted to kill him. McLoughlin laughed at him and then gave him the flogging of his life.

"I know, Pierre," he said, "all of you plan to kill me. Go ahead, if you can, but you will find you have a man, not a woman, to deal with."

Feelings among the men grew more intense. Most of them signed a paper pledging themselves to kill "the master." Finally, McLoughlin realized that he was through.

On the evening of his death, he sent for one of his men, one Antoine Kawanope, and said to him: "You are not to drink at this time, as I am going to die tonight, and I want you to help me in what I am going to do."

He then called his Indians together and got them so drunk that they all lay on the floor, dead to the world. He next sent for all his white men and ordered them to drink. When Pierre protested that he could not drink as much as McLoughlin poured out for him, McLoughlin insisted, half playfully, until Pierre emptied his cup. But Pierre poured the liquor on his shirt front instead of drinking it all.

Antoine had come to Pierre's room earlier in the evening and warned him. "My uncle, take care of yourself tonight," Antoine had said. "The master is going to die."

Pierre asked: 'Who is going to kill him?" And Antoine answered: "The blue men," meaning the Kanakas. And so Pierre drank but little and Antoine and McLoughlin not at all.

After McLoughlin had left the room, Antoine overheard him say to his wife, "I am going to die tonight. Very well, if I die, I must fall like a man."

In a little while, McLoughlin and Antoine went out together. Some fifteen shots rang out. They came back, armed themselves and went out again. Pierre afterward reported that McLoughlin sent Antoine one way and had started alone toward Urbaine's house when he was killed by a shot fired from the corner of the house toward which he was going.

Pierre said that Laperti, Urbaine and Simon were all concealed in the corner when the shots came.

Who killed him? No one knows. Laperti maintained he had not fired his gun. Simon maintained he was not at the corner at all. Urbaine claimed he had no gun. Martineau, who lived at Urbaine's house admitted that he fired twice, but claimed that he had fired into the air.

No one ever was punished for the murder. Sir George Simpson and Mr. Douglas, who came to the fort to investigate, invoked the theory of "self-defense," probable the first and only time in the history of murder investigations, without knowing who the person or persons were who killed the victim.

TOM WINBOURNE, Scappoose, Oregon

~ 310 ~

Marooned Group Nearly Starves

In 1843, my great grandmother and a party of friends were barging down the Columbia River on a raft. A strong wind suddenly sprang up when they were on Cascade Rapids, below what is now Bonneville, Oregon.

Their raft was capsized by the churning waters, but fortunately they were close to shore, so they were all safe, for the time being. All that was saved from their load of supplies was a buffalo hide, some clothes and an old kettle.

Sheer walls rose on either side of the party, and they saw it would be impossible to escape. A vicious storm was raging and they began to feel the cold. A fire was started by Indian strategy, and presently the increasing pangs of hunger attacked them. But there was no food--that is, until someone remembered the buffalo hide. By this time, they were hungry enough to eat anything, so the hide was boiled in the kettle and choked down by the starving party.

After four days had passed, friends at Vancouver, Washington became worried and went to Dr. John McLoughlin for help. McLoughlin sent out an Indian guide to look for them, and they were finally found, huddled together and nearly starved.

The Indian gave them food which he had brought with him and then hastily returned for help.

After they had spent seven days and seven nights isolated, a bateau (large canoe) reached them and they were taken to Vancouver. Despite their hardships, the days of cold and hunger, none of the party died and all safely recovered from these harrowing events.

AUDREY CRAWFORD, Mulino, Oregon

~ 311 ~

Making Sauerkraut and Cabbage "Spears"

My grandfather, Willie Mueller, delighted in telling me stories of the adventures and experiences he had with his father, Hugo, during their challenging move to Oregon and the exhausting life they lived after they finally stepped foot onto the fertile soil of their beautiful Willamette Valley homestead in the Silverton hills. The following story is about making sauerkraut.

Sauerkraut (sour cabbage) was a very popular food item for this family of German ancestry. The Mueller family wouldn't leave Missouri until they had a barrel, or more, of freshly made sauerkraut tied securely on the back of one of their canvas covered wagons. Also a quarter pound, or more, of cabbage seeds had to be carefully collected and hidden away for future planting in Oregon where the warm summer sun and Oregon mists provided ideal growing conditions for this versatile member of the kale family. Every part of the plant (except the roots) were used in some way.

Sauerkraut is relatively easy to make as it requires only shredded cabbage heads (using a "kraut cutter"), salt and a clean barrel. It takes very little attention during the required two months waiting period for the fermentation process to turn sweet greenish-white cabbage into sour cabbage. Interestingly it doesn't require refrigeration during storage and it has been said that it's good for scurvy—which may or may not have been a problem for them.

Sauerkraut can be served either hot or cold, by itself, or with various meats and sausage including pork, goose and duck. It is especially delicious prepared with apple-smoked bacon chunks, diced sour apples and yellow onions, crushed garlic, ground caraway seed, apple juice or cider, and a little white vinegar. The large green leaves are used to wrap various sausage dishes and then either fried or baked for a fresh flavor and a crunchy texture.

Grandpa Willie enjoyed working alongside his father during the whole process of making sauerkraut using clean wooden barrels. The field harvested cabbage had to be washed; the outer leaves removed, and then the heads cut into halves and then into quarter sections. The center cores were then sliced from the cabbage wedges and dropped into salted, cold water for preparation later. These were the cabbage "spears" of which I explain later in this story.

Many of the German families in the wagon trains brought along their own "kraut cutter;" a shallow rectangular wooden box with cutting blades in the bottom. As the cabbage was pushed over the blades, thinly sliced shreds dropped through the hole in the bottom of the cutter box into a barrel. Layers were then generously sprinkled with lots of salt and firmly pressed down causing the cabbage shreds to give up their watery juices.

When the barrel was three-fourths full, with 2-3 inch layers of cabbage and salt, a large plate was placed on the cabbage mixture and weighed down with a suitably sized, cleanly washed rock causing the juices to rise up and cover the plate. A cloth was then placed over the barrel and the mixture allowed to ferment for about a month. At this time, the scum and mold buildup over the plate could be skimmed off, the plate removed and the kraut exposed for sampling to determine how well the fermentation process was going. Usually re-covering and waiting another one to four weeks was necessary to develop the maximum flavor desired.

But it wasn't ready until great-grandfather Hugo tasted it and exclaimed, "Ya! Das goot!" (Yes! That's good!). Only then was Grandpa and the other family members allowed to line up for their own sampling. Great-grandfather always insisted that "you kids" wash their hands with soap and water before reaching into the barrel for their first juicy handful.

"Oh, it tasted so good," Grandpa Willie told me. This must have been one of his favorite childhood memories.

When it was finally ready, the sauerkraut could be taken out, as needed, and excess juices allowed to drain off. Rinsing could be done, but a lot of the salty flavor would be washed away in doing so.

Now, let's get back to the cabbage "spears" (white core wedges) soaking in the cold, salted water. They are not normally included with the shredded cabbage for fermenting, they are usually cooked the same day as a special side-dish at their family dinner. The trimmed cabbage leaves could be chopped and also be included in the recipe, if desired.

Grandpa said he liked the spears fried quickly with a little smoked bacon grease, chopped onions, a splash of apple juice and seasoned with (more) salt and pepper. "They are crunchy and chewy," he said, "and flavorful."

He also remembers seeing four or five barrels of sauerkraut, in different stages of fermentation, lining the walls of their Silverton, Oregon fruit cellar. Also several large demijohns of apple juice "working" to make vinegar, flour sacks of potatoes, carrots, beets and turnips, and an abundant assortment of winter squash and pumpkins, all stacked carefully in the dimly-lit back corners of the room, ready for winter. "They made a strange mixture of earthy smells", he said, but he loved sneaking into the cool cellar on a hot day to raid the barrels of their salty kraut.

I remember Grandpa Willie used to tell me, "Cabbages are beautiful!" If he meant growing in the field, I agree—they are!

Sauerkraut isn't--really!

Fred Mueller, Tangent, Oregon

"Northwest Empire Builders"

PETER FRENCH

PART 2 of 2

"The Strange Fate of the Northwest's Greatest Cattle Empire"

By ANNE SHANNON MONROE, Author of *"Singing in the Rain"* and other fine Oregon books. April 21, 1935

By the beginning of the 1880s, the vast Central Oregon cattle land was no longer the all but exclusive paradise of California cattlemen. The Malheur Indian Reservation was thrown open to white settlers, the Indians removed to Fort Simcoe Reservation in Washington, and Camp Harney military station abandoned.

A Government Land Office was established in Lakeview, nearly two hundred miles across sand and barrenness from Harney Valley, and settlers were flocking in. The "last West" was open for settlement, government surveys were being made, and a big settler rush was on. Titles of many kinds were being handed out, for homesteads, desert claims, timber claims, and, under the swamp act, also for state lands.

The government's agent at Lakeview accepted the filing of the rider who had the fastest horse—the second arrival could only file a contest, and immediately a fight would be on. The long race across the desert was dangerous, difficult and often disastrous. Disputes arose on the way. The settlers were a mixed variety—good, bad, and indifferent.

Sheep men came in with their herds and disputes arose over grazing privileges. Swamp lands presented the least immediate difficulty, as applicants had only to describe the parcel desired, promise to reclaim it, and pay a dollar an acre for possession. Much of the land from Klamath, Oregon to the Blue Mountains and westward to the Cascades was designated as "swamp." The buyer did his own classifying and took chances on getting legal title later.

Constant appeals were being made to the government, and "special agents" were sent out from Washington, D.C. to look into matters and make a report. These "reports" seemed nearly always to favor the cattleman when the dispute was between cattleman and settler. The settler, losing out, would move on to another location, or sit tight and fight further for his rights, according to his own disposition. There followed "bad blood," threats, feuds and legal appeals. The law courts were busy.

Pete French continued on his way undisturbed, still acquiring land. The old saying that he and John Devine would never be satisfied till they owned "all that joined them" seemed true in his case. He bought more land along the Blitzen River, also indemnity school land. He had his employees take up homesteads, which he purchased from them for a few hundred dollars, as soon as they had a title.

He bought out new settlers, and when they proved obstinate about selling, he found ways to persuade them to listen to reason. The life of a small settler, with his few head of stock, became difficult. His stock would "wander," and be hard to find. Ultimately the time came to accept what he was offered and move on. That's about all he could do. Homesteads were dotted here and there all through what Pete French considered his land. Some settlers would never give up. Ed L. Oliver was one of these.

Barbed wire had been invented, and fences were now more dangerous to range cattle. Fence cutting became one of the crimes. Pete French kept the borders of his great ranch constantly patrolled by armed men. Often there were serious altercations—someone usually got hurt.

He considered the settler as someone in his way. The settler looked upon him as a monopolist. French wanted an uninvaded open range, the settler wanted a home. Pete had fought through Indian wars, hard winters and primitive conditions, but his real fight was now on. His troubles thickened.

His wife, who never stayed long in the country, coming in on visits only from California, divorced him. We have "Bruss" Byrd to thank for his impressions: "It was just that she was a city-bred girl, a lovely lady and a born socialite. It was just too lonely for her on the great old P Ranch with never another woman about. She couldn't stand it. And Pete's whole heart was in the country with his horses, dogs and cattle. Town life was too cramped for him. So they had to separate, and he had to lose his little boy."

She went back to California to live, and is still living, as I am told by Maurice Fitzgerald, another of the old-timers, now past 84, and also living in California. Their son, a semi-invalid from injuries received in a training camp, is still with his mother in Oakland.

In 1883, Dr. Hugh Glenn, Peter French's partner and father-in-law, was murdered by his bookkeeper in California. French was now in complete control of the French-Glenn properties. They had become a corporation.

Cattle rustling was one of the minor problems. Smaller men were said to be getting their start in this time-honored way. "Every old-timer had taken a few in his younger days," one of these told me philosophically. "But, as he prospered, he grew law-abiding and respectable; resenting it in others."

To add to the spirit of outlawry, an old forgotten military road grant came to light. The Willamette Valley Military Wagon Road Company, as I understand from Lawrence A. McNary, attorney, was given the grant somewhere around 1862 or 1863.

The requirements were only technically complied with, but a backing company of Paris, France, Lazard Freres & Company, made the loan and purchased the land in 1875, or thereabouts. B. J. Penga of Eugene, Oregon received the original grant. Later the entire grant, extending clear across the Central Oregon country, was sold to James. J. Hill, a Northwest empire and railroad builder.

In the meantime, many had settled on this land and made improvements. Along about 1890, evictions began. Colonel C. E. S. Wood of Portland was the lawyer who went into the country to settle with the occupants, and he is said by everyone to have been "just and honest" in making settlements. But still the people, many of them, still felt aggrieved. It was home. And they didn't see why they should give it up. Just another trouble on top of so many.

The feud started between Pete French and Ed L. Oliver along in 1888 over Oliver's refusal to be evicted from his land, which was in the midst of a French "field." Fields in those days amounted to whole sections. Oliver wouldn't go or be bought out, and Pete wouldn't consent to his staying. "A surly fellow, that Oliver," one of these early cattlemen told me. But he probably had plenty to be surly about.

But none of these disputes and difficulties deterred the ever-hopeful homesteader. Covered wagons continued to creak and lumber their way down the hillsides and on across the open country, bringing in families. Children's heads stuck out everywhere and mothers looked wearily on, wondering when they could "light" and start a home.

Vaqueros smiled knowingly. They guessed the Lord knew which side of the earth he wanted up. Settlers couldn't last—all this distributing of sod. But they were tolerant, and even kind, often contributing a sheep, half a beef, sometimes a milk cow.

Sentiment for a town grew. Monts Curry had started a settlement store near the present site of Burns, Oregon and at the edge of Pete Stinger's ranch, which a Scot, George MacGowan, bought out in conjunction with Stinger. They decided to start the town there, but MacGowan wanted it named for his favorite poet and Stinger wanted it named for himself. After some compromising on other details, the town was christened Burns.

The cattlemen had a store at old Camp Harney, where there was already a nucleus of camp buildings, and they wanted the town there. Surveyors had created Harney County out of Grant—the original county being larger than many Eastern states—and they wanted the county seat as well. But for once, the settlers won out. Burns soon became a going concern with half a dozen saloons, two stores and a livery stable.

Talk of a railroad was now in the air. More secrecy. More uncertainty. Engineers slipped about with their rods and chains, tantalizing to newcomers who'd like to "settle" near where the railroad was likely to run. This kept them uneasy. There were many whisperings.

Some claimed to be "in the know," but nobody knew, so tips were worthless. Whisperings, plottings and plannings went on in the saloons, which were the settlers' only meeting places, their clubs. Tension tightened up "Bill" Hanley. In one of his characteristic speeches, he expressed it: "The same as when cattle is worked up to a stampede. Everyone got under the atmosphere of uneasiness. Somethin' had to happen. Somethin' did happen. Feuds blazed out into gunfire—the gun days were in. No man at breakfast knew but what he might be stretched out in six feet of earth by dinner time."

And dapper Pete French went right on in his planned way, listening to none of the local gossip, smiling, maybe at some of it, at its futilities, for he had the outside man's view and understanding, where they were mostly a buzzing hotbed, guessing among themselves.

Busy with fences, busy with birds, busy with cattle, and dogs, and horses, busy with lawsuits. He had fifteen lawsuits on the docket when he was killed. Busy with ditches and drainage, busy acquiring more land.

Government surveyors had run a second meander line along the southern shore of Malheur Lake, for the waters of the great bird lake had receded. French had long ago gained possession of this shore. He claimed riparian rights, title out to the middle of the lake. And now, to the strip of land between the two surveys.

But settlers also claimed it, had made homes there. Commissioner Sparks of the Cleveland Administration had permitted them to file claims and to occupy them until the matter of title should be decided. There was a long delay, and the settlers felt that the matter was as good as decided in their favor.

But in the general agitation, this question again came up. "Special agents" came out from Washington D.C. to investigate and make a report, for the settlers had appealed to the Government to decide their claims and give them title. A little later, the entire strip of lakeside property was decided in Pete French's favor. More than once, after that, it was said, he was a target for a settler's bullet.

Strange whisperings of charges of chicanery passed from one to another. One story that rolled on and on and gained countenance was that a peculiar-looking equipage had been seen moving slowly along over the disputed territory—a boat set on a wagon bed, with a "special agent" in it. A dirty trick by which the agent could truthfully report to Washington, D.C., that he had "gone over every foot of the ground in a boat," which, of course, made it a "swamp" instead of agricultural land and the property therefore belonged to Pete French, who had bought it under the swamp act, instead of the property of settlers who had homesteaded it.

Resentment was hot and evictions were again under way. All over the great country, by some little stream where a "settler" was trying to get a start, by a far-away choice spring, in a small "happy valley," where a wife and tousled kiddies made a shack into the semblance of a home, the news spread. Men tightened their gun belts, set their jaws grimly and prepared for war.

No use to appeal further to the Government, Pete French would see the "special agent" first. No use to bring suit, Pete French would win. He was a banker and could command unlimited capital. Such loans, as they could manage, were short, his were long. While they must sell at what the market offered, he could afford to wait for a better market. Pete had every advantage of brains, money, the law, and he had outside influence. They were wholly local. And so, the gun became the only answer, as they saw it.

Ed L. Oliver, homesteader, held the gun, as it happened. There was the formality of an arrest and trial, but it was only a formality. Judge Lionel Webster of Portland went to Burns on the case, made an impassioned plea to a jury composed of the rank and file of settlers, and the case was dismissed. Oliver later left the country, then to Umatilla County, it is said.

The title to these lake lands is only today being settled. They've reached their "last court."

Men still live who say of Pete French, always with a sort of sadness, "Yes, I knew him." Mostly men in their eighties. Some of them were boys in his last days, with a boy's keen memory. "Bruss" Boyd of Lake Oswego, Oregon says Pete loved boys. "He took me to his ranch when I was a little shaver, talking along and visiting in a chummy way. I remember an old chair in the 'White House' made of cows' horns. The legs and feet were of hoofs, the arms were horns. But wasn't I proud when he told me I could sit in it!

"He was always so pleasant. He lived a wonderful life, but couldn't live cooped up. That was the way to live. How puny all our lives seem today, compared with the lives of those men. Yes, Pete French was a better man than many give him credit for." And his eyes grew tender, and I asked no more questions of him.

Dr. W. Clair Brown, now living in Corvallis, Oregon, a dentist for years in Burns, has similar memories. "He was fond of boys," he told me. "Many times he took me home with him, and he was always splendid company. He called me 'Claro,' which is Spanish for 'Clair.' He never got out of patience with me—confided some of his affairs—trusted me to deliver important mail. I loved him, very much."

He smiled. "I remember the gold fillings in his teeth—big, but not too conspicuous. Always, he was pleasant-mannered, spontaneous in his appreciation, but could be pugnacious and strong-willed. He showed an enterprising intellect. A great builder and financier."

Then there's "Bill" Hanley's testimony of Pete's kindness when he first went into this country and arrived all ragged and dusty with his little bunch of cattle at a French-Glenn camp. "Get your plate, boy, and get you something to eat."

Men who knew Pete French can't tell dispassionately of him even today, I find. Thought of him opens up the old romantic days of early Oregon, of their youth in the bunchgrass and sagebrush, when life was young and hard, and hopeful. There is something very suggestive of the loyal heart of the man for his own little boy and these youthful friendships.

Lawrence A. McNary, who remembers Pete French as he used to come into The Dalles, says: "He was a product of his times, representative of the business ethics of his day, and a brilliant man."

And so he paid the penalty of "business methods" that carried beyond the power of lesser men to cope with him. He seems a very lonely figure with it all, and we, some way, as did the little boys who loved him, have a strange drawing to him also.

Today, nearly forty years after his murder, the old P Ranch, his pride, and his downfall—having seen towns develop, railroads come, irrigation get under way—is not to be a part of all this development, but is to go back to the water birds, where Pete French found it—to become a governmental bird reserve. From now on, only the laughing loon, the whirring duck, the snowy egret, the honking goose, and the graceful white swan will break the still, sunny air or be silhouetted against the matchless blue sky that meant the best in life to this young man who came out of California at the age of twenty-four--penniless. Yet, he left a fortune of millions and the largest estate ever put together in the Northwest--at only forty-eight.

By ANNE SHANNON MONROE, Author of "*Singing in the Rain*" and other fine Oregon books, April 21, 1935

~ 312 ~

Pie Thief Gets Hot Pepper Cure

In the early days, my mother lived near an Indian settlement in Southern Oregon, close to the California line.

On regular baking days, she would put her freshly baked pies, and other hot food, out on the wide, flat rail of the back porch, to cool. Later, when she went to get this food, usually some of it was missing.

One day, just after she had put several pies out to cool, she saw an old Indian stealthily sneak up to the porch, grab two of her pies, and quietly, slip back on to the path, taking huge bites out of one of the pies. Mother resolved right then to cure him of his thieving habits.

The next day, she made one large pie, and before putting on the top crust, sprinkled a generous layer of cayenne pepper over the filling. When this pie was baked, it was put in the usual place on the porch.

Then she hid near a window and watched for her visitor. In a short time, he appeared, grabbed the pie and stole quickly away.

After that, no more of mother's foods disappeared from her back porch.

KATHERINE G. NELSON, Klamath Falls, Oregon

~ 313 ~

Pioneer Doctor Scalped by Proxy

My father, Dr. John C. Kellogg, crossed the plains by ox-team from Michigan in 1852, and at the time of this story, was living at Admiralty Head, (now Fort Casey) on Whidby Island, across from Port Townsend, Washington.

Sometime previously, an encampment of northern Indians on Whiskey Spit, opposite the mill at Port Gamble, had become a nuisance with their stealing and raiding of clotheslines. When the mill owners ordered the Indians to leave, they refused, so the government cutter, then at Port Townsend, was asked to get rid of them. The cutter anchored broadside to the Indian village and ordered them to leave, but they only laughed.

The captain ordered the cannon fired, killing several Indians, including a chief, and breaking up many of their canoes. The Indians fled into the woods and the cutter returned to Port Townsend, briefly, and then sailed back to San Francisco. Soon the Indians came out of hiding, picked up their dead and departed.

Many months later, the Indians returned to avenge the death of their chief and decided to kill my father, as a doctor was considered a "tyee" (chief) by the Indians. When a number of them arrived at my parents' home, and asked for my father, mother told them he was away for several days visiting a distant patient. The Indians waited for three days for his return and finally made camp on the shore at Ebey's Landing, some three miles distant.

Here they talked with Thomas Hastie, a lad of eighteen who worked for Colonel Isaac Ebey. The boy bragged about what a "hias tyee" (big chief) the colonel was, and his bragging cost that gentlemen his life.

After talking with young Hastie, the Indians decided Colonel Ebey would be a more satisfactory "tyee" in place of the doctor.

One night, after dark, the Ebey family heard the dogs barking, and fearing the Indians were stealing the clothes off the lines, the colonel stepped to the door to investigate. As he stepped onto the porch, the Indians shot and instantly killed him.

A.R. KELLOGG, Salem, Oregon

~ 314 ~

Scout Rescues Captive Girl

On one of the scouting trips of Bill Drannon, who was a protégé of Kit Carson, a famous Indian scout, Drannon met an Indian girl who told him of a white girl who had been held captive, for many years, by another Indian tribe.

Drannon decided to attempt a rescue, and the Indian maid secretly got a message to the white captive, telling her to meet the scout in a huckleberry thicket near the Indian camp. When Drannon met the girl there, she seemed afraid of him at first, but was persuaded to climb on the horse with him and set out for the safety of a white settlement.

They arrived at the home of my grandfather, Levi Harper, and stayed overnight there before going on. Grandfather said the girl's face had been tattooed and painted so that it could hardly be told she was white.

She told Grandmother her name, which was Olive Oatman, and said she and her younger sister had been captured by the Indians several years before, when her mother and father had died in a massacre. The sister had failed to survive the rigors of Indian life.

Olive was taken to California, where unsuccessful attempts were made to remove the tattooing from her face. She found relatives there, and later married. You can only imagine the stories she could tell of those dreadful years.

MRS. A. E. TORGERSON, Silverton, Oregon

~ 315 ~

Indians Evince Sense of Humor

My Grandfather Johnston was a blacksmith and veterinarian in Pendleton, Oregon, in the early days, and told of witnessing an episode which seems to disprove the popular belief that Indians lack a sense of humor.

One day, an Indian from a nearby encampment appeared to ask Grandfather's advice about a horse he had just taken in trade. The Indian had learned that the animal was not as young as represented by the horse trader, from whom he had gotten it, and that it had numerous other defects not noticeable at first glance. Grandfather could only tell him that his fears were well founded and that the horse was practically worthless.

A group of Indians had gathered as Grandfather was examining the horse. As he gave his verdict, there was an angry muttering among them. It was evident that they were in a bad humor. Just then, the trader rode up astride the pony he had taken from the Indian the day before. He was half drunk, but dismounted and started arguing with the Indians.

When they closed in upon him, however, he seemed to realize the mood they were in. He turned and leaped toward the pony. As his foot hit the stirrup, the saddle slipped under his weight, sliding under the pony. The horse shied sideways and the trader sailed through the air, and landed on the back of his neck on the hard ground.

The ominous attitude of the Indians quickly disappeared in the hearty laughter they enjoyed at the trader's discomfort. That fall evidently jarred him to his senses. With his belligerence gone, he agreed to make good the transaction by exchanging the old horse for a healthy three-year-old gray.

M. WOODWARD, Portland, Oregon

~ 316 ~

Feathers Good Hiding Place

My grandfather, William Coates, often tells of an incident that took place when he was about ten-years-old. His father, one of the earliest pioneers, had built a cabin in the forest, some distance from any other settlers.

In the spring, he left his wife and children alone for several days while he went to help another family build their cabin.

Remembering the Whitman massacre, the mother worried constantly about a surprise attack by the Indians, and, being afraid to sleep in the cabin, she had all available bedding carried some distance away, where she decided to spend the nights.

One evening, just at dusk, she had set out with her brood of six, when she remembered that their sole weapon, an ancient pistol, had been left behind. Her oldest son, Bill, was sent back after it.

He had no more than reached the cabin than he heard hoof beats, and glancing out, saw half a dozen warriors, very near their remote cabin. There was no time to run, and seemingly, no place to hide, until his eyes fell on a large barrel in which feathers were stored to be used in making bedding.

Grandpa lost no time in vaulting into the barrel. There he crouched and tried to hold the tickling feathers away from his nose. He could hear the Indians rattling kitchenware and tossing onto the floor whatever articles they considered not worth carrying away.

Finally, after what seemed hours, but was probably but a few minutes, the Indians moved on. He clambered out of the barrel, sneezing and half suffocated ... but safe.

SYLVIA L. PETERS, Eugene, Oregon

~ 317 ~

Pony Substitutes for Slave Maid

My father, nephew of the late George Huntington, who was for years a member of the police force in Portland, Oregon, told me of an incident which occurred when he was a small boy in Grays Harbor, Washington.

In those days, the Indians were still fighting among themselves, the Quilliute tribe from the north and the local Westport tribe particularly. Prisoners taken in battle were usually held as slaves, which was terribly humiliating to the bucks, as they were forced to do manual labor, normally delegated to the women.

On this occasion, a great local chief (Chief Cutler, I believe) was killed and according to their customs, there must be a living sacrifices made at the graveside. A young Indian woman slave, then attached to the chief's household, was chosen for the great honor. She learned of the selection and fled to my father's home for protection.

Somewhere, the Indians had secured great bolts of vividly colored ribbon, which they tied to the chief's painted pony's mane and tail.. Then they ran the horse back and forth along the ocean beach with the streamers flying nearly a hundred feet behind for everyone to see. My father said it was a very colorful and barbaric spectacle.

In lieu of the human sacrifice, the tribesmen had decided to kill the pony so that the chief might still have it in the happy hunting ground.

The following morning, when the crowd had dispersed and the excitement was over, the young slave girl returned to the village, but was not punished, in any way, for running away from her certain death.

LAWRENCE O. FRY, Oakville, Washington

~ 318 ~

Woman's Shooting Impressed Indians

In the early days, in California, the Indians, while not really hostile warriors, they were mean, would steal, and if they could get liquor, were all-around bad men.

My mother was quite young, had the care of her widowed brother's child, besides two babes of her own. My father's business kept him away every day, and sometimes at night.

The Indians annoyed her by begging for food, became rude and took anything they wanted. She became so frightened that she refused to stay alone, even in the daytime. One Sunday, a crowd of white men were gathered in front of our house, playing horseshoes, gambling with cards and shooting at a target some distance away. My father ran into the house and told my mother to come out and shoot at the target.

Father said, "There are a lot of Indians, especially the bucks you are afraid of, scattered around in the brush. Come on, I want them to see how well you shoot your gun." When she came out with the gun, the men cheered. She put the rifle to her shoulder, squeezed off a shot and hit the bulls-eye on the target with her very first try.

The men cheered wildly, the Indians gave a war whoop and rode away, never to bother her again, although she was alone the greater part of the summer.

M. C. McDANIEL, Portland, Oregon

~ 319 ~

Tooth-Shedding Scares Indian

Hank Miller crossed the plains in the early 1880s and settled in Western Oregon. For several years, the white settlers had been annoyed by prying Indians, who at night frequently stared in windows and at times appropriated poultry and small livestock without regard for the ownership of the settlers.

Grandfather Miller, soon after his son Hank had moved west, followed him to the new land. Upon his arrival, he learned of the annoying practices of the Indians, and as he sat one evening, near the fireplace, he saw a brown face pressed against the window, eyes staring at him intently.

Calmly, Grandfather Miller rested his head on the back of the rocking chair, pretending to be asleep, his face turned directly toward the peering eyes of the intruder. Suddenly, his mouth fell open, his upper false teeth dropped down into his mouth, and with a sudden movement forward, at the same time sending forth a sound like a vigorous sneeze, he blew out his teeth directly toward the window.

The face disappeared and there was a loud disturbance outside. The Indian, making a hasty retreat in the dark, fell into the rain barrel at the corner of the house.

From that night on, the Millers had no more trouble with prying eyes at their windows--and no more missing livestock.

BURRELL S. CRAIG, Eugene, Oregon

"When Oregon Went Berserk"

EPISODE 5 of 6

An Account of Ten Spectacular Years (1855-1865) When the Northwest was Host to War, Greed and Death

By JOHN W. KELLY, Staff Writer,
The Oregonian, October 11, 1936

Introduction

When the hostile Indians were suppressed and the country east of the Cascades in Oregon and Washington was thrown open to entry by the whites, a great cry was heard throughout the Northwest—"Gold!"

Miners by the thousands flocked into the area, making scores of fabulously rich strikes. For a time the red men, resenting this influx, carried on a guerrilla warfare against the newcomers, killing many until the miners in self-defense organized and drove the Indians away.

Now, however, came another difficulty—the arrival of outlaws and gunmen to pillage and rob, carrying out their crimes almost without restraint, until the organization of the Vigilantes who brought to a close those turbulent years of Oregon history.

EPISODE 5

With the Gold Rush Came Men Too "Smart" to Work for It

The scum of the earth gravitated to Portland, Oregon, congregated at The Dalles up the Columbia River, and then seeped over the mines east of the Cascades in the thrilling, riotous days of the Oregon gold rush. No sooner was the great Indian uprising crushed and whites permitted to enter the previously forbidden land spreading east of the Cascade Mountains, gold was discovered. Lots of it!

Everywhere was the yellow metal. Prospectors and miners by the tens of thousands flocked to Portland to outfit for the gold fields. With them came the bad eggs, outlaws, and killers ready to prey on the industrious miners who had struck it rich.

Boon Helm was one of the first arrivals. He was tough, remorseless and with an utter disregard of life, his own or another's. General Harney, in command at Fort Vancouver, had scarcely declared the interior open to settlement than Helm came to Portland, then went to The Dalles, where he fraternized with a crew of professional gamblers who were living off the soldiers who constituted the major part of the population. Pickings being small, Helm, with seven gamblers carrying paraphernalia of their profession and leading a race horse, started for Salt Lake City.

Terrible were their adventures in deep snows in the Blue Mountains. Indians attacked and killed six of the card sharps. Boon Helm and one gambler escaped and pushed on over mountains and sagebrush desert, through snow, until weakened for lack of food. This problem was solved by Helm. He turned cannibal, he boasted later. Boon Helm persevered and staggered wearily into Salt Lake City, where he joined a gang of horse thieves which operated into California and Oregon and had ramifications later into the Rogue and Willamette Valleys.

Ferdinand J. Patterson, gunman, came to Oregon with a record. He was involved in a duel at Yreka and was plugged. Later, at Sailor Diggings, in Jackson County, he was again too slow on the trigger. In Portland he refused to drink a toast to "the Union" and shot and killed a man named Staples, who proposed the toast. Patterson fled to the Aragoni Hotel with a crowd in pursuit, eventually making his escape. Following the gold seekers, he went to The Dalles, loafed there, and then went to Boise Basin, Idaho, where he killed ex-Sheriff Pinkham.

Henry Plummer, who organized crime, went to Portland with California pursuers on his track. Plummer fooled the California officers by sending back word that he had been executed in Washington Territory. Plummer also joined the scum of the earth in the sink hole of iniquity that was The Dalles. He met in the gambling dens of the village such chaps as James Romaine and Dave (Doc) Howard, who gambled for a living and did not hesitate to cheat. Another acquaintance was William Page, who lived across the Columbia River in Klickitat, Washington. All these desperadoes left a trail of blood in those gold-crazed days and flourished until their Nemesis overtook them, as is hereafter related.

If Portland had its bad element, The Dalles was worse. It was wild and woolly, gamblers, short-card sports, horse thieves, fugitives, prostitutes, and murderers. Indians still rankling over their failure to exterminate the whites and half-breeds elbowed one another on the only street. Shootings and stabbings were a daily occurrence. It was a motley crew in those winter months when snow-bound they impatiently waited for the ice to go out of the Columba and the roads to the mines again become passable.

Gambling was high. Returning miners risked their pokes of dust laboriously panned from the creeks, usually losing their all. Consorting with the criminal element was Jacob Dixon, former sheriff of Shasta County, California, a good man gone wrong. Fate was beckoning him to Boise Basin, as Fate was leading the other evildoers.

Also at The Dalles was Hill Beachy, planning a stage line, and Lloyd Magruder, trader. All of these men were to write history, give color to their day, yet their names are now forgotten, to be found only in the yellowed files of the newspapers of the time. They were principals in tragedies which were the talk of every mining camp from the Rocky Mountains to the Pacific Ocean.

The rope came into play late in November, 1862. Tom the Spaniard, a Powder River desperado, stabbed and killed John Desmond and William Lytia over a card game at Auburn, Baker County, Oregon. The Spaniard fled, but was caught in Mormon Basin, returned to Auburn and was the principal attraction at a necktie party. During the lynching by Vigilantes, friends of Tom the Spaniard started firing into the self-appointed hangmen, wounding three, while a friend of Tom was killed in the returning volley. This appears to be the first lynching during the gold excitement. It was a pattern for hundreds which followed.

Violence was unrestrained in the subsequent year. Henry Plummer had drifted on to 'Bannock, making it his headquarters. He was elected sheriff, and as head of law enforcement he staffed his office with desperate men. Plummer was a master mind, a cunning executive, and a fine organizer. Boldness of his imagination is attested by the fact that he made crime a racket on a very large scale. Plummer's organization of horse thieves, highwaymen, robbers and cutthroats increased until he had 130 members, all oath-bound. He headed a secret society of outlaws--and presided as sheriff.

How would history have been changed if his lawless reign continued? This iniquitous order of outcasts killed and robbed 120 citizens and many stages before they reached the end of their rope—which can be taken literally. The 120 crimes are of record; how many more were perpetrated is problematical.

No modern racketeer or super-criminal could teach Sheriff Plummer any tricks. His gang was ubiquitous; they operated in every camp.

"Innocent" was the password of Plummer's gang; identification signs were wearing the necktie in a sailor's bowknot and instead of having a beard, as most miners did, these road agents wore a mustache and goatee—"imperial" was the name of the chin adornment. They frequently disguised themselves as Indians, thereby shifting suspicion for murders and robbery on the innocent. These bandits were known as "chiefs," "road agents," knights of the road," but were just plain horse thieves, murderers, robbers and counterfeiters of gold dust.

George Noble of Oregon City was robbed of 100 pounds of gold dust between Florence and Oro Fino in December of 1862 before Vigilantes were organized at the Florence mines on Salmon River.

Nelson Scott, David English and William Peoples held up a freight shipper, taking 1,400 ounces of gold. They were arrested in Walla Walla and lynched. These three highwaymen were members of Plummer's gang.

The most famous of the crimes of the Plummer organization was the Lloyd Magruder murder. Magruder, who had operated as a trader of goods at The Dalles, left Lewiston, Idaho in August, 1863, with his pack train for Beaver Head, where he sold goods and his mules for $80,000. With Magruder on the return trip were Charles Allen and William Phillips, both from the Willamette Valley, they having $20,000 in gold. In The Dalles, Magruder had met Doc Howard, Romaine the gambler, and Bill Page the trapper from Klickitat, Washington.

Chris Lowey, who had been the blacksmith with the Mullen expedition, which had accompanied Governor I. I. Stevens of Washington Territory, was permitted to work his passage back to Lewiston with Howard, Page and Romaine. This quartet of villains were members in good standing with the Plummer gang. They explained they wished to get back to The Dalles. Page tended the stock; Romaine was cook for the outfit.

Between the Clearwater and Bitter Root Rivers, as the caravan of 40 animals proceeded toward Lewiston, the tragedy took place. In a night camp Lowey killed Magruder, while Doc Howard and Romaine murdered Allen and Phillips. The bodies were rolled over a precipice. All but eight horses were slaughtered and thrown over the cliff. Fire consumed the equipment. Wearing moccasins, the murderers trampled the snow to give the appearance of an Indian attack, should bodies be found before spring.

Intending to head for Puget Sound in the western part of Washington, the outlaws abandoned the plan, as traveling was bad, so they rode into Lewiston. Arriving at Hotel de France October 19, eighteen days after the crime, the quartet placed their mounts in a stable operated by Hill Beachy. Page bought four seats in the stage for Walla Walla, giving such names as Brown and Smith. Stage Agent Beachy became suspicious; he recognized the passengers not as Brown and Smith but as Doc Howard and Romaine, whom he knew in The Dalles. He was further suspicious because Magruder was overdue and he recognized the saddles on the horses left by the killers as Magruder's property.

By this time the desperadoes were in Walla Walla and bought tickets for Portland. Beachy, A.P. Ankeny and seven others went in pursuit. When the posse tracked the murderers to Portland, the later were on their way to San Francisco, and Beachy's party continued the chase. In San Francisco the gold was taken to the mint for coinage; then the robbers secured cover, Howard and Romaine registering at the Lick House.

A detective by instinct, Beachy located and arrested Howard and Romaine and then rounded up the rest of the fugitives. The prisoners bribed a police captain to permit their escape but the policeman pocketed the bribe and double crossed the killers. Back in custody, the party returned to Portland, Walla Walla, and to Lewiston where Vigilantes demanded his criminals, but Beachy refused to surrender his prisoners despite threats. Page turned state's evidence and revealed the whole story. Lowey, Howard and Romaine were hanged legally on March 4, 1864.

Beachy's expenses for bringing in the gang were $6,244. He is the same Beachy who attempted to operate a stage line from Boise Basin to California through Southeastern Oregon but was routed by hostile Indians.

Vigilantes were secretly organizing. Eventually they founded a network extending from the mines in Oregon, across Idaho to into Western Montana. They had detectives in every gold camp and a system of espionage such as was not parallel until spying became a fine art during the world war. It is estimated there were over 1,000 in the organization which gridironed the men in the gold fields. They gathered information secretly, would swoop down and hang their man and in fifteen minutes be on their way--reports the *Walla Walla Spokesman* of April 15, 1864. In December, 1863 and January, 1864, Vigilantes hanged twenty-one. That was just the beginning. Along in 1864, the Idaho Vigilantes took a "breathing spell" after twenty-seven unpublished hangings.

To realize the operation of the Vigilantes in the old Oregon country it should be noted that the famous and much-publicized Vigilantes of San Francisco had but four men in 1853 and four more in 1856. The Northwest rope had quietly swung that many into eternity on a single night or day without the publicity accorded their predecessors in San Francisco. Usually the irate citizens had formed the societies of Vigilantes who were content to string up their victims, but there were occasional departures from the established custom. In 1863, a house owned by Sheriff Plummer in a Montana camp was literally blown to pieces with dynamite, then the Vigilantes lit a fire with the lumber and placed the dead body of the suspect on the pyre.

Despite the loss of members of the crime syndicate, Sheriff Plummer carried on, confident that tracks were so well covered that none of the robberies and other public outrages could be traced to his door. Reports of the activities of the Vigilantes worried him very little. He received accounts of local robberies and horse stealing and the passing of counterfeit gold dust but waxed indignant, swearing oaths that he would run offenders to earth and exact justice.

For a considerable time his Jekyll-and-Hyde role was not suspected, but such duplicity did not continue indefinitely, and the detectives of the Vigilantes were collecting clues and fragments of evidence and weaving a rope which was eventually to choke the life out of this monster.

The climax of the era of desperate deeds was drawing to a close and Oregon's ten most thrilling years would soon be memories. But there was still work to be done by the gangs in spite of the threat of swinging from a tree with a rope around their neck.

What happened to Sheriff Plummer and his followers and the coming of law and order will be related in the next and final episode of "When Oregon Went Berserk."

To be continued . . .

~ 320 ~

Settlers Foster Indian Romance

My father, Daniel Bridges, brought his family from Santa Rosa, California, in 1871, to the home of my uncle, B. F. Owen, then living in a small log house in Scott's Valley, Oregon. Almost the entire valley was then owned by two sons of Charles Applegate, John and Albert.

Although my uncle and aunt had a family of six children themselves, with true pioneer hospitality they welcomed us into their already full home, until my father could build a log cabin for his own family on Red Hill.

The Applegates were always good friends with Chief Halo, leader of the Indians there. Uncle Charlie Applegate and Aunt Melinda, his wife, were held in high esteem, even affection, by all the Indians.

One morning, when we came into my aunt's living room, there, by the fireplace, sat an Indian woman with a few-weeks-old papoose. My aunt told us that this was "Sally-Ann," and added, "She is a daughter-in-law of an Indian chief." Afterwards, my Aunt Jane told us all about Sally Ann's romantic marriage to BeEll, a son of Chief Halo.

So many years have passed since the story was told that I have forgotten the name of the tribe of Indians Sally Ann belonged to, but she had been sold to an Indian somewhere in the Willamette Valley--because her father wanted more ponies than BeEll was able to muster up.

However, Sally Ann refused to accept her father's choice of a husband, preferring BeEll, and ran away through the mountains, on foot all the way, and arrived at the home of my aunt after nightfall. As Sally Ann could speak pretty good English, and my aunt knew some Chinook, Sally Ann explained the situation to my Aunt, who took her in.

Finally, BeEll, who always consulted Uncle Charley, or some of the Applegate family, in any emergency, talked the matter over, and Uncle Charley, Uncle Jesse, Uncle Lindsey, William Wilson and others made a treaty with Sally Ann's relatives, enough ponies were gotten together to satisfy the demand, so that BeEll and Sally Ann could be married.

Sally Ann had a large family and one of the girls was named Melinda, after the wife of Charles Applegate. Another daughter was named Laura after the wife of John Applegate who still lives in Yoncalla, Oregon.

EMMA BRIDGES MILLER, Yoncalla, Oregon

~ 321 ~

Settler Escapes Death in Creek

In the 1860s, when The Dalles, Oregon military road was the most direct route between The Dalles on the Columbia River and old Fort

Boise on the Snake River, Burnt Ranch was a stopping-off place for those who followed the wagon tracks. On Burnt Ranch, west of the junction of Bridge Creek and the John Day River, three men were living at the time of the episode narrated here.

One day, during the summer of 1862, a party of Indians out for a little excitement, happened by the place, saw it was occupied and prepared to kill its occupants. However, the killing was forestalled when the whites surrendered the cabin to the marauding band without a struggle.

After ransacking the contents, ripping up several feather mattresses, and knocking the head off a barrel of molasses, the Indians discovered that their paleface hosts had made for the tall timber. Looking about for something to vent their emotions on, in the absence of the men, one of the Indians spied a grizzled old tabby cat, which was immediately doused in the molasses and rolled in the feathers. It looked more like a chicken than a cat.

Two of the men were successful in covering up all signs of their hasty retreat, leaving George Masterson as the sole prey of the Indian band. Fleeing up Bridge Creek about two miles, with his pursuers rapidly nearing him, George jumped into the creek and crouched under an overhanging brush covered bank that gave just room enough for him to keep his nose above the water. He remained in this damp and unpleasant hideout several hours while the Indians unsuccessfully scoured the creek bank.

At the approach of darkness, the disgruntled Indians gave up the search, allowing Masterson to escape from his forced bath onto dry land.

ORVILLE WILLIAMS, The Dalles, Oregon

~ 322 ~

Indian Woman's Finery Shocks Guests

For several years, my father was pastor of a small church in Salem, Oregon, where my parents had arrived in 1885 from their former home in Illinois. Upon their arrival in Salem, Father volunteered to get someone to help Mother with the work of getting settled. Mother was astonished when he returned home accompanied by a large, very obese Indian woman, who, it seemed, was the only person available at the time. The woman, who said her name was Kate, proved to be a good worker, but needed constant supervision to keep her boundless energy in the right channels.

After they were settled, Mother invited the ladies of the church to her house one afternoon. She was very desirous of making a good impression upon them, so took extraordinary care that everything was just as it should be. She got Kate to make the house spotless, while she herself prepared the refreshments for the afternoon get together. As Kate was working, she came upon a bundle of odds and ends that had been discarded, mostly old clothes, worn beyond repair. She asked if she might have them and Mother assented.

Finally, everything was ready. Kate had been so eager to be present that mother did not have the heart to refuse her. So, much against her better judgment, she at last agreed to let Kate stay, saying that she might help serve the refreshments.

The guests began to arrive, and Mother heard a clatter in the kitchen and knew her aide was on the job. It was nearly time for the refreshments. Mother opened the kitchen door and told Kate she might bring the tray.

Here came Kate, her chubby face abeam, the tray of sandwiches and cake held high, blissfully unaware that the concerted gasp from the ladies present was not caused by admiration, as they beheld, proudly worn on top of her other finery, Mother's discarded pink corset that had been among the old clothes given Kate that morning.

The effect was heightened by the fact that she had laced it with a piece of bright red ribbon, the ends of which fluttered out behind her ample hips as she calmly went about the business of serving the speechless guests.

MRS. VICTOR JONES, Portland, Oregon

~ 323 ~

Teepee Cover Saves Pioneers

In the year 1875, my grandfather and grandmother crossed the plains to Oregon. In the wagon train in which my grandparents traveled, there were about forty wagons.

One day, in a skirmish with Indians, a blazing firebrand was hurled onto Grandfather's canvas wagon top, setting it afire. The canvas was completely destroyed. Having given the Indians a sound beating, the pioneers hastily gathered up their scattered goods and traveled on their way. The next day, the pioneers passed by the Indians' deserted camp. Grandfather tore down the best looking teepee, which was greatly decorated, and used it to re-cover his damaged wagon.

Several days later, as they were traveling through some very hot country, a large band of Indians appeared. Before the pioneers were aware of what was happening, the Indians were yelling like mad and displaying their weapons. They didn't have time to prepare for the attack and their ranks were in disarray when suddenly the charging warriors stopped in their tracks. They seemed to be looking at Grandfather's makeshift wagon top.

Then, as suddenly as they had appeared, they wheeled their horses and galloped off. They were soon lost to view. The travelers were mystified by this strange behavior as they gave thanks to God, gathered up their reins and again started westward.—without further incidents from Indians.

LAWRENCE W. GILLIAN, San Diego, California

~ 324 ~

Wife's Relatives Plague Trader

My grandfather, Charles Carlton, came to Oregon with a wagon train in 1860, which stopped for repairs for a couple of days at a small stage station run by a white man who had an Indian wife.

As was the Indian custom in those days, the wife's relatives had moved in on this trader en-masse, and etiquette forbid him to refuse to provide for them and consequently the place was covered with them, large and small. They evidently felt that as long as their white in-law was prospering, there was no reason for them to not share his good fortune.

The morning that the wagon train was ready to move, the trader saddled his horse, and said he would accompany them several miles on their trip.

They started out. The miles passed and they halted for an afternoon rest, but he did not turn back. When they resumed the journey, he was still with them. Not until when camped for the night did he tell that he was not going back and had arranged with the driver of one of the wagons to pack all of his personal belongings in the wagon. He had left the stage station and its contents to his wife and her relatives.

He continued the trip with them and apparently considered it a good bargain that he had ridden himself of his pestiferous kinfolks at the cost of his business.

C. J. IRWIN, Portland, Oregon

~ 325 ~

Indian Scorns Farm Lessons

In the early 1870's, the Dee family was left fatherless on a homestead in Washington Country. Widow Dee was very able as head of the family. She did the plowing, grubbing and heavier tasks, while the four children were taught to weed, hoe and cultivate the sizable family garden.

Indians camped thereabouts in the summer, and Widow Dee soon tired of their begging vegetables from the garden. She determined to introduce the art of gardening to all begging Indians. When that season rolled around again, and the Dee garden was at its best, an Indian appeared, and, pointing to the garden, said, "Potato," and produced a sack from under his blanket.

Widow Dee said, "No. You take hoe. I'll show you how to make garden and grow your own potatoes. Next year you come, I give seed, you plant them, up come vegetables, skookum; you big, strong, make big garden, plenty good eats. You see my babies, they make this garden."

The Indian stood erect and listened attentively, his dark eyes flashing angrily. When Widow Dee tried to pass the hoe to him, he haughtily said, "Me buck, me no squaw," and hastily strode away—with his sack empty.

J. DOELEM, Portland, Oregon

~ 326 ~

This Indian Woman Was Boss

My uncle, Jim Weatherby, ran a trading station in Eastern Oregon in the 1880's, where he outfitted prospectors, cattlemen, and all the miscellaneous gentry of that locality, including many Indians.

He once told me of an Indian woman who came into his place, one day, wanting to see some shoes. He had a pair of high laced woman's shoes, and these immediately took the lady's eye. However, upon learning the price, she did not have the money to pay for them. So she departed, leaving them behind, although obviously reluctant to do so. Sometime later, a big buck Indian appeared at the station. "Squaw wantum shoes," he said. Uncle Jim told him the price, but he shook his head. "No got money. Squaw say me work."

Knowing in what little esteem Indians held their womenfolk, as well as their natural aversion to work, Uncle Jim was astonished when he realized that the Indian really did wish to do enough work to pay for the shoes. Although doubtful, he finally agreed that if the Indian would work three days, he could have them. He set to work immediately, but it soon became evident that he was doing so, under duress as it were, and that he had no enthusiasm for his tasks.

Therefore, when the Indian woman reappeared later in the day, Uncle Jim told her that he was afraid he would have to call the bargain off, as her husband was shirking on the job. She promised him she would remedy that at once--and she did.

And thereafter, for the remainder of the three days, the Indian worked like a good fellow, but Uncle Jim noticed the squaw always lurking in the background. When the time was ended, she appeared triumphantly and carried away her shoes. Her husband, weary and subdued, followed her.

KENNETH DAY, Portland, Oregon

~ 327 ~

Old-Timer Recalls Table Rock Battle

During the very early days of the West, 1846–47, in the vicinity of Jacksonville, Oregon, where many Indian wars have taken place and everyone now has a mine in their back yard, or under their house, or street, my grandfather Hodges, in his youth, fought Indians with the Oregon Volunteers under the command of Joe Lane.

Grandfather was often sent out on scout duty (which was to ride on ahead, trying to locate the Indian bands and then reporting back). One morning, Grandfather was sent out and saw several Indians coming, but

unfortunately, they saw him at the same time, and before he could turn back to give the warning, they shot, missing their aim, but killing the horse instead.

He jumped free of the falling animal, and, being very fleet of foot, it didn't take him many seconds to get to the tall timber. Hearing the shots, the whites arrived in a very short time. Grandfather jumped on the back of one their horses and they chased the Indians all the way to Table Rock, shooting as they rode.

To escape, the Indians ran up on top of Table Rock, but put themselves in a trap as the whites surrounded the rock. Surrender was the only alternative for the Indians.

The chief seemed to realize that this was their last stand. Surrender here also meant surrender forever. This was to be the white man's country and the last frontier of the West. Their Indian life would be changed--forever.

MISS LULA HEARD, Portland, Oregon

"Northwest Empire Builders"

HENRY W. GOODE

He Made Northwest Lights Shine Brighter

By HENRY E. REED, an Executive of the 1905 Lewis & Clarke Exposition in Portland, Oregon. April 28, 1935

A year and a few days separated the coming of the telephone and the electric light to Portland, Oregon. The young city quickly adopted these modern conveniences, but there was a difference in its initial reception of them.

When the phone was proposed in the spring of 1878, it was regarded as a "perfect nuisance." It interfered with the time-honored lung exercise of the pioneers of shouting the length of the streets and across the river. To help Alexander Graham Bell's contraption along, W. T. Shanahan and George H. Himes consented to make their stores the termini of an experimental line.

People talked and heard over the wire and were convinced. The City Council granted a franchise for the "American speaking telephone," and the exchange was opened June 18, 1878. Portland was the seventh city in the United States, perhaps in the world, to have a commercial exchange. New Haven, Connecticut, being the first. Within two years, two companies, serving 250 customers, were operating.

The age of light and power dawned when the steamer *State of California*, 59½ days from Philadelphia, by way of Cape Horn, berthed her 307 feet of length at a Portland dock, May 25, 1879. The "*State*" had two electric lights in the engine room and four in the cabin.

It was a great night on May 28th when a public exhibition of the lights was given aboard. Over five hundred people marveled at "the light that needed not to be started with a match and could not be blown out". When they descended the gangplank to come uptown for a toddy at the Oro Fino or the Gem, or oysters at Keith's, the gas jets and kerosene lamps on the street corners just did not seem to fit any longer into the picture. That night, they were started on their way out, together with their attendants, the picturesque lamplighters.

The following summer, another new steamer for the Pacific Coast trade, the *Columbia*, arrived with larger and more complete electric light equipment, including incandescent lamps. She put a reflector behind an arc light and shot a beam to the western hills that caused many to believe that an Aurora Borealis had broken loose from its moorings.

Schoolboys who were better behaved than to throw rocks at the telephone wires to make them "sing," speculated about electricity. William H. (Billy) Meeker, who was a classmate of mine in the Harrison Street School, wrote a composition on the subject when he was in high school in 1881.

In the old public school days, "exercises" were held on Friday afternoons. There was, for each class, a varied program of compositions, declamations, dialogues and recitations. Sometimes fond parents came to see their hopefuls perform.

Master Meeker soared one Friday afternoon and predicted that the streets of Portland would someday be lighted by electricity brought from Oregon City by long-distance transmission line. The town was talking across its length and breadth by telephone, but to bring electricity thirteen miles, and make it work. That was certainly something else.

If Meeker had been a grown man with a beard or sideburns, he would have been ridiculed out of town. But Billy was only a kid, and the essay passed out of mind with the usual faint smiles and shrugging of shoulders.

About eight years afterward, to be exact, June 2, 1889, Portland was lighted in the way that Master Meeker had foretold. It was the first city of the world to be lighted in this manner. The slender, studious lad from present Southwest Arthur Street was right after all.

Electrical prospects in Portland, brought from California in the 1880's, Parker Farnsworth Morey, a native of Maine, energetic, positive, and resourceful. He sought a franchise from the city to supply Bull Run water for Portland from the snow melt on Mount Hood, but was blocked by the private water monopoly, and the city government's decision to control the Bull Run source themselves.

Turning to electricity, Morey and others organized the United States Electric Light Company which put the first arc lights on the streets of Portland in 1885. The name of this corporation was changed to Willamette Falls Electric Company when the water power at Oregon City was harnessed.

At this point, the subject of this sketch can be introduced. Henry Walton Goode came to Portland in 1890 as manager of the Northwest Thomson-Houston Company. He had been a Westinghouse man before locating here and made his headquarters in St. Paul, Minnesota. Shortly after he arrived, the Thomson-Huston and Edison General Electric companies were merged to form the General Electric Company.

Morey interested the General Electric people in his enterprise and changed the name of his Willamette Falls company to Portland General Electric Company. In other words, it was the General Electric Company of Portland.

Morey thought highly of Goode and promptly picked him for Vice-President and General Manager of Portland General Electric Company (PGE). This was in 1892. Goode, then thirty years old, was in an important place for a man of his years, and smooth-shaven at that.

Morey retired from the presidency in 1899, and Goode succeeded him. At the start, the Pratts of Standard Oil connection, who dominated the affairs of Portland General Electric Company, were friendly to Goode. For some reason they cooled, and often without notice or reason, they countermanded orders for machinery which Goode had placed with Eastern factories.

When Goode was elected President and Director-General of the Lewis and Clark Exposition, the Pratts woke up to the fact that the man at the helm in Portland was a live wire and their friendship returned.

More than anything else in the electric business, Goode was a salesman. He was not an electrical engineer. However, he knew his job. Morey was inclined to be combative. Goode was just the opposite. He was quiet, unassuming, gracious, soft spoken and never in a hurry. From his Virginia ancestry of two centuries standing, he had inherited an intensely proud spirit.

Goode's plans always had a definite objective in view, and to that he worked. His aim was to make PGE a popular public utility. When he was called to the presidency, the company was charging twenty cents a kilowatt hour for light. He knew that business could not be developed under such a handicap, so he reduced the rate to fifteen cents and then to 9.74 cents.

Light and power were serious problems for the Lewis and Clark Exposition. The Exposition had no money for a plant and neither of the two power companies then operating in Portland had sufficient plant capacity. Goode went to New York and told his big stockholders that it was the duty of PGE to take care of the Exposition's needs. A new plant costing $300,000 would be required.

Such would be the growth of Portland, said Goode to the stockholders that the output of the new plant would be quickly absorbed and even more capacity would be needed in the future. Grudgingly, Goode was permitted to have his way, but was told that he would be held accountable for the result of the expenditure.

After the Exposition, Goode, with the backing of the Clarks of Philadelphia, organized Portland Railway, Light & Power Company in succession to PGE. It was a gigantic corporation with $30,000,000 capital, and reached for the control of the light, power and the city and suburban electric railways of Portland and vicinity.

At the very beginning of what promised to be a brilliant career in the electrical world, death put forth his hand. While in the East on business, Goode was stricken by pneumonia, and died in Atlantic City, New Jersey, March 31, 1907, at the age of forty-five. He was born in Newcastle, Indiana, September 26, 1862.

Mr. Goode did not seek service with the Exposition. He was drafted. The office of Director-General was an important one, and after the financing had been completed, the site selected and Oregon's aid safely past referendum, the pressing question was--who would be appointed to fill it?

Many were considered, some of them from the East, but the preference of the Board of Directors was for a local man. In the summer of 1903, someone mentioned Harry Goode and the choice was quickly made. A year later, when Harvey W. Scott withdrew from the presidency, Goode succeeded him.

Goode did not take long to fit into his new position. He knew little or nothing about expositions, but a lot about how business should be conducted, and soon was carrying on like an old hand. First of all, he gathered about him, as heads of the principal divisions, men who he could trust, and from whom in return he expected truth and confidence.

His goal was that the Exposition should be complete on the opening day. It was 98% complete, and what was unfinished could not be noticed.

He all but slept on the Exposition grounds the two weeks prior to the opening day, so intent was he that everything should be in order.

The scope of the Exposition seemed to enlarge from day to day. As at first projected, it was a small, local show, not very much larger than the mechanics' and industrial fairs to which early Portland was accustomed. When Oregon made a liberal appropriation, the Exposition became state-wide, and when the United States Government voted to participate, it blossomed out as a national affair.

This broadening out called for more money than the stock subscriptions, which were paid up 97%, could be expected to provide. This came from sales of exhibit space and from concessions.

As the Exposition expanded, the budgets of the departments were increased, but there always was kept in view the reasonable probability that the funds to be expended would come into the treasury.

The story of 1905 has been often told, and it suffices here to say that the result exceeded all expectations. The attendance was far greater than the early estimates. Whereas in 1903, not to exceed five thousand Eastern people were expected to come, the railroads brought 122,500 in 1905.

The Exposition was an institutional and a financial success. The Portlanders who subscribed nearly $418,000 stock in 1901, thinking that they would never again see a penny of it, and not caring either, were returned 21%.

The finale came on the night of October 14. While thousands of people were milling about in the heavy rain, waiting for the turn of the switch that would extinguish the lights for all time, the officers and directors sat down to a dinner in the New York building with Theodore B. Wilcox as toastmaster. When Goode's turn to speak came, he did not exult. In a few words, he complimented and thanked his staff, and closed by observing that while much might be said about the Exposition, it was all included in the single statement, "We have held an exposition and have delivered the goods."

There is plenty of grief connected with the organization and holding of an exposition. Portland had its share of it. A good deal of it was caused by doubters, who could see nothing but failure, followed by business stagnation in Portland. Much the greater part originated with critics who thought that they knew better than the management how the thing should be done.

Goode as President and Director-General was the target of the doubters and critics. If he was even annoyed by them, he never showed it. He kept his head up and pushed on to his objective. Those of us who were associated with him frequently wondered what, between his double shift in the electric company and in the Exposition, was keeping him on his feet.

I have often thought that the strain of the Exposition period, when over five hundred luncheons, dinners, receptions and dedications were attended, undermined Goode's health and opening the way for the attack of pneumonia that carried him off.

There were bad half hours in the construction and operating periods. The darkest moment was in the first week of June, just after the opening. The first day's attendance was disappointingly small, due it was later ascertained, to the parade that was held downtown, which caused people to believe that there would be a crush at the gates and so they stayed away.

And then came the rain. The operating cost was $3,650 a day, and for several days, the intake did not average 60% of this amount. It looked as if the town had turned its back on the show. Goode was concerned, but in his usual philosophical way he merely remarked, "Wait till the rain stops."

When the weather settled, the people flocked to the Exposition, and from that time forward, the result never was in doubt. The Exposition grossed nearly $1,525,000, and after holding a good show and paying all its bills, returned about $84,500 to stockholders.

There was nothing particularly eventful in Goode's career with Portland General Electric Company from the time he entered its service until formation of Portland Railway, Light, & Power Company. First as Vice-President and General Manager and later as President, he merely carried on. The period of business depression following 1893 was not favorable to large expansion of plant capacity.

The organization of Portland Railway, Light, & Power Company reflected Goode's confidence in the future of Portland and its tributary territory. He foresaw sustained growth in population and industry and intended that his company should be prepared at all times to deliver adequate service.

He planned to play an active part in the city's civic and business life, and had he lived, would have been an outstanding leader. He was a man that Portland could ill afford to lose.

The electric service to the Exposition was Goode's special pride. Wonderfully beautiful effects from 100,000 lights made the Lewis and Clarke Exposition grounds a gem at night. Nothing like it had ever before been seen on the Pacific Coast.

So perfect was the installation that when the lights were turned on for trial two weeks before the opening day, not a detail was lacking. Electricity was used also to supply water for irrigation, sanitation, fire protection and for pumping water every day into Guild's Lake to keep it at a constant level.

What was gratifying to the Board of Directors and a contributing factor to the financial success of the Exposition was that the charge of this service was remarkably low. Goode saw to that. When Portland General Electric Company named its price for light and power, its competitor, the Oregon Water Power Company, was put out of the running.

By HENRY E. REED, an Executive of the 1905 Lewis and Clark Exposition in Portland, Oregon

~ 328 ~

Indian Covets Dinner Call

When my grandfather crossed the plains to Oregon in pioneer days, Indians were still very hostile and much feared by the emigrants.

One day, the scout of my grandfather's wagon train saw a band of Indians approaching and hurried back to sound a warning. The wagons were drawn up in a circle, and they awaited an attack, but none came.

However, the Indians were known to favor night for their attacks, so a watch was kept and camp fires were built. All night they watched, but no attack came. The next day, it was decided to pool what food they had, and when a meal was prepared, somebody beat on a big iron kettle with a large spoon to tell the guards to come and eat. While they were eating, a lone Indian rode into camp. The men seized their guns.

But it turned out that all he wanted was to trade some skins for the "dinner call." After arranging the trade, he rode away, beating on his kettle like a child with a new drum. Incidentally, the travelers learned that the Indians of that district were friendly and the whites had little to fear.

JOHN DOANE, Marshfield, Oregon

~ 329 ~

Rescued Indian Shows Gratitude

In 1860, my grandparents lived in a log house near Celilo Falls, on the Columbia River in Oregon. The Indians have one certain spot below the falls where they fished for salmon, with great success I might add.

White men were greeted with rocks and clubs if they were seen fishing from this place. However, one morning, Grandfather decided to try his luck at salmon fishing, and, as no one was in sight, he took his pole and gaff hook and went to this forbidden spot.

Soon, he heard a cry for help, and, looking down, he saw an Indian trying to climb back up the slippery rocks. His head was a mass of blood and he seemed to be in terrific pain. Suddenly he let go of his hold on the rocks and started floating downstream. As he passed, Grandfather reached out with his gaff hook and gently pulled the semi-conscious man to shore.

Half dragging and half carrying him, he finally got the injured man home, where he and Grandmother nursed him back to health--several days before he went back to his own people.

A year later, the same Indian returned, bringing fresh and smoked salmon, and many small tokens, to my grandparents, to show his gratitude for what they had done for him. He became a true friend, and each year, during the salmon fishing season, made his appearance at the log house with more delicious fish.

MRS. ROCHELLE DEERING, Oregon City, Oregon

~ 330 ~

Woman's Wig Frightens Indian Woman

My grandfather, with my grandmother and four children, settled in Benton County, Oregon, in the middle 1840's.

One day, an Indian woman came to the door to ask Grandmother if she would teach her how to bake biscuits, as Grandmother had sent biscuits over to the Indian camp as a gesture of friendliness. Grandmother explained that biscuits should be baked in an oven, which she probably didn't have, but she would still be happy to teach her.

The woman was invited in and the culinary lesson began. As Grandmother stepped to the porch where the milk was kept, a puff of wind came up and lifted her wig. The Indian woman uttered a cry of horror, muttering something about being scalped by an unknown force, and went running out of the house.

It took quite some persuasion by Grandmother to get the woman back into the house to resume the cooking lesson. Grandmother also found and gave her an old, un-used, heavy, iron "Dutch oven" to bake them in.

MISS L. JOHNSON, Portland, Oregon

~ 331 ~

Chinese Innkeeper Parts With Queue

In the early 1880's, citizens of Prineville, Oregon, objected to having the town's hotel run by two Chinese men, Ah Doon and Moy Doon, brothers, who had come to Prineville originally to work as house boys.

The hotel, known as the Jackson House, was owned by Ben Allen, stockman and banker, considered the richest man in Crook County. Animosity was created when Johnny Dauthit, editor of the *Ochoco Times*, published a humorous article entitled, "*Ah Doon and Ah Ben*," that provoked a fistic attack on the sagebrush editor by the banker/hotel owner Ben Allen.

Soon after the fight, a group of stockmen hotel patrons called on banker Allen with a demand that he find a white landlord for his hotel. The banker told them the matter of renting to Chinese was purely a business proposition with him. He then adroitly turned the conversation to other channels.

A few days later, the U.S. mail stage, on the 125-mile trip to The Dalles, Oregon, had just left Prineville on a stormy December morning, when it was stopped by four masked riders. Ah Doon was a passenger, starting on a trip to San Francisco, California.

When the stage was halted, three of the masked "bandits" dismounted. Ah Doon was yanked roughly off the seat. His long queue severed with a keen-edged knife. He was then told to never show his face in Prineville again upon penalty of death.

At the next stop, which was Hay Creek, Ah Doon, more indignant that frightened, excitedly gave details to two friends, Charles H. Lewis, then teaching school on upper Trout Creek, and Frank Summerville, son of an early-day merchant and postmaster at Hay Creek.

Many regarded the affair as a practical joke on the part of some rollicking cowboys. Others, in the know, felt that inspiration for the unique holdup could be traced directly to the cool rebuff banker Allen accorded the stockmen.

Ah Doon did not heed the banishment order or death threat. Instead, he came back to Prineville with a haircut and a stock of general merchandise. With his brother, My Doon, and Wah Tye, a young Chinese lad born in Portland, he continued in business at Prineville until just before the Spanish-American War, when the trio sold out and went to China to become importers and distributors of American merchandise.

ROBERT BALLOU, Oregon City, Oregon

~ 332 ~

Indians Battle Among Selves

The first Indian fight in Crook County, Oregon, occurred in the summer of 1866, on Dry Creek, about thirteen miles from Prineville.

Dr. McKay, a half-breed Indian (who afterward became quite noted as a surgeon), was camped on what is now known as McKay Creek with a band of Warm Springs Indians. With him was Billy Chinook, who formerly served as a scout and guide for General John C. Fremont and Kit Carson, when they passed through this territory in 1843.

McKay ordered Billy Chinook to take twenty-five men and reconnoiter for any other Indian bands. The following day, they discovered a band of Piutes on Dry Creek. After counting their fires and wigwams, they decided there were no more, so far as numbers were concerned, than they had themselves.

The orders were not to attack, but if the Indians were found, to return and give the alarm. But the opportunity was too favorable, and they disobeyed orders. The first Piute campfire started in the morning was to be the signal for the whites to attack.

Accordingly, as the early fire appeared, a rush was made. Although surprised, the Piutes made a gallant defense, but the whole band numbering thirty-two bucks, women and papooses, were killed or captured.

My father, Lewis Hodges, one of the earliest settlers in Crook County, says that the Indians did not bother the whites much in the early days here, that the tribes fought mostly among themselves--but everything changed.

STELLA HODGES, Prineville, Oregon

~ 333 ~

Tree Monument to Early Hero

An interesting landmark, which stands on the Old Overland Trail, near Fallon, Nevada, is an immense lone cottonwood tree. It stands as a monument to the man who unknowingly planted it, Emmet McCain, a pony express rider who carried the mail between Sand Springs and Fort Churchill.

In 1861, while McCain was riding his route with the mail, he was pursued by Indians. In his mail pouch were important government documents, and as a rider's first thought was always of the mail, McCain wanted to save that, at all costs.

He was crossing the Carson Sink where the ground was damp and swampy in places. Hastily dropping the mail pouch into the mud, he trampled it out of sight with his horse's hoofs. In his hand was a cottonwood switch he had cut while crossing the Carson River. He jammed this into the moist earth beside the mail pouch to mark its location.

He was overtaken and went down under their fire.

Rescuers found and removed the mail pouch, but left the slender switch beside it undisturbed. It took root in the damp soil and grew into the beautiful tree which stands there, alone, until this day.

K. D. EVANS, Portland, Oregon

~ 334 ~

Powder Blast Scares Indian

My great-grandfather Hastings was an early settler in the Willamette Valley in Oregon, where he took up a donation land claim. There were many Indians living nearby, and for some time after Grandfather and his family settled there they were bothered by the Indians, who would steal anything they could carry.

Grandfather cured them of this habit, however, and at the same time acquired a reputation as a first-class medicine man himself. It happened accidentally and without the least intention on his part.

He was clearing land one day, taking out stumps on a piece of land that had been cut. He had just put some blasting powder under a stump, set the fuse afire and retired to a safe distance to await the blast. He noticed an Indian coming across the field directly toward the smoldering fuse.

Grandfather yelled a warning, but instead of stopping, the Indian started to run--straight toward the stump, which was due to blow up any moment. Again Grandfather shouted and started after him, trying to make him understand his danger. But the frightened Indian only ran faster.

He was almost up to the stump when the charge exploded. The blast knocked him down, but he was not seriously hurt and he had scrambled to his feet by the time Grandfather reached him. He stood there trembling, scared half to death, begging Grandfather not to hurt him anymore. And then, Grandfather noticed that he had been carrying an axe he had picked up with the intention of carrying off.

This was the reason he was trying to get away. He was convinced that Grandfather had seen him making off with the axe and had stopped him by some kind of white man's powerful magic.

CLELLA STILLWELL, Portland, Oregon

~ 335 ~

Indian Girl Rejects Parent's Choice

Early one morning, about the year 1858, a young Indian maid came running to our door, begging us to hide her, as her father had sold her to an old blind Indian for thirty ponies.

Much against their better judgment, my parents put her between a corner bedstead and the wall and threw back the covers. Soon the Indians stopped by to inquire about the run-away girl. Father, first treating them to bread and molasses, called his own hounds and addressed them in his most guttural German. He told the Indian girl's father that the dogs understood, and, if she had not escaped, they would find her.

Then the Indian mounted his own horse and hunted for her until nightfall before he gave it up, after making many threats as to what he would do to her if he should find her.

A week passed before Father had a chance to smuggle her to Oregon City, into the care of a friend, Sydney Moss, where she worked in seclusion while Mr. Moss negotiated, in her behalf, among his Indian friends.

That fall, a "hello" brought my mother to the door to be greeted rapturously by the young Indian girl who leaned back and pointed to a stalwart young buck riding with her, leading thirty fine ponies and six dogs.

With much glee, she assured my mother that this one was not blind. Asked if she were not afraid to go home, she said, "No, all Father wants is the price--and no one cares what becomes of the old blind Indian!"

MINERVA THESSSING OLDFIELD, Milwaukie, Oregon

"When Oregon Went Berserk"

EPISODE 6 of 6

An Account of Ten Spectacular Years (1855-1865) When the Northwest Was Host to War, Greed and Death

By JOHN W. KELLY, Staff Writer, *The Oregonian*, October 18, 1936

Introduction

The years preceding and following 1860 were indeed "roaring years" for Oregon. The conclusion of the Indian wars and opening of Eastern Oregon and Washington to settlers brought the discovery of gold and the influx of thousands of miners.

On the heels of the prospectors came gamblers, outlaws, and murderers to plague the land until the formation of the Vigilantes.

This is the last of a series of articles on the historic era "When Oregon Went Berserk."

EPISODE 6

No Degrees of Crime—Any Crime—One Punishment—Hanging!

During 1864, Vigilantes were being organized in every settlement and mining town in Eastern Oregon, Eastern Washington, Idaho and

Western Montana—throughout the area of the gold discoveries in the old Oregon Country. Throwing open to settlement the interior country, the region east of the Cascade Mountains, following the suppression of the great Indian uprising, resulted in gold finds on every creek and stream. With the prospectors and miners came the murderers, horse thieves and robbers who were so well organized into a secret outlaw gang that law-abiding citizens resorted to the rope to make life and property safer.

Vigilantes reached their peak and decline in 1864-65. By the end of the latter year the old Oregon Country was fairly well cleansed of its criminal element. Having lynched twenty-one in the months of December and January, the Vigilantes began taking in more territory.

Sheriff Henry Plummer, leader of 130 "chiefs" and "road agents," who had killed and robbed one hundred men, was captured finally by Vigilantes, and, on a cold day in February, 1864, was hanged at Bannock, being one of 27 strung up. The sheriff begged for his life. He had the ability to organize the law-enforcement agencies into a gang of oath-bound desperadoes, but Plummer was craven at heart.

Another victim of that Roman holiday of the Vigilantes was Boon Helm, who had journeyed from The Dalles to Salt Lake City in the dead of winter when General Harney opened the up-country after the punishment of the Indians. Helm joined with a gang of horse thieves in Utah who accepted this cannibal. Boon Helm naturally gravitated to the crime syndicate of Sheriff Plummer. Newspaper reports say Helm died "shouting three cheers for Jeff Davis." The Oregonian said Helm had committed several murders in the mines in the eastern part of the state.

On the physical body of Sheriff Plummer was a list of eighty-five names of gang members and a record of their murders and robberies. He was systematic. On Plummer's list were the names of Doc Howard and Jim Romaine of The Dalles, William Page of Klickitat, and Chris Lowey, all of whom were hanged for the Lloyd Magruder murder three weeks after Plummer was left dangling from a tree. Magruder had been a trader at The Dalles.

Men of Touchet and Copper River organized Vigilante committees in Washington and started for the Snake River area to put the fear of death in the hearts of bandits. Similar committees were formed along the Walla Walla River.

W. J. Connell, a farmer at Payette, Idaho, across the river from Ontario, resented having his horses stolen. Accompanied by two friends, he pursued the thieves into the vicinity of La Grande, Oregon, found their hideout, and attacked--killing three. The fourth man, the leader, was wounded. From this man Connell obtained names of horse thief organizations which were active even into the Rogue, Umpqua, and Willamette River valleys, with their secret grips, signs and passwords. Then Connell shot him down. Armed with this information, Connell announced that he was ready to recover any horses reported stolen. He had the roster of the society of thieves and where the members could be located.

In addition to highwaymen and horse thieves the diggings were infested with counterfeiters. They counterfeited only gold dust. Payette, Idaho organized its vigilance committee in an underground warehouse, and then began looking for the counterfeiters. These latter scattered, some going to the Grand Ronde Valley, others to the bustling and rich camp at Auburn, Baker County, Oregon. Still others went to Walla Walla and down the Columbia River to The Dalles.

The criminals who operated in the Burnt River and Payette River areas were well organized and had complete equipment for masquerading as Indians. This Indian disguise gave origin to the designation of highwaymen as "chiefs." Vigilantes also disguised as blanket Indians causing additional confusion. Through their connections with the law "enforcement" officers, the gangsters caused the false arrest of members of the "committee of safety" at Payette, Idaho. They were then taken to Boise, identified and later released.

Vigilantes from Walla Walla chased horse thieves from that section into the Blue Mountains near Umatilla and did a hanging job. Occasionally the self-appointed executioners were in error. They lynched William Stoughton on the Umatilla River, later discovering that he was innocent. Passions flared and men saw red.

April 12th, 1865, two men were captured at Wallula for horse stealing and hanged near the Walla Walla River. April 16, Walla Walla vigilantes hanged a cattle thief. April 18, a Negro horse thief was lynched. He had served a term in the Oregon Penitentiary and had killed another Negro man in Boise Basin. When *The Oregonian*, April 21, said fifteen were hanged at Walla Walla, citizens there were indignant and charged *The Oregonian* with gross exaggeration—only six were strangled to death.

Despite the activities of the hanging crews, the outlaws were continuing their banditry. A man named Updike had been elected sheriff of Boise Basin, and he followed in the footsteps of the late Plummer. Desperadoes in the basin held complete sway. There were sixty violent deaths and not one conviction. Incendiarism was added to other outrages. One town was almost completely wiped out. Any man with a poke of gold was not safe.

Fate was weaving a web for Ferdinand J. Patterson, gambler. Born in Texas, Patterson went to California in 1850, was shot at Yreka and at Sailor Diggings and later killed a man named Staples in Portland in 1861. In Boise he scalped his lady friend while attempting to cut off her hair. Patterson also had killed Sheriff Sumner Pinkerton in Idaho City. Vigilantes decided the killer had lived long enough, so they moved to present him with the gift of a necktie of rope.

Officers kept Patterson safe in jail until he was tried—and acquitted. Then Patterson moved to Walla Walla, where he thought the climate would be healthier. Tom Donovan, watchman of a hotel, on orders from the Payette Committee of Safety, assassinated Patterson. Donovan was tried, and the jury, which included members of the Vigilantes, disagreed and Tom went to San Francisco. There he was arrested and returned to Walla Walla, via Portland, only to be released.

A robber gang began operating near Boise City and in Port Neuf Canyon, near Fort Hall. Ben Holladay's stage coaches were being held up, passengers were robbed and strong boxes looted. The road agents disguised themselves as Indians. Hay at Holladay's stations was burned; horses stolen. Holladay was mad. He had good and loyal employees and they helped arouse the sentiment for reprisals against the highwaymen. Holladay's mail contract with the U.S. government carried his stages to Burnt River, across the Blue Mountains to Grande Ronde and Walla Walla.

Detectives of the vigilantes eventually unmasked Sheriff Updike as the leader of the gang of outlaws. From a tree on Sirup Creek, south of Boise City, swung the body of the sheriff on an April day. On his chest was a pinned a notice: "Aider of murderers and thieves. This fatal example has no terror for the innocent, but let the guilty beware and not delay too long and take warning." The card was signed "XXX."

Down Sirup Creek next day were found the remains of Jacob Dixon, former sheriff of Shasta County, California. Again "XXX" signed a note, which, according to the *Owyhee Avalanche*, read, "Counterfeiter, horse thief, road agent generally."

The legal law-enforcement agencies were no longer in the hands of outlaws, such as horse thieves, highwaymen, chiefs and their ilk. The organized bandits were disappearing. Secret, silent and swift were the avengers. At times the Vigilantes were too enthusiastic and refused to draw a distinction between a gambler and a gunman. There were no degrees of crime and but one punishment for every offense, whether major or minor—hanging.

Bold and self-satisfied the Vigilantes became. In the *Walla Walla Statesman*, they published a notice announcing they had been organized for more than a year, boasted of amending their former plan of organization so that they could "act more expeditiously and with greater certainty in ferreting out the perpetrators of the crimes—no matter what grade—and the interest of all good, well-disposed and law-abiding persons; and we make no distinction between officer and private, rich or poor, or Vigilante or anti-Vigilante. All are subjects for our action in the way of crime, and will receive equal justice at our hands."

That published notice gives an idea how seriously the Vigilantes were taking themselves. They were arresting officer, judge, jury, prosecutor, and executioner. Many times the three middle positions were ignored.

Swan song of the Vigilantes, that published announcement may be considered, and brought to a close the most sensational era of the old Oregon Country. High-handed and ruthless the committees of safety were, whether on the banks of the Walla Walla, the Clearwater, the Snake, the Owyhee, or Burnt rivers. It was a time and age when the up-country was no place for softies; life was hard and cheap.

A strange commentary on that period was the relative ease with which the criminal class voted associates into office. This was accomplished by the simple practice of a few men knowing what they wanted and acting in correlation against an unorganized majority. The outlaws assumed leadership and with none to dispute them they readily elected their peace officers at the miners' meetings.

While the transient prospectors stood mutely around, the desperados proposed the Plummers and Upkikes for sheriff and by victorious vote carried the election. It was as elementary as that. A half-dozen horse thieves could elect a friendly sheriff before a hundred puzzled gold hunters knew what was going on.

In the light of events and the piecing together of fragmented clues, it would appear that the outlaws from The Dalles to Bannock and from Salt Lake City to the Willamette Valley were more or less in a loosely connected federation of criminal societies. The membership roll of Henry Plummer carried the names of desperados from Portland to the western slopes of the Rocky Mountains. The roster of the horse thieves taken by Connell from the lists in Grand Ronde Valley revealed a group intermingling with the Plummer crime syndicate. Horse thieves preyed in Western Oregon, Northern California, Northern Nevada, Western Utah, Idaho and Eastern Oregon and Washington. Stealing a horse was more serious than stealing an automobile today.

Probably some bandit with a flair for the dramatic conceived the idea of an oath-bound society for mutual protection. Secret signs and pass-words followed logically. It was natural that the gamblers should join the bandits and highwaymen in a common cause against their prey, the miners and traders with gold.

In the face of such organization it required desperate courage for the first committee of safety to be formed. More than one Vigilante was rubbed out by friends of some victim of a necktie party, or in Auburn at the lynching of the Spanish killer from Powder River. Donovan, who disposed of Patterson at Walla Walla by order from the Vigilantes, met death at the hands of Patterson's friends.

Guarded sacredly to the present day is the roster of the Vigilantes. Names of a number of leaders became known, for on occasion they performed their job publicly and without masks, but in the written records available, no general identification is made. Connell wrote a manuscript recounting his experiences, but he was careful not to involve others.

Thus the span of a decade closed with the disbanding of the self-appointed crusaders and reformers. For ten years the old Oregon Country had experienced one thing after another; an era of Indian outrage, of fabulous gold discoveries, of outlaws representing law and order, and of the avenging Vigilantes. It required but a few lynchings by the San Francisco committee of safety to make a peaceful community. Ten times that number were swung east of the Cascades in the gold fields.

And of Auburn, where Vigilantes first appeared, not a trace remains today no matter where you may look in Baker County. It is symbolic of that era, living only in memory of a few old-timers (who have since passed on) and the ancient files of dusty newspapers.

JOHN W. KELLY, Staff Writer, *The Oregonian*

~ 336 ~

Dead Man's Glasses Save Pioneer's Life

My grandfather, who came across the plains in a wagon train in 1868, once told me of an encounter they had with Indians while making the trip. They were on the Snake River in Southern Idaho when the Indian's attacked.

Before the travelers could assemble into a protective formation, the Indians had killed several of them. Grandfather's partner went down in this first attack and Grandfather stopped to aid him. He was beyond human aid, however, as an arrow had penetrated his chest killing him almost instantly.

Grandfather saw the chief, who had been riding at the head of the band of Indians, stop his pony and scalp this man. He waved his gruesome trophy aloft with a yell. Then, before mounting again, Grandfather saw him stoop down and take off the pair of glasses his partner was wearing and put them upon his own nose.

Outraged, Grandfather forgot his own danger for the moment and rode straight toward the chief, who turned to meet him. He had an arrow in his hand ready to fit in the bow, but the glasses must have been out of focus and confused him, for he fumbled with the arrow and dropped it. Grandfather immediately shot him from his horse.

Afterward he realized the foolish chance he had taken. He knew he would have been killed just as his partner had been if the Indian's sight had not been hampered by his friend's spectacles.

CHARLES OBER, Portland, Oregon

~ 337 ~

Plug of Tobacco Repulses Indian

Early settlers in the West had to be diplomats as well as frontiersmen in order to succeed in their personal struggle to establish themselves. An illustration of this is told, how a thoughtless gesture cost my father his home.

He settled in Klamath County, Oregon, when it was still inhabited mostly by Indians, and white settlers were very scarce. After much work, he succeeded in hauling a large wagon load of lumber, from a distant sawmill, to build a house.

On the day before he was to start on the house, an Indian passed by. Father stopped what he was doing, sat and talked with him for a while. As they were talking, Father pulled a plug of tobacco out of his pocket, cut off a chew and offered the plug to the man who accepted it and cut a large chew for himself.

He put it in his mouth and they talked for a few minutes more until Father noticed that the man had swallowed the tobacco. Not realizing that this was the Indian's first encounter with chewing tobacco, Father thought little of it until it became clear that the man was in distress and getting sick to his stomach.

The Indian stopped talking abruptly and stalked away quickly, not wanting Father to see how the tobacco had affected him.

That night, the lumber that father was going to use to build his house was completely destroyed. He later learned that the Indian, thinking Father had tricked him, had returned--and for revenge set it afire .

C. GREER, Portland, Oregon

~ 338 ~

Woman Rescues Settlers' Flour

Among the very early shipwrecks on the Columbia River Bar was the schooner *Woodpecker*, wrecked on Clatsop Spit in 1848. It had a cargo of flour for the settlers on the Clatsop plains.

The settlers, knowing that she would soon go to pieces, set about to save the flour, at that time priced at $12.00 a fifty pound sack. The weather was unsettled and they could work only a short time during the last part of the ebb tide, as the waves were breaking over the schooner most of the time.

On the second day, they had succeeded only partially in cutting open the hatch when they were driven away by a strong wind and incoming tide. They found it impossible to make a landing on the beach and were forced to take shelter in Tansy Creek.

In the party were B. C. Kindred and his two sons. Mr. Kindred was a pioneer of 1845 and had taken up a donation land claim near what is now known as Hammond, Oregon. They were congratulating themselves on having secured seven sacks of flour and were content to wait for the turn of the tide and decreasing winds, later in the evening.

Mrs. Kindred, becoming worried about the non-arrival of her husband and boys, went down to the beach to look for their boats. In the meantime, the flood tide had completed the work begun by the men and had broken up the deck and floated out the entire cargo.

When Mrs. Kindred reached the beach there was not a boat in sight, but she saw something that looked like a flock of white birds riding the waves. The tidal waves were bringing the *Woodpecker's* cargo ashore.

Later in the evening, Mr. Kindred and the boys landed with their cargo of seven sacks to find 360 sacks landed and stacked on the beach by Mrs. Kindred, who was still watching for and stray sacks that might come within her reach.

JOHN DOANE, Marshfield, Oregon

~ 339 ~

Horse Raiders Change Minds

The Bannock-Piute Indian raid in Eastern Oregon and Idaho in June and July of 1878, was taken advantage of by wandering, pilfering bands of renegade whites and half-breeds who infested the country traversed by the hostile Indians. These unprincipled wretches butchered cattle and sheep, taking only the choice portions and leaving the balance as carrion for buzzards and coyotes. Homes of fleeing settlers were pillaged, horses stolen and many crimes committed by these renegades. Naturally the blame was laid onto the hostile Indians.

One such party of twenty-five outlaws, under the leadership of the notorious horse-rustler "Rattlesnake Jack," thoroughly combed the hostile regions and landed in Wyoming with over three-hundred stolen horses.

An attempt by several well-known citizens of Pendleton, Oregon to "grab" a bunch of these stolen horses from the Indians had a very ludicrous termination.

A report had been circulated that a large band of Indian cayuses and stolen horses was being guarded by a few Indians on the open prairie about five miles northeast of Pendleton. This was an opportunity not to be missed to get a few horses from the Indians, just for the taking, and at the same time, even up past scores.

Half a dozen men obtained mounts and rifles and sallied forth to accomplish their goal. Among the men attempting this "coup" were James Jacobs, Samuel Tillard and J. H. Turner. Jacobs rode one of his thoroughbred race horses. The others were all on good mounts except Tillard and Turner. These two were each astride mules they had hired from a freighter.

About an hour after their departure, a streak of dust on the north hillside and a broken line of mounted men rapidly descending the hill into town, minus any extra horses, indicated that something unforeseen had taken place.

Tillard and Turner, on their faithful but slow-going mules brought up the rear. As they afterward recounted their exciting experiences; they had discarded their useless rifles and could almost swear that there was an Indian jumping up and shooting at them from behind every sagebrush during that five-mile run. They also had suddenly arrived at the conclusion that they really didn't want any horses after all, and were only interested in returning home--by the most rapid transit possible.

J. L. SHARON, Vancouver, Washington

~ 340 ~

Pioneer Sheriff Has Troubles

My grandfather, John Gordon Baker, came to Oregon in 1843 and settled on a donation land claim near McMinnville, becoming the first settler between the north and south forks of the Yamhill River.

He became the first Sheriff of Yamhill County, under Oregon's Provisional Government, and held the post four years. Many unusual experiences happened to him as the law-enforcement officer of this new and unsettled area.

In 1852, a man named McCormack was tried, found guilty and sentenced to serve three years imprisonment. However, from the lack of either a state or county prison, the judge remanded the prisoner to the care of the sheriff, to be kept until the County Commissioners could meet and provide some sort of incarceration. Grandmother often had to watch McCormack while Grandfather went about other duties.

However, when the commissioners met, they neglected to take action in the case, so the judge gave my grandfather private instructions that the vigilance should be relaxed and, to relieve the sheriff of the task of keeping him, the prisoner allowed to escape.

Such was the working of justice in pioneer days.

M. WINIFRED BOYD, Portland, Oregon

~ 341 ~

Indian Woman Frightens Herder

I don't claim to be one of the old scouts that killed Indians by the score, but I did actually shoot at one Indian, and my poor aim saved me a lot of trouble.

When I was a lad of about sixteen years, I signed up to go on a horse drive with some other boys, all older than I. They told me so many stories about Indians that my nerves were all on edge. We had one-hundred-fifty horses, and night herded them, with two boys each night, by shifts, one until midnight, and the other from midnight until morning.

My first night came as we were southeast of Pendleton, Oregon, near the Blue Mountains. When I started out with the herd, the boys warned me to be on the lookout for Indians and keep my six-shooter handy. It was just before dark, as I was slowly riding around the herd, when I heard the horses on the opposite side of the herd squeal and start to mill. I rode around the herd and saw a lone Indian riding away with two horses. I pulled my gun and quickly fired two shots, then rode back to camp and yelled, "Indians!"

The boys all mounted and gave chase. Then came back laughing. What I thought was a wild Indian was only a young Indian woman leading two of her pack ponies. Luckily, I hadn't hit her.

OWEN THOMPSON, Camp Sherman, Oregon

~ 342 ~

Woman Recovers Stolen Bossy

The first white settlers to take up a donation land claim, farthest south in the Willamette Valley, were John Killin and his brave wife.

They owned a cow, which furnished the principal part of their living. She was kept, staked out, where the grass was best. One evening, when John went to bring her in at milking time, he found the rope cut and the cow had disappeared. They suspected that Indians had stolen her.

Next morning, Mrs. Killin insisted that her husband find the cow and bring her back home. John found tracks, which he followed to an Indian village, about five miles distant, where he saw his cow staked out, peacefully grazing. He asked the Indians for her but was told he could not have her, so he returned home without the cow.

His spunky little wife said, "We've got to have that cow John. What will we do with a baby coming and no milk?" Next morning, Mrs. Killin didn't say much, and John took his ax and went to work in the woods, as usual. His wife took her big butcher-knife and started for the Indian village.

She was tired and cross after her long walk, and when she saw the cow staked out, she went straight to her, cut the rope, threw the loose coils of the rope over her arm and started off, leading her cow. Some Indians yelled at her, and a young brave started toward her, but she waved her long knife at him threateningly and he stopped. Mrs. Killin and her cow kept getting farther and farther away from the village.

The other Indians jeered at the young brave, but he said, "White woman have heap strong heart." The Killins kept their cow and were not further molested by their Indian neighbors.

MINNIE ROOF DEE, Portland, Oregon

~ 343 ~

Emigrants Rescue Foot Traveler

My grandfather, Charles E. Fendall, left for Oregon in the spring of 1843 under the guidance of Captain John Nesmith. The greater part of the journey, he rode astride a horse, and he was one of the hunters for the party, his skill with the gun resulting in the replenishment of many empty larders.

While on one of his hunting expeditions, ahead of the train, he was surprised to see a young man, about his own age, with a pack on his shoulders, making his way toward the east--not west. The young fellow informed him his name was Sitton. (Later he was known all over the Willamette Valley as "Uncle Doc" Sitton.)

He had left with an emigrant train earlier in the spring. Sitton told my grandfather the story that one night, while on guard duty, he aroused the train by shooting at what he believed to be an Indian, but when the incident was investigated, he had shot the wagon train captain's mule.

The captain was very angry and ordered him back across the plains--alone and on foot.

Grandfather gave him a ride back to the Nesmith train and they were buddies from then on. On their arrival in Oregon, they spent the winter on Panther Creek near McMinnville--and a few years later married sisters.

JACK FENDALL, Willamina, Oregon

"Northwest Empire Builders"

SIMON BENSON

The All-Steam Bunyan That Was a Mighty Logger

By STEWART H. HOLBROOK, A personal acquaintance of Mr. Simon Benson. May 12, 1935

Two somewhat heretical opinions acquired early in life, and from which he deviated not one inch, so long as he was engaged in business, played no small part in Simon Benson's amazingly successful career.

One was that he would not always be able to buy fine virgin timber for $5.00 an acre. The other, that bull teams and skid roads were not necessarily the ultimate method of cheap and efficient logging.

Coming to the United States from his native Norway in 1867, Benson stopped ten years in Wisconsin on his way to the Pacific Coast. Ten years was long enough for a shrewd young man to see what was taking place in the lumber industry of this country.

He observed that the tall spruce of Main had been pretty much felled years before, and that the horde of loggers had swept through New York and Pennsylvania like a forest fire and on into the Lake states, where even then the excellent white pine was falling like wheat before the onslaught of axes and saws.

Young Benson had never seen such logging in Norway. Over there, the forests had been logged, true enough, and for many centuries, yet new trees had always been planted as the old ones were cut. Here in now, American loggers were as a host of locusts, driving swiftly westward and leaving nothing behind them but stumps and a few rusting cantdogs on river bottoms.

Thus, when the young immigrant came to Portland in 1879 and sighted the mighty stand of Douglas fir which grew almost down to the very porch of the Overland Hotel at First and Couch Street, he knew what to do. The time, place and the man had been brought together.

In 1852, Simon Bergerson was born on a little farm near Lillbraner in south central Norway, one of four brothers and three sisters. Early in 1861, his oldest brother, and later his sister, emigrated to America and settled in Wisconsin. They saved their money and by the spring of 1867, they had done so well, they sent passage money to the folks at home who immediately took ship for the new world and Wisconsin.

About the first thing the Bergersons did was to have their name changed to Benson. Simon Benson once told a writer, "We wanted to be good Americans and have a good American name, a name which could be remembered and pronounced without difficulty.

"I still think that all foreigners who come here to live should simplify their names if they are hard to pronounce. If not on their own account, then for the sake of their children. I don't believe in keeping up any old world names, or traditions, or prejudices."

The trip to America cost the Bensons $10 a head and required five weeks. Simon got a job working on a farm near Black River Falls, Wisconsin soon as he had arrived there. The farmer told him he would pay him $2 more a month as soon as he could speak English. Within three months, young Simon had qualified and his pay was raised to $20 a month.

Until 1874, Benson worked in logging camps during the winter and in sawmills the rest of the time. Then, in 1875 he met and married Esther Searles at Lynxville and started a small general store at that place. The store did very well, as long as it lasted. In 1879, it was destroyed by fire—building, stock and records. With his wife and baby Amos, he struck out for Oregon, where he had heard such timber a man had never seen before.

Leaving wife and baby at the Overland Hotel in Portland, Benson went out to look for a job. Someone told him a lot of logging was being done near St. Helens. On the boat for St. Helens, he got to talking with a man who turned out to be John Beavis, a logging operator, who had a camp on Tide Creek. He hired out to Beavis at $40 a month. Two months later, Beavis raised his pay to $60.

Benson's wife and son now came to join him at Tide Creek, and Benson spent the winter felling tall Douglas Fir; taller stuff than he had ever seen in Wisconsin or Norway.

Along with his muscle work, young Benson did some thinking. In the spring, which was 1880, he made a very small down payment on a timber tract of 160 acres, for which he agreed to pay $5 an acre, or $800 in all. On this land stood not less, and probably more than 6,000,000 feet of fir which had been growing there since before the first Spanish explorers sailed up the West Coast.

In the best pioneer tradition, young Benson cleared a space in the dark forest, built a cabin and made a garden. Then he went to Sam Miles of St. Helens. Miles had a lot of cattle. Benson told Miles, "If you will let me have six of those unbroken steers, I will break them to work. If I find I can't pay you for them, you can have your steers back and you will get more for them as oxen than you would for beef."

Benson took the steers to his clearing, slapped homemade yokes onto them, cut himself a goad stick, and within a month they knew which was "Buck" and which was "Star," while young Benson had, no doubt, learned the magic words and terms which drive the devils out of unruly steers and make them into skid road oxen.

A cautious storekeeper from St. Helens came out to look the outfit over, listened to the glowing plans of the ox-teamster and agreed to let him have supplies on credit. The young, would-be logging operator then hired a man for $30 a month and board. Soon there was the crash of falling firs, followed by the clanking of chains and bellowing of oxen as the first turn of logs creaked and rolled over the skidway down to the broad Columbia River. The Benson Timber Company was in the making.

For the next three years, Benson sold his logs to the old North Pacific Lumber Company of Portland. He paid for his claim and all the equipment and still put some money in the bank.

Late in 1883, Mrs. Benson became ill. Physicians advised a change to a drier climate. Benson sold his Columbia County holdings for $5,000 and took his family to Colfax, in Eastern Washington, where he took a job as foreman in a sawmill. The climate, however, did Esther Benson no good and she died in Colfax in 1891..

After paying doctors' bills, Benson had just enough money to carry him and his family, now a boy and two girls, to his old stomping ground in Columbia County. He might have been broke, but his credit was still good. He got some timber at Reuben, now known as Goble, and went to logging on a larger scale than heretofore. In two years, he had paid for everything and had $3,000 in the bank.

The Portland firm of Ordway & Weidler, which had been buying Benson's logs, offered to sell him a stand of 4,000 acres of timber in Cathlamet, Washington district, but Benson did not have enough money to swing the deal. Thereupon the three went into a partnership, with Benson in charge of the logging. This was in 1891.

Benson had seen enough of bull team logging to know that it was slow and expensive. Although they thought they could scarcely afford the risk of trying something new, Benson came to Portland and picked up a batch of second-hand rails, some trucks and a small locomotive, which had seen better days, by far, but which would still run.

He paid $6,000 for this collection of old iron. It cost the group another $4,000 to lay a mile of steel into the Cathlamet timber. $10,000 shot, and not a log in the water. One can easily imagine the shaking of heads by solid, conservative businessmen who knew it was God's plan to log timber with oxen and not with a steam locomotive. It was heresy of the worst kind.

It was good-paying heresy, though, and four years later, the partners had paid for everything and were $20,000 in the clear. The rising firm now undertook to buy and pay for what many old-time Columbia River loggers will tell you was the finest logging show ever seen since King Solomon sent his lumberjacks into the cedars around Lebanon.

It was near Oak Point on the lower Columbia, and loggers who helped cut it, still talk about that logging show. Benson and his partners paid 50 cents a thousand board feet for it.

But the lumber market went to pot. "General" Jacob Coxey, and his army, had been repulsed at Washington. Gene Debs' "rebellion" had been put down by General Miles in Chicago, and the smoke of the battle of Homestead had wafted away. Yet the country was to struggle through three more years of hard times.

First Ordway sold his interest to Benson and Weidler. Then Weidler sold his half to Benson for $33,000. To acquire sole title to the firm, Benson borrowed $18,000 from the Portland produce firm of Everding & Farrell.

With a lone hand, Benson decided to carry his machinery heresy even further than logging by locomotive. He sold the last of his oxen, those which had been used for yarding logs to the railroad, and put the money, with much more, into donkey engines.

All that doesn't sound like much in 1935, yet in 1896 it was the next thing to trying to fly in a machine. It is true that donkey engines had been tried out in the woods, both in the lake states and here on the coast, but the results had been costly and discouraging. Benson had no trouble in buying his donkeys cheap.

What happened next was told to this writer a few years ago by Mr. Benson himself:

"My camp at Oak Point was the first all-steam logging show in the Pacific Northwest," he said. "By using steam, I reduced my logging costs by more than half. With railroad and oxen, my total cost of putting logs in the water had been $4.50 a thousand feet. With donkeys and railroad, the cost was only $2.15. I cleared $75,000 during my first year at Oak Point."

Benson continued logging at Oak Point until 1908, and then moved across the Columbia River into the country back of Clatskanie, Oregon. Here he had acquired a vast timber tract of 46,000 acres, on which was standing 2,500,000,000 board feet, or an awful lot of timber. This stand had not been bought in one purchase, but in piecemeal from homesteaders.

"Whenever a settler wanted to sell his homestead," Mr. Benson has told, "I would pay him from $1,500 to $2,000 for it. Most of the logging operators laughed and said I was crazy to pay such fabulous sums. It wasn't long before any homesteader who wanted to sell out would come to me. I always bought."

During the years Benson continued to buy and use the newest and best equipment that was to he had. Every kind of appliance that had any sort of promise to it at all was sure of a welcome at Benson's camp. When bigger donkeys were built, he bought them. The wire rope on the ground lead was the strongest available. No better grub was served on the river.

Employees were treated as human beings. Wages were always just as high, and sometimes a bit higher than at other camps. I didn't get this particular information from Mr. Benson, but from men who used the wire rope and ate the food and got the wages.

Six dollars per thousand feet was pretty much the standard price of sawlogs on the Columbia River early in the century. Benson went after the export trade, which required special lengths and sizes, receiving from $10 to $12 a thousand for his logs. California was on a boom. Benson thought the coastal freight rates too high.

Down in the quiet of Wallace Slough, on the Columbia, Benson, with O. J. Everson and J. A. Fastabend, went to work building a strange seagoing monster. It was the very first of the long line of Benson log rafts, different from any ocean-going log rafts which had gone down to the sea before.

The raft was cigar-shaped and contained a million board feet of logs. It also contained piling, timbers and several hundred thousand feet of sawn lumber. When it was towed into San Diego harbor, not a whit the worse for its 1,100 mile trip, the natives there thought Leviathan had arrived. Workmen quickly took the raft apart, picked out the sawn timbers and lumber, whacked up a good-sized sawmill and soon the remainder of the raft was being converted into lumber.

When the first Benson raft put out of Wallace Slough, there was the same wagging of heads among solid, conservative businessmen as there had been when Benson put steam into the woods. But year after year, the Benson rafts have left the Columbia and arrived at San Diego, most of them carrying between 4,000,000 and 5,000,000 board feet of logs each. Only two of them got into trouble on the way, but they were salvaged by being towed into Santa Cruz.

"The rafts saved me $2 a thousand on freight, or around $150,000 a year," was the way Mr. Benson once explained.

In 1910, Benson sold his timber holdings, logging equipment and the mill at San Diego for $5,000,000, and thought he had retired. But he hadn't. He built the hotel in Portland which bears his name. It immediately began losing money faster than he ever had made it, he has often told, so he took over the management himself.

He must have applied to the hotel the same efficiency he brought to the woods, for in three years' time it was out of the red and making a good profit. He then sold it for close to a million dollars.

All Portlander's know the drinking fountains on downtown street corners which were given to the city by Mr. Benson, but not everyone knows the story back of them.

"One of the troubles I had in my logging camps," Mr. Benson told the writer, "was the Monday morning hangovers of loggers getting drunk Saturdays and Sundays in Portland. There wasn't a place in town where a man could get a drink of water unless by asking for it in a restaurant or store, something people do not like to do.

"I thought that if good, clean, cold water was put where anybody could drink it, a lot of men who ordinarily would have gone into a saloon for a glass of beer would drink the water instead. That's why I built the fountains." They are now known as "Benson Bubblers."

Fearing, rightfully, that such beautiful spots up the Columbia River Gorge as Multnomah and Wahkeena Falls were sure to attract hotdog stands and mammy's chicken shacks, Mr. Benson bought the land around the falls (400 acres) and deeded it to the City of Portland as a public park.

When he saw, as he did very early, that the automobile was to supplant the horse, just as the donkey engines had supplanted the oxen of the skidroad, he became an active and generous worker for paved highways, especially one along the Columbia River Gorge. He served as Chairman of the first Oregon State Highway Commission.

Although Simon Benson had done very well in life on the meager formal education he received in a district school in Norway, he was not, as are so many "self-made" men, contemptuous of education. An education to him meant a better way of doing things, rather than the abstract benefits which are derived from the higher classical learning.

Vulgarly speaking, he would seem to have come to the same skeptical conclusion, only much sooner, which is currently creeping into the minds of pedagogues, namely, that many an able housewife, plumber and electrician has been ruined by the Greek and Latin and esthetic dancing piped into them early in life. So, the Benson Polytechnical School was founded in Portland with a generous endowment from the logger who monkeyed with locomotives, donkeys and oceangoing rafts. The school is very much a going concern.

Simon married Pamelia Loomis in 1894. They had two sons, Gilbert and Chester. For the past several years, Mr. Benson has lived in Beverly Hills, near Los Angeles, California, where his mansion is one of the show places. Also in California are two sons, Amos and Chester. A daughter, Alice, is married and lives in Chehalis, Washington. The other married daughter, Caroline, lives in Vancouver, Washington.

At 83, Mr. Benson retains all the identical energy which marked his rise to the position of "tyee logger of the Columbia River." As this is being written, another of the long and continuous line of Benson-type log rafts is being put together for its trip south. Not far from Portland, in any direction, you can hear the snort and toot of a logging donkey, but you will listen in vain for the bellowing of skidroad oxen.

And there isn't any more virgin timber to be had at $5 an acre.

Simon Benson died in Los Angeles, California, August 5, 1942 at age 90. He was buried at River View Cemetery in Portland.

By STEWART H. HOLBROOK

~ 344 ~

Governor Was Full of Scraps

When the first Territorial Governor of Washington, Governor Isaac I. Stevens (1853-1857), first entered Olympia, the state capital, no sirens shrieked to announce his entrance. He had pushed ahead of his own party, and when he arrived alone, tired and hungry, he sought the only place that looked like a dining hall, but he was refused admission.

"We're goin' to have a doin's here," said the chef, "and we can't feed strangers 'till after it's over."

"Well, see here, I'm hungry. Can't you give me some of the scraps at the kitchen table?"

"Oh, yes, I guess we can do that."

After eating his dinner scraps in the kitchen, the governor walked out into the street. There he got into conversation with a man who complained about the slow arrival of the new governor. "I suppose I am the man you are looking for," Stevens admitted.

Satisfied that the small, travel-stained man was really the new governor, the man beat frantically on a circular saw that hung on a nearby post. This was the prearranged signal. Men came quickly from cabins and from their boats. They filed into the dining hall and placed the governor at the head of the table, but he sat, unable to eat a mouthful.

He was too full of scraps!

RUBY D. WHEELER, Aberdeen, Washington

~ 345 ~

Teamster Hides Watch on Horse

In the early 1870s, before the advent of a railroad on the west side of the Willamette River in Oregon, products raised for shipment in southern Yamhill County were hauled by team to Dayton, and from there, by boat to Portland. After grain harvest, nearly anyone who was able to drive a team could get a job hauling wheat, as the farmers were anxious to get their grain hauled before the fall rains set in.

A neighbor of my father hired one of my brothers, then about 12 years of age, to drive one of his teams. An itinerant worker who called himself Billy Barlow was also employed as driver for one of the wagons.

One day, while on one of their trips with a load of wheat to Dayton, they went to a general merchandise store in Dayton and looked at their stock of watches. Barlow told the merchant that after he sold his wheat, he would return and purchase a watch and chain.

A short way from Dayton, homeward bound, Barlow and my brother were overtaken by the merchant and an officer. The merchant accused them of stealing a watch and chain from his store and had come to search them.

After searching thoroughly their persons and wagons and not finding the watch, they were allowed to go on. When they arrived at the Harrison ranch that evening, Barlow went to the team my brother had been driving, and to the astonishment of the boy brought forth the watch and chain, which he had tied securely under one of the horse's manes.

He drew his wages the same evening and disappeared.

JOHN M. UMPHLETTE, Amity, Oregon

~ 346 ~

Daughters Offered as Doctor's Fee

One of the first Knights of the pill and lancet clan (doctors) to practice in Curry County, Oregon was a certain Dr. Hubbard. The good doctor was an adventurer who visited the main colony at the Rogue River during the spring of 1854 with the inspiration of raising a company of volunteers to aid William Walker in his conquest of Nicaragua. The following incident is the only record of his services to the community during his brief stay on the Rogue River.

An Indian chief, who lived a few miles up the river, attracted the doctor's attention, largely due to the fact that the old warrior had received a wound in the face, at the siege of Battle Rock which had almost closed his mouth when it healed. The chief was unable to talk and had to force his food through the small opening with his fingers

Dr. Hubbard finally succeeded in persuading the Indian that his white doctor magic would cure his troubles, and made good his promise by performing an operation that was highly successful.

A few weeks later, the old Indian chief turned up at the doctor's home, his face entirely healed, with his wife and two young daughters in tow. He made the doctor understand that he wished to present him with both daughters for services received.

Hubbard thought fast and quickly declined the offer by explaining that he already had a wife and no white man could have two. However, he hinted that his house guest, a young chap named Colt, was unmarried and could use a wife.

Colt promptly took to the woods on his horse and remained hidden until the old chief had left with his family. The doctor declared that romance must be dead when a lonesome young gold miner refuses the hand of a young princess, offered in gratitude by the ruling chieftain of the Rogue River Indian nation.

JACK C. WOODRUFF, Bandon, Oregon

~ 347 ~

New-Fangled Gun Scares Indian

During the early pioneer days, my uncle, Jim Weatherby, conducted a trading post in a small Eastern Oregon mining camp. He told me an amusing incident that happened in his place shortly after the new double-action revolvers were invented, taking the place of the old single-action guns.

Uncle Jim bought a supply of these new guns to sell at his post. They were quite a curiosity, at first, and nearly everyone who came into the place stopped to examine them. Consequently, he thought nothing of it when, one morning, as he was alone in the store, and Indian stopped to look at one of the weapons. Uncle Jim obligingly showed him how the action worked, explaining that it was now not necessary to cock it with the thumb and that a pull on the trigger was all that was necessary. He even put some live ammunition into it.

While he was thus engaged, a miner, plainly the worse for liquor, came into the store and wandered over to the hardware counter. Uncle Jim finished explaining the gun to the Indian and handed it to him to examine for himself. But the Indian had evidently missed some of the vital points on the training, because the first thing he did was to pull the trigger.

The gun discharged with a deafening roar and the bullet banged into a tin teakettle the inebriated miner had been inspecting, knocking it to the floor with an awful clatter. The poor fellow let out a yell and jumped back, just as the Indian dropped the revolver on the floor, where it discharged again, narrowly missing him.

The Indian tore out of the door, close behind the frightened miner, who looked back and saw him coming. This served only to increase his speed as he ran down the town's one street yelling, "The Indians are on the warpath!"

The Indian, unaware that he was the cause of the other's fright, and knowing only that he wanted to get out of that vicinity as soon as possible, came sailing along just one step behind the miner. While Uncle Jim, who was really the damaged party, stood in the doorway too weak from laughter to attempt to stop them as they disappeared from sight--still going strong.

KENNETH DAY, Portland, Oregon

~ 348 ~

Paint Betrays Horse Thieves

"Let your guns rest on your saddle horns and dismount. You're under arrest."

Such was the terse order given a couple of men from the Modoc lava beds one June day in 1874, suspected of entering a stable and riding off with a span of milk-white horses, a mare and a gelding, belonging to Uncle Bill Rogers, living near McMinnville, Oregon.

When the flurry succeeding the theft had partially subsided, although fences, barns and blacksmith shops, and the like, were being plastered with glaring posters for the arrest of the thieves, with a $500 reward attached, the twain crossed the Cascade Mountain Range, there to meet their Waterloo on the Deschutes and the hands of Lewis Garrison and W. C. Hembree, Yamhill County deputy sheriffs, armed with double-barreled sawed-off shotguns.

But for the gelding casting a shoe, and the resetting of it by a blacksmith at Lower Soda, Uncle Bill would have lost his horses for good, for at that time, Oregon was well filled with white horses answering the description of the stolen span.

While shoeing the gelding, the smith caught an unusual odor--that of fresh paint. This led to an important discovery, the existence of a covered-over scar. The smith lost no time in apprising the two deputies who chanced to be in Lebanon at the time, and the chase over the mountains was on.

Garrison and Hembree reached the bridge, where they went into hiding. As the unsuspecting outlaws cantered out on the bridge, Hembree rose from beneath the east approach, Garrison closed in from behind, and the jig was up.

When taken to Salem, both outlaws pleaded guilty and were given twenty year sentences. "Uncle Bill" Rogers was my father.

TOM H. ROGERS, McMinnville, Oregon

~ 349 ~

Trade Brings Dire Results

An old lady who crossed the plains to Oregon, when a young girl, once told me of her only vivid recollection of the trip; due, no doubt, to a child's love of the ridiculous, this incident stayed fresh in her mind while other, more dramatic events encountered on the long trip, were forgotten.

On the plains, the wagon train encountered a band of friendly Indians, one of whom admired a bright red blanket belonging to her father. He offered to trade a buffalo robe for it and her father agreed.

The Indian left to get the robe. As he was returning with it, another member of the train which had heard the bargain, intercepted him, and, seeing that the robe was a large, beautifully tanned one, persuaded the Indian to exchange it for a blanket belonging to him. The girl's father, rather than cause trouble, said nothing about it.

Before daybreak, the next morning, there was a commotion from the wagon where this fellow and his wife were sleeping. Their neighbors saw that they were industriously trying to get rid of the vermin that had crawled onto them from the buffalo robe. But this was not easily accomplished, and it was several days before the two quit scratching--and much longer before the wife let her husband forget the incident.

JENNIE GRAY, Portland, Oregon

~ 350 ~

Joe Meek's Position Made Big Difference

In the year 1856, an uprising of the Warm Springs Indians was threatened, and a call for volunteers to suppress them was made at The Dalles, to which eighty men responded. Each man was equipped with a muzzle-loading rifle, ammunition and a small supply of food. The volunteer was responsible for bringing his own blankets, his boots and a knife, if desired. A sturdy Indian pony was also issued to each.

Joe Meek, the famous mountain man, guide and trapper of the early Northwest, who was chosen Captain of the group, was somewhat swelled up over his commission. He concluded it would be impossible to maintain the dignity of his position—and Meek's large build, on an Indian pony, so he chose a large, gray, and somewhat stubborn mule for his mount.

After scouting for several days, and since there had been no signs of the warlike tribe, they decided to return home. As the volunteers were crossing an open stretch of country, on the farther side of which was a belt of timber, one of the scouts, glancing back, saw a band of about five hundred Indians, on their ponies, coming at full speed toward the whites.

Joe Meek took in the situation at a glance, and gave the order to make for the timber and stand off the Indians from there, as he could see that the enemy would be too many for them in an open field fight. The command was instantly obeyed. The men began to yell and the ponies began to travel as fast as possible.

Meek's dignified mule was slowly being left behind. He kept dropping farther and farther back, until there were fifty long yards between him and the last volunteer. This was too much for Joe. Waving his arms, he yelled at the top of his voice, "Halt! Halt! You damn cowards. What in hell are you running for? Stop and let's clean 'em up!"

The men either didn't hear or pay any attention to the order, but kept going straight ahead for the timber. By that time, the Indians were close enough to shoot. One old brave, rising up on his pony, shot an arrow which hit Meek's mule in the hind quarter, near its tail. The plodding mule gave a loud snort, doubled up and began to travel like the wind.

The distance between Captain Meek and his men lessened and the mule grew more and more excited. Meek and the gray mule charged right through the group and headed for the tall timber ahead. Meek began waving his arms and yelling, "Come on boys. For God's sake, run. There's more'n a million of them."

This time, the men obeyed the command. They reached the dense cover just in time, and, after some hard fighting, drove the Indians off. They returned to The Dalles, where more volunteers were called for at Portland, and, with the addition of the regular Army, the number of defenders numbered about one thousand. Then the Indians were only too willing to smoke the "peace pipe."

The gray mule recovered from the arrow wound, but this time Meek picked out a very fast, spirited horse for his new mount.

This story was told by my father, who came to Oregon in 1853. He was one of the group of eighty men mentioned in the account.

A. F. FELLOWS, Salem, Oregon

The stories they lived and shared
are the stories we read today.
Let us not forget what they did.

By Gentry W. Cutsforth

Most Memorable Story Quotes

1. "Malinda! Go in the house and take off those—those pants!"
2. "R-r-run? How the hell could I r-r-run?"
3. "Kill a steer, cut his hide into strips and splice them to the rope!"
4. "Are all white women stuffed with feathers?"
5. "If I go to Oregon, that flagpole goes with me!"
6. "We didn't believe him, so we strung him up too!"
7. "I will stay by the boy, live or die!"
8. "Bet you marry the first girl you get into that buggy!"
9. "I'll blow a hole in your head big enough for a rabbit to jump through!"
10. "I didn't do nuthin', twas the ox that saved ye!"
11. "No pushee, no pullee, allee same go like hellee!"
12. "You sure made that feller beller!"
13. "I have only once to die!"
14. "I could be happy with a man like him!"
15. "Stay with the oars or we shall all perish!"
16. "You got cattle or horses, me hunt 'em—heap shame hunt hogs!"
17. "If you don't let me loose, I'll—I'll swear!"
18. "Eda is the youngest. Get her out first!"
19. "Cook heap big kettle beans—eat all time—in two days all well!"
20. "Heap skookum, huh!"
21. "Oh Missy Co'bet, see plitty kitty?"
22. "Nobody in Tillamook will know what 'due process of law' means!"
23. "You don't know me, but I know you!"
24. "Run for your life man. Run!"
25. "A hangin' is no place for children!"
26. "We started out for Oregon; let's stick with our first choice!"
27. "She yelled like two Indians!"
28. "Huh! Her no half-breed. Her quarter-breed!

65102839R00219

Made in the USA
San Bernardino, CA
27 December 2017